PRO/CON VOLUME 18

COMMERCE
and TRADE

Published 2004 by Grolier,
an imprint of Scholastic Library Publishing
Old Sherman Turnpike
Danbury, Connecticut 06816

Library of Congress Cataloging-in-Publication Data

Pro/con
   p. cm
   Includes bibliographical references and index.
   Contents: v. 13. U.S. History – v. 14. International Development – v. 15. Human
Rights – v.16. Education – v. 17. New Science – v. 18. Commerce and Trade.
   ISBN 0-7172-5927-7 (set : alk. paper) – ISBN 0-7172-5930-7 (vol. 13 : alk. paper) –
ISBN 0-7172-5929-3 (vol. 14 : alk. paper) – ISBN 0-7172-5931-5 (vol. 15 : alk. paper)
– ISBN 0-7172-5928-5 (vol. 16 : alk. paper) – ISBN 0-7172-5932-3 (vol. 17 : alk.
paper) – ISBN 0-7172-5933-1 (vol. 18 : alk. paper)
   1. Social problems. I. Scholastic Publishing Ltd Grolier (Firm)

HN17.5 P756 2002
361.1–dc21

                                                                    2001053234

Printed and bound in Singapore

SET ISBN 0-7172-5927-7
VOLUME ISBN 0-7172-5933-1

For The Brown Reference Group plc
Project Editor: Aruna Vasudevan
Editors: Chris Marshall, Phil Robins Lesley Henderson, Jonathan Dore,
Mark Fletcher
Consultant Editor: Dean Baker, Director, Center for Economic and Policy
Research, Washington, D.C.
Designer: Sarah Williams
Picture Researchers: Clare Newman, Susy Forbes
Set Index: Kay Ollerenshaw

Managing Editor: Tim Cooke
Art Director: Dave Goodman
Production Director: Alastair Gourlay

GENERAL PREFACE

"All that is necessary for evil to triumph is for good men to do nothing."
—Edmund Burke, 18th-century English political philosopher

Decisions

Life is full of choices and decisions. Some are more important than others. Some affect only your daily life—the route you take to school, for example, or what you prefer to eat for supper—while others are more abstract and concern questions of right and wrong rather than practicality. That does not mean that your choice of presidential candidate or your views on abortion are necessarily more important than your answers to purely personal questions. But it is likely that those wider questions are more complex and subtle and that you therefore will need to know more information about the subject before you can try to answer them. They are also likely to be questions where you might have to justify your views to other people. In order to do that you need to be able to make informed decisions, be able to analyze every fact at your disposal, and evaluate them in an unbiased manner.

What is *Pro/Con*?

Pro/Con is a collection of debates that presents conflicting views on some of the more complex and general issues facing Americans today. By bringing together extracts from a wide range of sources—mainstream newspapers and magazines, books, famous speeches, legal judgments, religious tracts, government surveys—the set reflects current informed attitudes toward dilemmas that range from the best way to feed the world's growing population to gay rights, from the connection between political freedom and capitalism to the fate of Napster.

The people whose arguments make up the set are for the most part acknowledged experts in their fields, making the vast difference in their points of view even more remarkable. The arguments are presented in the form of debates for and against various propositions, such as "Should Americans Celebrate Columbus Day?" or "Are human rights women's rights?" This question format reflects the way in which ideas often occur in daily life: in the classroom, on TV shows, in business meetings, or even in state or federal politics.

The contents

The subjects of the six volumes of *Pro/Con 3—U.S. History, International Development, Human Rights, Education, New Science,* and *Commerce and Trade*—are issues on which it is preferable that people's opinions are based on information rather than personal bias.

Special boxes throughout *Pro/Con* comment on the debates as you are reading them, pointing out facts, explaining terms, or analyzing arguments to help you think about what is being said.

Introductions and summaries also provide background information that might help you reach your own conclusions. There are also tips about how to structure an argument that you can apply on an everyday basis to any debate or conversation, learning how to present your point of view as effectively and persuasively as possible.

VOLUME PREFACE
Commerce and Trade

Commerce and trade—commerce is the specific part of trade comprising the exchange of commodities or goods—are integral parts of the global economy. Trade occurs when a country's output of a particular good exceeds domestic demand so that the country can export that good. Exports can be mass-produced goods, such as computers, or specialized products, such as diamonds.

In the 18th and 19th centuries international trade increased as European countries expanded their empires into Asia, Africa, and South America. By the end of the 20th century trade had become truly global as transportation became quicker and cheaper. Today the United States is the world's largest economy, and trade and commerce are vitally important to the country's wealth.

Issues in international trade

There has been much discussion about free trade. Classical economics promoted free trade, in which the international market is not restricted by government intervention such as laws or taxes. In the early part of the 20th century, however, many western countries abandoned free trade and adopted protectionist policies. Such policies aimed at using tariffs and quotas to protect the domestic economy from imports in an attempt to combat depression.

Since World War II ended in 1945, western nations have again encouraged free trade in a spirit of economic cooperation. International institutions have been set up to facilitate trade, including the General Agreement of Tariffs and Trade (GATT) and the World Trade Organization (WTO). Many people believe that such organizations favor the developed world and make developing nations poorer. Advocates of free trade also believe that liberal trade policies can lead to political openness and so encourage the growth of democracy.

Another key issue in trade is globalization, or the spread of the activities of large corporations around the world. Advocates of globalization believe that it encourages efficiency and creates jobs. Opponents argue that the process favors richer nations and encourages poor nations to exploit their workers or use child labor in order to produce cheap goods that are then sold in the developed world.

While many people believe that free-market economic policies are a good thing, others highlight the dangers of unregulated trade. For example, should companies be punished for supplying arms to regimes that support terrorism? Should the United States trade with countries with poor human rights records? Or should western countries ban imported goods made by children?

Pro/Con

Commerce and Trade looks at 16 topics related to international trade and commerce. It asks many questions about issues to do with international trade and the United States—including monopolies, trade unions, the dollar, and NAFTA—and puts forward both sides of the arguments in a clear and informed way.

HOW TO USE THIS BOOK

Each volume of *Pro/Con* is divided into sections, each of which has an introduction that examines its theme. Within each section are a series of debates that present arguments for and against a proposition, such as whether or not the death penalty should be abolished. An introduction to each debate puts it into its wider context, and a summary and key map (see below) highlight the main points of the debate clearly and concisely. Each debate has marginal boxes that focus on particular points, give tips on how to

present an argument, or help question the writer's case. The summary page to the debates contains supplementary material to help you do further research.

Boxes and other materials provide additional background information. There are also special spreads on how to improve your debating and writing skills. At the end of each book is a glossary and an index. The glossary provides explanations of key words in the volume. The index covers all 18 books, so it will help you trace topics in this set and the previous ones.

marginal boxes
Marginal boxes highlight key points of the argument, give extra information, or help you question the author's meaning.

summary boxes
Summary boxes are useful reminders of both sides of the argument.

further information
Further Reading lists for each debate direct you to related books, articles, and websites so you can do your own research.

other articles in the *Pro/Con* series
This box lists related debates throughout the *Pro/Con* series.

background information
Frequent text boxes provide background information on important concepts and key individuals or events.

key map
Key maps provide a graphic representation of the central points of the debate.

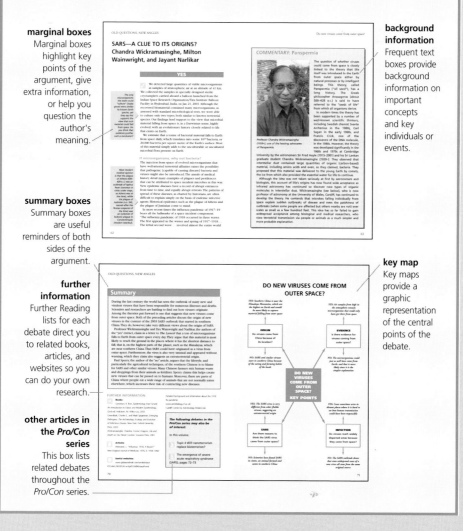

5

CONTENTS

PART 1
TRADE AND THE ECONOMY

Throughout history individuals and groups have exchanged goods and services with other people. In early societies such exchanges took the form of barter, the trading of one good or service for another. From around 1,200 B.C. cowrie shells (mollusk shells) were used as a form of currency, and this system was found in parts of Africa until around the mid-20th century. Bronze and metal coins became a means of economic exchange in various parts of the world from Europe to East Asia from around 1000 B.C.

The introduction of paper and metal money, coupled with the development of a banking system and other financial institutions, made trade between countries far more easy. Today virtually all international trade is carried out and measured in terms of money.

The development of trade

Since ancient times trade has been central to the development of communities, which arose around both trade routes and sources of tradable commodities such as coal, timber, or grain. Some of these places grew into thriving cities that attracted a diverse range of businesses and industries and with them new people seeking employment and income.

Initially trade by wagon, horseback, or boat was slow and could be highly unreliable—goods rotted or were stolen, boats sank, harbors silted up, and wars, sometimes over trade rights, closed sources and routes of supply.

In the early Modern Age many European countries grew rich partly through trade in natural resources, spices, and slaves. Trade routes crossed much of the globe, connecting China to western Europe and Scandinavia to the shores of the Black Sea. Nations, such as Spain, Portugal, and the Netherlands, led the effort to find new trade routes and new goods with which to trade. A theory emerged, later called "mercantilism," that nations should accumulate capital from abroad in the form of resources and from the income earned by exports. Followers believed that nations should also protect their domestic economies and capital holdings by limiting imports.

In 1776 the British economist Adam Smith (1723–1790) published what is arguably still one of the most influential economics books ever written. *The Wealth of Nations* challenged the assumptions behind mercantilism as Smith proposed what would for 200 years become the accepted economic orthodoxy among the world's industrialized countries: free trade. Smith argued: "If a foreign country can supply us with a commodity cheaper than we ourselves can make it, better buy it off them with some part of the produce of our own industry, employed in a way in which we have some advantage." Unhampered by quotas or tariffs, trade could benefit every nation by allowing countries to concentrate on the production of their most efficient goods and services. Economists later refined Smith's theories, and supporters often argue that the benefits of free trade extend beyond economic efficiency. The Heritage Foundation, for example, concluded in 2001 that countries that were more open to trade also tended to maintain higher environmental and labor standards.

they are a natural part of what is termed the business cycle. Topic 2 examines if recessions are inevitable.

Other variables

A free trade system can be affected by other factors. One example is the creation of a monopoly, in which control over an industry is consolidated in the hands of one individual or company. Such big businesses can experience economies of scale, which

---

"The evidence shows that increased trade leads to increased economic growth, which raises labour and environmental standards."

—AARON SCHAVEY, POLICY ANALYST, CENTER FOR INTERNATIONAL TRADE AND ECONOMICS, HERITAGE FOUNDATION (2001)

But many nations, including the United States, also practice a degree of protectionism, using tariffs or quotas to limit imports and protect domestic firms. In the 20th century, too, communist states experimented with planned economies, in which government policies controlled all economic activity. Topic 1 examines whether free market is the best system to encourage world trade.

A common criticism of free trade is that it leaves poor countries, in particular, vulnerable to fluctuations in the international economy, such as a rise in prices caused by a shortage in supply of goods.

Some economists ask whether it might be possible to avoid fluctuations in the international economy through the intervention of international financial bodies; others believe that

make production cheap and lead to lower prices for consumers. But monopolies can cause a rise in market prices, restrict consumer choice, and prevent technological innovation from occurring.

Some people argue that other factors can disrupt free trade. Strong unionization can be equally harmful by working to limit employers' freedom. In some countries labor unions have grown immensely powerful. Their fight to improve the working conditions of their members, critics argue, can force up costs of production through unrealistic demands. But advocates argue that they are essential in protecting workers from exploitation. Topics 3 and 4 in this section examine whether monopolies are always bad and if labor unions can adversely affect economic growth.

Topic 1
IS A FREE MARKET THE BEST WAY TO ORGANIZE WORLD TRADE?

YES
FROM "THE CASE FOR FREE TRADE AND LOWER TAXES"
AN INQUIRY INTO THE NATURE AND CAUSES OF THE WEALTH OF NATIONS (1776)
ADAM SMITH

NO
"FREE TRADE IS NOT FREE, MR. PRESIDENT"
THE AMERICAN CAUSE, MAY 2001
PATRICK J. BUCHANAN

INTRODUCTION

Since the late 18th century the idea of free trade has dominated classical Western economic thought. It inspired the dynamic economics of the Victorian age and still inspires such international bodies as the World Trade Organization (WTO). Increasingly, however, free trade faces objections from opponents who believe that it is unfair and inefficient.

The term "free trade" generally means an economic system under which governments do not interfere in the movement of goods between countries. Its opposite is known as protectionism. Governments have methods by which they traditionally try to provide their home producers with an advantage over foreign competitors. Among these measures is the imposition of tariffs—taxes on imports—which makes goods entering the country become more expensive than home-produced ones.

Free trade was most famously advocated by Adam Smith (1723-1790),

the father of classical economics, in *An Inquiry into the Nature and Causes of the Wealth of Nations*, published in 1776. Smith, a Scottish economist and philosopher, argued against the prevailing economic theory of mercantilism, which aimed to increase a nation's power by amassing gold and silver. To that end governments used protectionist methods to limit imports and thus prevent bullion going overseas, and encouraged national self-sufficiency. Smith, however, thought it ridiculous for a country to struggle to produce goods it could import more cheaply. In his view it would be more beneficial to society as a whole if each country produced what it was good at or had ample supplies of and then traded freely with others for its other needs. That would be the fairest system for all nations, he argued.

In the 19th century the idea of free trade took hold in Europe, particularly in Great Britain, where trade barriers were dismantled. Free trade benefited Great Britain, which was the first country to industrialize and therefore needed plenty of tariff-free export markets for its goods. The United States, by contrast, had a developing industrial sector at the time and used tariffs to cushion it from competition with established industrial nations. Britain persisted with free trade until the early 20th century, when it also turned to tariffs to counter other countries' protectionist polices and to help its industries recover unchallenged from World War I (1914-1918).

> *"Free trade is not a principle, it is an expedient."*
>
> —BENJAMIN DISRAELI (1804–1881), BRITISH POLITICIAN AND OPPONENT OF FREE TRADE

After World War II (1939-1945), and under the leadership of the United States, the idea of free trade made a comeback—there was a feeling that protectionism had worsened the Great Depression of the 1930s. In 1947, 23 countries signed the General Agreement on Tariffs and Trade. GATT encouraged its members to negotiate the reduction of tariffs and other trade barriers. In 1995 GATT was succeeded by the WTO. Many people object to the WTO's advocacy of free trade, which they say is unfair to developing nations.

So is a free market the best way to organize world trade? Free trade supporters argue that the competition for sales in open markets brings lower prices and a wider choice of goods. For developing countries, meanwhile, free trade can bring a boost to economic growth. With trade restrictions removed, they argue, the way is open for foreign companies to invest in a developing country—by setting up a factory, for example, which hires local labor and so stimulates economic activity. Supporters also argue that protectionism does not work. Evidence suggests that it harms domestic consumers. As in the Great Depression, the existence of such barriers to trade might worsen economic problems.

Opponents of free trade, however, view matters differently. In the United States, for example, critics blame the 1994 North American Free Trade Agreement (NAFTA) for job losses, asserting that it enables companies to move factories to Mexico, where labor is cheaper. At the same time, they say, free trade is bringing about the collapse of domestic manufacturing industries because imported goods made by low-cost labor are so cheap that home producers cannot compete.

Critics also disagree that free trade benefits developing countries. Too often, they say, lowering trade barriers leads to a flood of imports, the profits on which go to the foreign producers. They argue too that free trade pacts can give corporations too much power. For example, under NAFTA a company may sue a government if it enacts a law that can reduce its profits—even if the law is to protect health or the environment.

The following articles examine the debate further. The first is an extract from Adam Smith's *Wealth of Nations*, the first expression of the concept of free trade. The second, by right-wing ideologue Patrick Buchanan, attacks free trade for eroding the United States' economic independence.

THE CASE FOR FREE TRADE AND LOWER TAXES
Adam Smith

This extract is taken from Adam Smith's Wealth of Nations *(1776), which is generally considered to be the first masterpiece of political economic thought.*

How should an economy be judged? By the health of individual sectors or by its overall health?

YES

By restraining, either by high duties, or by absolute prohibitions, the importation of such goods from foreign countries as can be produced at home, the monopoly of the home-market is more or less secured to the domestic industry employed in producing them. Thus the … high duties upon the importation of corn, which in times of moderate plenty amount to a prohibition, give a like advantage to the growers of that commodity. The prohibition of the importation of foreign woolens is equally favorable to the woolen manufacturers. The silk manufacture, though altogether employed upon foreign materials, has lately obtained the same advantage. The linen manufacture has not yet obtained it, but is making great strides towards it. Many other sorts of manufacturers have, in the same manner, obtained in Great Britain, either altogether, or very nearly a monopoly against their countrymen….

That this monopoly of the home-market frequently gives great encouragement to that particular species of industry which enjoys it … cannot be doubted. But whether it tends either to increase the general industry of the society, or to give it the most advantageous direction, is not, perhaps, altogether so evident….

A pointless struggle

The natural advantages which one country has over another in producing particular commodities are sometimes so great, that it is acknowledged by all the world to be in vain to struggle with them. By means of glasses, hotbeds, and hotwalls, very good grapes can be raised in Scotland, and very good wine too can be made of them at about thirty times the expense for which at least equally good can be brought from foreign countries. Would it be a reasonable law to prohibit the importation of all foreign wines, merely to encourage the making of claret and burgundy in Scotland? But if there would be a manifest absurdity in turning towards any employment, thirty times more of the capital and industry of the country, than would be necessary to purchase

The Scottish economist Adam Smith in a drawing dated about 1780.

COMMENTARY: Protectionism

The basic premise behind free trade is that it is beneficial for a country to specialize in what it can produce best and trade with other countries to get goods at a lower cost than it would take to produce them at home. Supporters of free trade argue that when there is a period of general free trade, the world is more prosperous and peaceful. When governments adopt protectionist measures, such as raising the taxes or tariffs on imported goods and imposing limits or quotas on the amount of goods governments allow to enter a country, world trade drops, and that leads to economic depression.

The Great Depression

The economic model at the time of the Great Depression—the severe world slump of the 1930s—depended on international free trade, a stable currency, and a competitive economy. However, perfect competition was lacking in a period that was prone to monopolies and was characterized by war and political disturbance. The United States has traditionally used tariffs to protect its industries from foreign competition. After the stock market crash of 1929 Congress passed a controversial tariff law—the Smoot–Hawley Tariff Act—in 1930. The act was passed despite a petition advising against it signed by more than 1,000 prominent economists. During World War I (1914–18) agriculture outside Europe had grown considerably. With the postwar recovery of the European agriculture sector there was a period of overproduction during the 1920s which led to declining farm prices. The intention behind the Smoot-Hawley Act was to protect domestic farmers against foreign agricultural imports.

Collapse of world trade

Calls then came from all sectors of the U.S. economy for protection, and tariffs were raised to historically high levels. Within a year more than 25 other governments had passed similar laws. The international economy relied on the U.S. market for European imports. The raising of tariffs led to a chain reaction as all industrialized governments resorted to protectionist measures. Between 1929 and 1934 world trade plummeted by around 66 percent. The collapse in world trade contributed to the length and severity of the Depression. The situation was exacerbated by countries leaving the gold standard, the system that facilitated international trade by allowing currencies to be freely exchanged in gold.

Critics argue that the Smoot–Hawley Tariff caused the Great Depression. It certainly marked a low point in terms of U.S. support for free trade. Since then the United States has become a champion of free trade, supporting the General Agreement on Tariffs and Trade (GATT), the North American Free Trade Agreement (NAFTA), and the World Trade Organization (WTO).

from foreign countries an equal quantity of the commodities wanted, there must be an absurdity, though not altogether so glaring, yet exactly of the same kind, in turning towards any such employment a thirtieth, or even a three hundredth part more of either…. As long as the one country has those advantages, and the other wants them, it will always be more advantageous for the latter, rather to buy of the former than to make. It is an acquired advantage only, which one artificer has over his neighbor, who exercises another trade; and yet they both find it more advantageous to buy of one another, than to make what does not belong to their particular trades.

"Artificer" is now a largely archaic term for an inventor or skilled craftsman. However, the term is still used for certain skilled trades—for example, ordnance artificer, a position involving the handling and testing of weapons and ammunition.

Who benefits from import restrictions?

Merchants and manufacturers are the people who derive the greatest advantage from this monopoly of the home-market. The prohibition of the importation of foreign cattle, and of salt provisions, together with the high duties upon foreign corn, which in times of moderate plenty amount to a prohibition, are not near so advantageous to the graziers and farmers of Great Britain, as other regulations of the same kind are to its merchants and manufacturers. Manufactures, those of the finer kind especially, are more easily transported from one country to another than corn or cattle. It is in the fetching and carrying [of] manufactures, accordingly, that foreign trade is chiefly employed. In manufactures, a very small advantage will enable foreigners to undersell our own workmen, even in the home-market. It will require a very great one to enable them to do so in the rude produce of the soil. If the free importation of foreign manufactures were permitted, several of the home manufacturers would probably suffer, and some of them, perhaps, go to ruin altogether, and a considerable part of the stock and industry at present employed in them, would be forced to find out some other employment. But the freest importation of the rude produce of the soil could have no such effect upon the agriculture of the country.

A "grazier" is a person who raises cattle or sheep— grazing animals— to sell at market.

Smith wrote at a time when agriculture dominated the economy. Does it matter so much today?

FREE TRADE IS NOT FREE, MR. PRESIDENT
Patrick J. Buchanan

This article was published on the website of the American Cause, an educational organization funded by conservative Patrick J. Buchanan (1938—) to promote "national sovereignty, economic patriotism, limited government and individual freedom." Buchanan is a columnist and politician.

This article was written in 2001. The U.S. trade deficit with China at the end of 2002 was $103.1 billion. American exports to China were worth $22 billion, but the United States imported Chinese goods to the value of $125 billion. See page 17, Trade deficits.

Do you think that oil dependency also caused the invasion of Iraq in 2003? See Volume 13, U.S. History, Topic 15 Was the Persian Gulf War a war about oil?

NO

As Mr. Bush flies off to Quebec to tout a super-NAFTA from Patagonia to Prudhoe Bay, he has likely not seen the latest trade figures. They are worth a glance, if only for their size. In 2000:

• The U.S. merchandise trade deficit hit $450 billion, almost 5% of the U.S. economy.

• Our trade deficit in manufactured goods, $324 billion, is now 22 times as large as our trade surplus in agricultural goods.

• Imported manufactures now equal 62% of U.S. manufactures.

• Manufacturing jobs, 30% of U.S. jobs in 1953, are now 13%.

• America's biggest trade deficit, $84 billion, is with China. We buy about 40% of China's exports; China buys 2% of ours.

Not long ago, such trade deficits would have stunned U.S. statesmen. No more. To acolytes of the Global Economy, "Trade deficits do not matter." An article in the May/June *Foreign Affairs* ("The U.S. Trade Deficit: A Dangerous Obsession") instructs us: We must not let these huge deficits frighten us.

The meaning of trade deficits

Well, as Wellington said of the recruits sent over to Waterloo, they may not frighten Napoleon, but by heavens, they frighten me! What do these deficits mean to America?

A dangerous, deepening dependency on foreign nations for the vital necessities of our national life. America imported $89 billion in crude oil last year, half of all the oil we consumed. Oil dependency sucked us into war with Iraq [in 1990–1991], has forced us to give war guarantees to non-viable states in the Gulf, and is dragging the U.S. into the snake pit of Caspian Basin and Central Asian power politics.

COMMENTARY: Trade deficits

A country has a trade deficit when the value of the goods and services it imports exceeds the value of the goods and services it exports—in other words, it buys more on the international market than it sells. The United States has the largest trade deficit in the world. At the end of 2002 it stood at $435.7 billion. The last time U.S. annual international trade figures showed a surplus (the opposite of a deficit) was in 1975. Since then, although figures have fluctuated, the trend has been generally upward, and the deficit has jumped markedly since 1992. The trading partner with which the United States has its largest deficit is China—$103.1 billion at the end of 2002—which took over from Japan as the major creditor in 2000.

Among the causes of the U.S. trade deficit has been the general lifting of trade restrictions worldwide. One of the effects of such a move is to allow more imports than before to enter a richer country, while poorer countries that are doing the exporting may not be able to return the favor by buying the richer nation's goods—thus one side in the partnership does most of the buying while the other does most of the selling, and an imbalance develops. It is also usually the case that poorer countries pay their labor lower wages, so they can sell their goods cheaply. The relative strengths of currencies also play a part—if a selling country's currency is weak (that is, has a low value) compared to that of a buying country, then its goods will be inexpensive, and vice versa.

Experts are divided over whether a large trade deficit is a good thing for the United States or a disaster. Some believe the deficit gives cause for great concern because the country must sell its assets, in the form of stocks and government bonds, to pay for it. In time, these critics argue, the United States will be owned by foreigners. By contrast, others point out that when the United States has a large trade deficit, economic growth—in terms of the nation's output—is high.

Have we forgotten? Hamilton created the "American System" to end our reliance on England and Europe, because he and Washington believed economic independence was necessary for political independence. If we did not depend on Europe, they knew, we could stay out of Europe's wars. Is all that Made-in-China junk at the mall worth the loss of our economic independence?

A second cost of free trade is deindustrialization. When Spain, Holland and Great Britain lost primacy in manufacturing, to focus on trade and finance, their great days were over. Manufacturing is the muscle of a nation, the key to its productivity and wage growth. What benefit do we get from a $105 billion trade deficit in autos and trucks,

The "American system" was a federal economic plan drawn up in the early 19th century. It advocated setting high tariffs for the protection of U.S. industries. Alexander Hamilton (1755–1804) played a key role in how the government managed the national economy.

Patrick J. Buchanan challenged George Bush for the 1992 Republican presidential nomination.

a $48 billion trade deficit in clothing, and a $43 billion trade deficit in office machines and ADP equipment, all of which we used to make here?

Why take these high-paying jobs, the yellow brick road to the middle class for working Americans, and send them abroad?

Is manufacturing really a way for working Americans to improve their lifestyles?

Paying for China's arsenal

A third cost of free trade is the corruption of conservatism and the mass conversion of American capitalists into the pimps of hostile powers. Since 1990, China has amassed $400 billion in trade surpluses with the U.S. That cash hoard has financed the largest military buildup in Asia since Japan in the '30s. Beijing has used it to buy Russian destroyers, subs and Sunburn anti-ship missiles and Lavi fighters and Python air-to-air missiles from Israel. What is this Chinese arsenal for? To fight and kill the U.S. Pacific fleet.

American companies and consumers are giving China the dollars to put Shane Osborn and his crew at risk of their lives in the Taiwan Strait and South China Sea. The Clintonites are not the only ones corrupted by soft money. Conservatives who celebrated the Reagan "strategy of denial" toward Moscow now tell us that feeding the Asian tiger will domesticate it.

U.S. Navy lieutenant Shane Osborn was the pilot of an EP-3 Aries II surveillance aircraft that collided with a Chinese F-8 fighter over the South China Sea on April 1, 2001. He and his crew of 23 were taken into custody by the Chinese authorities for 11 days.

But when does that occur? Before, or after, Beijing has targeted 600 missiles on Taiwan and U.S. bases in Japan and Korea?

Love of money is the root of all evil, said St. Paul. To acolytes of our new religion of Economism, love of money is the way to convert the barbarian to democracy.

No more "Buy American"

Do not Americans see what is happening to their country? As our dependency grows, our bonds of unity dissolve. "Buy American!" is now stupid; buying cheapest is smart. Trade deficits have given Asians and Europeans the dollars to buy 10% of our stocks, 20% of corporate bonds, nearly 40% of our public debt. Our current account deficit is 4.4% of GDP, an unheard of figure that portends a collapse of the dollar after we have been denuded of our factories.

Should consumers be prepared to pay more to support U.S. firms? Who benefits?

Finally, there is the loss of sovereignty. As the European socialist superstate, the EU, demonstrates, every free trade zone calls into being a regime to enforce its rules. Global free trade leads to global government. Clinton understood this. Conservatives do not. They will wake up one day to find out that free trade is not free.

The European Union (EU) is an organization of 15 states, 12 of which now share a single currency, the euro. Go to http://europa. eu.int/index_en.htm to find out more.

Summary

Is a free market the best way to organize world trade? In the first extract Adam Smith, writing toward the end of the 18th century, begins by describing the benefits enjoyed by various manufacturing industries because of the duties imposed on foreign competitors. He then questions whether this "monopoly of the home-market" is an effective way to organize international trade. Taking the example of wine production in Scotland and France, he asks: "Would it be a reasonable law to prohibit the importation of all foreign wines, merely to encourage the making of claret and burgundy [French wines] in Scotland?" He concludes that it would be folly for Scotland to try to develop a wine industry when wine can be imported from abroad at a fraction of the cost. Instead, "they both find it more advantageous to buy of one another, than to make what does not belong to their particular trades."

Patrick J. Buchanan, writing at the start of the 21st century, views free trade as having an extremely negative effect on the U.S. economy. After detailing trade statistics for 2000, he lists four areas in which he believes the United States is being damaged by current economic thinking: (1) an increasing dependency on foreign countries for essential goods; (2) the destruction of domestic manufacturing industries; (3) the sale of large quantities of American assets overseas and the funding of potentially hostile powers through the purchase of their goods; (4) loss of sovereignty—in Buchanan's words, "Global free trade leads to global government."

FURTHER INFORMATION:

Books:

Gomes, Leonard, *The Economics and Ideology of Free Trade: A Historical Review*. Northampton, MA: Edward Elgar Pub., 2003.

Irwin, Douglas A., *Free Trade under Fire*. Princeton, NJ: Princeton University Press, 2002.

MacArthur, John R., *The Selling of "Free Trade": NAFTA, Washington, and the Subversion of American Democracy*. New York: Hill and Wang, 2000.

Roberts, Russell D., *The Choice: A Fable of Free Trade and Protectionism*. Upper Saddle River, NJ: Prentice Hall, 2000.

Stiglitz, Joseph E., *Globalization and Its Discontents*. New York: W.W. Norton & Company, 2002.

Useful websites:

www.census.gov/foreign-trade/balance
Census Board site giving U.S. trade balances by country.
www.wto.org
World Trade Organization (WTO) site.

The following debates in the Pro/Con series may also be of interest:

In this volume:

Topic 3 Are monopolies always bad?

Topic 5 Has globalization hindered the economic growth of developing nations?

Topic 14 Is protectionism good for U.S. business?

Topic 15 Has NAFTA cost the United States jobs?

IS A FREE MARKET THE BEST WAY TO ORGANIZE WORLD TRADE?

YES: The competition engendered by free trade leads to a wide variety of goods at low prices

YES: It is pointless struggling to produce something that another country can make more easily and, perhaps, better

CONSUMERISM
Does free trade improve the situation of the ordinary American?

EFFICIENCY
Does free trade lead to a more rational worldwide division of labor?

NO: Maybe so, but at the same time, floods of cheap imports are costing other Americans their jobs

NO: It can lead to the erosion of a nation's manufacturing industry and to a dangerous dependency on imports

IS A FREE MARKET THE BEST WAY TO ORGANIZE WORLD TRADE?
KEY POINTS

YES: Multinational companies may set up operations, generating employment opportunities for local people and thereby stimulating the local economy

YES: The European Union is effectively a superstate. Also, under NAFTA companies can sue governments if they make laws that might reduce profits.

BETTERMENT
Does free trade benefit developing countries?

INDEPENDENCE
Does joining a free trade zone rob a country of its sovereignty?

NO: It opens the way for a flood of imports, the profits on which go to foreign companies and do not benefit the local economy

NO: Although they cooperate economically, countries in free trade zones retain control of national decision-making

Topic 2
ARE RECESSIONS INEVITABLE?

YES

FROM "WHEN THE ECONOMY GOES SOUTH: WHAT HAPPENS IN A RECESSION"
REGIONAL REVIEW, VOL. 9, NO. 1, 1999
JANE KATZ

NO

FROM "THE HANGOVER THEORY: ARE RECESSIONS THE INEVITABLE
PAYBACK FOR GOOD TIMES?"
WWW2.GOL.COM/USERS/COYNERHM/HANGOVER_THEORY.HTM, DECEMBER 3, 1998
PAUL KRUGMAN

INTRODUCTION

A recession is a prolonged, but temporary, decline in economic activity or prosperity. A nation's economy is based on the production and consumption—that is, purchase—of goods and services. During a recession, also known as a slump, the economy contracts, or slows down. In other words, the demand for goods and services declines. As people buy fewer of their goods and services, businesses make cuts in production and reduce costs by paying their employees less or laying them off. As a result, consumers—the public—have less money and are also worried about their future well-being. They spend less, so the demand for goods and services drops even further. If a recession lasts for a long time and is especially severe, it is called a depression.

More than 20 recessions have occurred in the United States since 1900, the worst being the Great Depression of the 1930s. Recessions cause hardship to many people, often hitting the poor hardest. But many economists have debated whether anything can be done to prevent recessions from taking place.

The United States has what is termed a market economy, in which producers are usually allowed to charge what they want for goods and services, and consumers are free to buy—or not buy—those goods and services. This system gives consumers and producers a large degree of freedom. Such economies tend to follow a pattern of expansion and contraction—sometimes referred to as boom and bust—that economists are still debating the cause of.

The period of expansion usually lasts from six to ten years. Toward the end of this phase economic growth slows. Consumer demand for goods and services has peaked. At the same time, businesses can find neither new projects in which to invest nor available money with which to finance them. However, recognizing that such a point has been reached and that a recession is imminent is notoriously difficult without the benefit of hindsight. The recession phase usually lasts between six months and two years.

Economists who believe that recessions are inevitable point to the business cycle as the reason why, citing recessions as the price the economy must pay for a previous period of expansion. Once the limits of expansion are reached, the dynamics of the market economy insist that it go into reverse by shrinking production to meet a declining demand—seemingly the economy cannot simply stand still.

> *"It's a recession when your neighbor loses his job; it's a depression when you lose yours."*
>
> —HARRY TRUMAN,
>
> 33RD PRESIDENT (1945–1953)

Other commentators point out that recessions often seem to have been triggered by an event or combination of events taking place as the economy reached its peak. A triggering episode may be economic in nature, such as a stock market crash or a rise in the price of oil. However, it could equally be noneconomic, caused by a war or strike, for example. The effects of these events on the economy may be direct—higher oil prices mean higher production costs. But the impact may also be psychological—the threat of war causes uncertainty, making business

and the public jittery and cautious about spending money. But does the existence of triggering events make recessions inevitable? Some economists think so.

Even economists who believe that recessions are avoidable acknowledge that boom and bust are features of the economy—but only if they are allowed to be. Such people advocate economic action at a high level, by the government or the central bank—in the case of the United States, the Federal Reserve—to prevent the business cycle from taking its classic course.

According to one view, if the economy shows signs of expanding out of control—overheating—then measures should be introduced to slow it down. For example, interest rates might be increased, making it more expensive to borrow money, thereby discouraging businesses and the public from spending. Conversely, should the economy appear to be going into recession, interest rates might be lowered, encouraging people to borrow money and thereby stimulating demand for goods. The judicious use of such measures would, their advocates assert, bring an end to the extremes of boom and bust.

Economist Jane Katz, in the first article that follows, argues that while economists can attempt to reduce the risk of a recession, it is impossible to predict one or what its cause may be. However, in the second article economics professor Paul Krugman claims that recessions can be avoided if positive government action is taken. He takes particular issue with the "hangover theory" of recession—the idea that booms necessarily lead to slumps, just as drinking binges lead to hangovers.

WHEN THE ECONOMY GOES SOUTH: WHAT HAPPENS IN A RECESSION
Jane Katz

Jane Katz is an economist and editor of the Regional Review at the Research Department of the Federal Reserve Bank of Boston. She wrote this article in 1999.

YES

The modern American Economy is an impressive machine. Over this century, it has generated enormous advances in technology, absorbed millions of immigrants and women into the labor force, and seen massive investments in capital goods and a sharp rise in educational attainment, all of which have translated into huge increases in living standards. Yet, there are periods—more than 20 since 1900—where the economy contracts and production drops. For households and firms, the declines in employment and income that result cause considerable distress, both financial and psychological.

Why and how does this happen? What causes a healthy economy with a highly educated work force and a large store of modern equipment to falter? Why don't prices and wages adjust to reach full employment? Are these economic downturns inevitable? …

Rhetorical questions help explain to the audience the subjects you plan to address.

What happened last time: 1990–91

It has been nine years since the start of the most recent U.S. recession. It began, according to the National Bureau of Economic Research (the people in charge of dating the peaks and troughs), in July 1990, about a month before Iraq invaded Kuwait. It was relatively brief, ending eight months later in March 1991, although a sluggish early recovery made the downturn seem to last much longer and kept unemployment rising—up to 7.8 percent in June 1992—even as the economy started to come back.…

And, as cycles go, this one was milder than average. The downturn was relatively short, about eight months long as compared to an average of 11 months for recessions after World War II. The cumulative loss of GDP was also less than average. And the unemployment rate saw the smallest increase of any recession since the war. (New England, however, was hit hard.…)

A country's GDP (gross domestic product) is the total value of goods it produces and services it provides, usually calculated each quarter or each year. A country's gross national product (GNP) is its GDP plus the income it earns from foreign investments and minus the income foreign investors earn in its markets.

Compare this to the Great Depression of 1929, the most calamitous economic event in the United States this [20th] century. Within less than three years, the nation lost production equal to almost half of the entire output loss from all other recessions this century, according to calculations by U.C. Berkeley economist Christina Romer. Measured unemployment rates soared to 25 percent, with the true rate probably far worse, as many people just gave up looking for work. As MIT Professor Peter Temin observed, "Policies that avoid similar catastrophes may be more important than policies that fine-tune the economy."

MIT stands for Massachusetts Institute of Technology, which is situated, like Harvard University, in the city of Cambridge.

Proximate causes

To avoid catastrophes, it helps to know what causes them. In a paper prepared for a 1998 conference, "Beyond Shocks: What Causes Business Cycles?," sponsored by the Federal Reserve Bank of Boston, Professor Temin attempted to determine the dominant cause of each of the recessions since 1890. In particular, he looked for a break—a shock or change—to an important economic relationship that might have triggered the subsequent decline in production and employment. Such a break might come from a fall-off in demand (a drop in consumption or investment spending in response to a war or other event that erodes confidence) or events on the supply side (an increase in the cost of an important input such as oil). It might, as his MIT colleague Rudiger Dornbusch has suggested, originate with the Federal Reserve and contractionary monetary policy, which by choking off liquidity and raising short-term interest rates slows spending on housing, capital goods, and other interest-sensitive demand. Or it might be imported from abroad, as fallout from economic or financial distress that begins in a foreign country.

"Choking off liquidity" means reducing the amount of money in the economic system. The Federal Reserve can achieve this by selling government bonds and removing from circulation the money paid for them. With less money available to be spent or invested, economic activity slows.

   Temin examined evidence from the historical literature and concluded that there was no single underlying source for all of this century's recessions. About two-thirds had their origins in the domestic economy, the other one-third in external events, he decided. Roughly half could be attributed to a monetary event; half began with a shift in the supply of or demand for goods and services. Temin also looked for systematic differences in the causes of big and small recessions, and found none.

   But determining causation is a tricky undertaking, as Temin notes in his paper. Your underlying theory about how the economy works will matter; those (very few) who doubt on theoretical grounds that monetary policy is capable of affecting anything in the economy except prices would never ascribe any recession to actions of the Federal Reserve. It also requires separating out the "cause" from a chain of connected events, a subtle task and one that is open to interpretation

The Federal Reserve—"the Fed" for short—is the United States' central bank. Go to www.federalreserve.gov to find out more about the Fed and how it operates.

and subject to disagreement. For example, all recessions since World War II have been preceded by rising inflation that has, in turn, prompted tighter monetary policy. While many would argue that such policy was appropriate and should, in fact, be given credit for dampening business cycles over that period, Dornbusch and others argue that the Fed "caused" these recessions.

The federal funds rate is the interest rate that banks charge when they loan one another money and is controlled by the Fed. If this rate is increased, then the banks will sooner or later raise the interest rates they charge their customers—for loans and home mortgages, for example.

Assigning a single cause—even to any particular recession—may be impossible, for downturns often result from a combination of events. In 1990-91, for instance, you can look for causes as far back as March 1988. With the economy arguably at or near capacity, the Federal Reserve raised the federal funds rate and short-term interest rates soon followed. Around the same time, problems in the real estate industry meant that many bankers and bank regulators became cautious in approving loans, and the resulting "credit crunch" may have squelched some investment demand. Once Iraq invaded Kuwait in summer 1990, consumer confidence fell and the price of oil rose, resulting in declines in spending and personal income. And Robert Hall of Stanford has suggested that, with economic conditions hard to discern, the Fed reacted cautiously in lowering the federal funds rate later that summer. All these factors may have contributed to the subsequent recession; perhaps, none alone would have been enough.

A matter of vulnerability

The author is referring to a crisis that began in July 1997. The value of many Asian currencies dropped, so they could not afford to import goods. With imports down, the countries that export to Asia suffered, including Japan, Russia, and Latin America. The problem threatened to become global, but normality was beginning to return by mid-1999.

What does seem important is whether the economy is vulnerable—weakened enough so that it is unable to handle a disturbance that might have only mild consequences when the economy was more robust. In 1990-91, for instance, the economy was already slowing and, thus, may have been particularly sensitive to the spending drop that occurred around the time of the invasion of Kuwait. Perhaps the recent currency crisis that began in Asia and spread to Russia and Latin America could have triggered a recession in the United States if the domestic economy had been more vulnerable.

And it may be a mistake to look for recessions' causes only in economic factors. "Virtually all recessions have occurred around the time of some highly distinctive, not purely economic event such as a war, a massive change in the price of imported oil, a major strike, or wage, price, and credit controls," observes [former Federal Reserve Bank of Boston economist Stephen] McNees. "Recessions almost always come as a surprise," he reminds us, "though they seem easy to 'explain' after the fact." …

Since World War II, the nation's economic expansions have lasted longer and its recessions have become less frequent (although they are not noticeably shorter or less severe than those between 1886 and World War I). This is due partly to better macroeconomic policy. Tighter management of inventories and a growing share of employment in the less cyclically sensitive services industries may have also helped. Still, most economists think it unlikely that the United States has seen its last recession.

Some point out that economic "shocks" will always be with us. Wars, technological upheaval, foreign economic instability, and bad economic policy are probably inevitable, if ultimately unforeseeable. When they do occur, the economy, caught off guard, takes time to adjust.

A self-fulfilling prophecy?

Others see recessions as originating in the expansions that precede them. Victor Zarnowitz, for example, argues that business profits, investment, and credit conditions tend to interact in a way that turns booms into busts. In an expanding economy, high profits and a rising stock market encourage firms to invest, he notes. As the boom continues, firms may begin to undertake riskier and riskier investments and the danger of overconfidence grows. Eventually, growth begins to slow, and profits and investment decline as well. Business failures must be written off; credit markets may move to safer and more liquid assets, which can create a credit crunch. Investment and consumption spending fall off, as boom turns to bust. Just as overconfidence can lead to asset bubbles, "herd" psychology can amplify declines. As earnings reports disappoint, the stock market may also drop and exacerbate the downturn. Thus, the seeds of recessions may be sown in the expansions that went before.

Nor is there necessarily any way to prevent them. As Paul Samuelson has noted, financial economists have crafted clever new products—options and other derivatives—to improve efficiency in the pricing of specific financial assets, such as an individual stock, but no opportunity exists to make money by trying to correct mispricing in the general level of stock market prices.

So whether recessions are generated by "shocks" or they are inherent in the process of expansion, the next one is probably inevitable. And while it is possible to assess the economy's vulnerability and to implement policies that reduce its exposure to risk, there is no way to predict when the next recession will arrive or what its cause will be....

"Macroeconomic policy" is the way the government handles the country's economy. Among its branches are fiscal policy, which covers taxation and government spending, and monetary policy, which deals with such matters as interest rates.

A "derivative" is a type of financial product that is linked to another financial product, such as a stock. An "option" is a type of derivative: the right to buy a stock at a specified price during a specified time. Buying an option is cheaper than buying the stock itself. Also, if the price of the stock rises above the option price during the specified time, the buyer still gets the stock at the lower price. The buyer may choose not to use his option, which expires at the end of the specified time.

THE HANGOVER THEORY: ARE RECESSIONS THE INEVITABLE PAYBACK FOR GOOD TIMES?
Paul Krugman

The author stresses his contempt for the "Austrian theory" by comparing it to a long-discredited idea. Until the late 18th century phlogiston was believed to be a substance present in all combustible materials that was given off during burning.

A few weeks ago, a journalist devoted a substantial part of a profile of yours truly to my failure to pay due attention to the "Austrian theory" of the business cycle—a theory that I regard as being about as worthy of serious study as the phlogiston theory of fire. Oh well. But the incident set me thinking—not so much about that particular theory as about the general worldview behind it. Call it the overinvestment theory of recessions, or "liquidationism," or just call it the "hangover theory." It is the idea that slumps are the price we pay for booms, that the suffering the economy experiences during a recession is a necessary punishment for the excesses of the previous expansion.

The hangover theory is perversely seductive—not because it offers an easy way out, but because it doesn't. It turns the wiggles on our charts into ... a tale of hubris and downfall. And it offers adherents the special pleasure of dispensing painful advice with a clear conscience, secure in the belief that they are not heartless but merely practicing tough love.

A wrongheaded theory

Friedrich August von Hayek (1899–1992) was an Austrian-born British economist who taught at the London School of Economics. Joseph Alois Schumpeter (1883–1950) was Austrian minister of finance (1919–1920). He taught at Harvard from 1932 to 1949.

Powerful as these seductions may be, they must be resisted—for the hangover theory is disastrously wrongheaded. Recessions are not necessary consequences of booms. They can and should be fought, not with austerity but with liberality—with policies that encourage people to spend more, not less. Nor is this merely an academic argument: The hangover theory can do real harm. Liquidationist views played an important role in the spread of the Great Depression—with Austrian theorists such as Friedrich von Hayek and Joseph Schumpeter strenuously arguing, in the very depths of that depression, against any attempt to restore "sham" prosperity by expanding credit and the money supply. And these same views are doing their bit to inhibit recovery in the world's depressed economies at this very moment.

The many variants of the hangover theory all go something like this: In the beginning, an investment boom gets out of hand. Maybe excessive money creation or reckless bank lending drives it, maybe it is simply a matter of irrational exuberance on the part of entrepreneurs. Whatever the reason, all that investment leads to the creation of too much capacity—of factories that cannot find markets, of office buildings that cannot find tenants. Since construction projects take time to complete, however, the boom can proceed for a while before its unsoundness becomes apparent. Eventually, however, reality strikes—investors go bust and investment spending collapses. The result is a slump whose depth is in proportion to the previous excesses. Moreover, that slump is part of the necessary healing process: The excess capacity gets worked off, prices and wages fall from their excessive boom levels, and only then is the economy ready to recover.

Except for that last bit about the virtues of recessions, this is not a bad story about investment cycles. Anyone who has watched the ups and downs of, say, Boston's real estate market over the past 20 years can tell you that episodes in which overoptimism and overbuilding are followed by a bleary-eyed morning after are very much a part of real life. But let's ask a seemingly silly question: Why should the ups and downs of investment demand lead to ups and downs in the economy as a whole? Don't say that it's obvious—although investment cycles clearly are associated with economywide recessions and recoveries in practice, a theory is supposed to explain observed correlations, not just assume them. And in fact the key to the Keynesian revolution in economic thought—a revolution that made hangover theory in general and Austrian theory in particular as obsolete as epicycles—was John Maynard Keynes' realization that the crucial question was not why investment demand sometimes declines, but why such declines cause the whole economy to slump.

A breakdown in logic

Here's the problem: As a matter of simple arithmetic, total spending in the economy is necessarily equal to total income (every sale is also a purchase, and vice versa). So if people decide to spend less on investment goods, doesn't that mean that they must be deciding to spend more on consumption goods—implying that an investment slump should always be accompanied by a corresponding consumption boom? And if so why should there be a rise in unemployment?

John Maynard Keynes (1883–1946) was an influential British economist who urged government intervention to stimulate the economy in a time of slump. He advocated that the government finance major projects, such as construction, and hire unemployed people to work on them. These people would then spend their wages, creating a demand for more goods and pulling the economy out of recession. Keynes' ideas were influential at the time of the New Deal program set up to alleviate the effects of the Great Depression of the 1930s.

Most modern hangover theorists probably don't even realize this is a problem for their story. Nor did those supposedly deep Austrian theorists answer the riddle. The best that von Hayek or Schumpeter could come up with was the vague suggestion that unemployment was a frictional problem created as the economy transferred workers from a bloated investment goods sector back to the production of consumer goods. (Hence their opposition to any attempt to increase demand: This would leave "part of the work of depression undone," since mass unemployment was part of the process of "adapting the structure of production.") But in that case, why doesn't the investment boom—which presumably requires a transfer of workers in the opposite direction—also generate mass unemployment? And anyway, this story bears little resemblance to what actually happens in a recession, when every industry—not just the investment sector—normally contracts.

The author uses quotations from the works of his opponents to back up his argument. The first snippet is from Schumpeter, the second from von Hayek.

As is so often the case in economics (or for that matter in any intellectual endeavor), the explanation of how recessions can happen, though arrived at only after an epic intellectual journey, turns out to be extremely simple. A recession happens when, for whatever reason, a large part of the private sector tries to increase its cash reserves at the same time. Yet, for all its simplicity, the insight that a slump is about an excess demand for money makes nonsense of the whole hangover theory. For if the problem is that collectively people want to hold more money than there is in circulation, why not simply increase the supply of money? You may tell me that it's not that simple, that during the previous boom businessmen made bad investments and banks made bad loans. Well, fine. Junk the bad investments and write off the bad loans. Why should this require that perfectly good productive capacity be left idle?

If Krugman is right, why do you think economists still debate the question? Can it really be that simple?

Appealing to conservatives

The hangover theory, then, turns out to be intellectually incoherent; nobody has managed to explain why bad investments in the past require the unemployment of good workers in the present. Yet the theory has powerful emotional appeal. Usually that appeal is strongest for conservatives, who can't stand the thought that positive action by governments (let alone—horrors!—printing money) can ever be a good idea. Some libertarians extol the Austrian theory, not because they have really thought that theory through, but because they feel the need for some prestigious alternative to the perceived statist implications of Keynesianism. And some people probably are attracted to Austrianism because they imagine that it devalues the intellectual pretensions of economics professors. But moderates and liberals are not immune to the theory's seductive charms—especially when it gives them a chance to lecture others on their failings.

Few Western commentators have resisted the temptation to turn Asia's economic woes into an occasion for moralizing on the region's past sins. How many articles have you read blaming Japan's current malaise on the excesses of the "bubble economy" of the 1980s—even though that bubble burst almost a decade ago? How many editorials have you seen warning that credit expansion in Korea or Malaysia is a terrible idea, because after all it was excessive credit expansion that created the problem in the first place?

The term "bubble economy" has come to mean a period of overconfident economic expansion, characterized by the bubblelike inflation of prices for assets, such as land and stocks, to unrealistically high levels.

Time to take the easy way out

And the Asians—the Japanese in particular—take such strictures seriously. One often hears that Japan is adrift because its politicians refuse to make hard choices, to take on vested interests. The truth is that the Japanese have been remarkably willing to make hard choices, such as raising taxes sharply in 1997. Indeed, they are in trouble partly because they insist on making hard choices, when what the economy really needs is to take the easy way out. The Great Depression happened largely because policy-makers imagined that austerity was the way to fight a recession; the not-so-great depression that has enveloped much of Asia has been worsened by the same instinct. Keynes had it right: Often, if not always, "it is ideas, not vested interests, that are dangerous for good or evil."

Summary

Jane Katz argues that recessions are probably inevitable. According to her, research suggests that there is no single underlying cause for all the slumps of the 20th century. Recessions are often the result, she contends, of a combination of factors, including unpredictable events not linked directly to the economy, such as war and technological change. What is clear, she argues, is that recessions happen when an economy is weak and unable to withstand these unpredictable events. However, she points out, some economists believe that recessions simply result from the interaction of economic forces during the preceding expansions. Katz notes that since World War II (1939-1945) recessions have been less frequent, and periods of growth have lasted longer, and she puts this down partly to better government policy. She concludes that "While it is possible to assess the economy's vulnerability and to implement policies that reduce its exposure to risk, there is no way to predict when the next recession will arrive or what its cause will be."

Economics professor Paul Krugman disagrees that recessions are inevitable. He argues particularly against the "hangover theory"—that slumps are the unavoidable but necessary price we pay for economic expansion. Krugman argues that this theory has strong appeal because it turns economics into "a tale of hubris and downfall." Conservatives, in particular, adhere to it because they dislike the idea that government intervention in the economy could be beneficial. Krugman believes that the Great Depression of the 1930s spread partly because influential economists believed austerity was the way to fight the slump, instead of encouraging people to spend. He concludes that the Asian depression of the 1990s was "worsened by the same instinct."

FURTHER INFORMATION:

 Books:

Buchholz, Todd G., *From Here to Economy: A Short Cut to Economic Literacy*. New York: Dutton, 1995.
Krugman, Paul R., *The Return of Depression Economics*. New York: W.W. Norton, 2000.
Rothbard, Murray N., *America's Great Depression*. Auburn, AL: Mises Institute, 2000.

Useful websites:

http://howstuffworks.com/recession.htm
Howstuffworks explanation of recessions, featuring definitions of economics terms.
http://howstuffworks.com/stock.htm
Similar site dealing with stocks and the stock market.
www.nber.org
National Bureau of Economic Research site.

The following debates in the Pro/Con series may also be of interest:

In this volume:

Topic 7 Are International Monetary Fund financial assistance policies harmful?

Topic 13 Does a high dollar harm the domestic economy?

In *U.S. History*:
Topic 8 Was the New Deal "new"?

ARE RECESSIONS INEVITABLE?

YES: Evidence shows that the U.S. economy has often been hit by a recession after a noneconomic event, such as a war

YES: By carefully monitoring the economy and using fiscal policy, the government can keep a recession at bay

NONECONOMIC FACTORS
Are recessions caused by noneconomic factors, such as wars?

MANAGING THE ECONOMY
Should the government intervene to prevent recessions?

NO: Economic factors, such as investment and profits, are far more likely to trigger a recession

NO: The government should leave well alone and let markets and the business cycle run their natural course

ARE RECESSIONS INEVITABLE? KEY POINTS

YES: Only through recession and a period of austerity can excess capacity be used up and wages and prices be brought back to sensible levels

YES: Recessions are needed to prevent the economy from "overheating"

BUSINESS CYCLES
Are recessions a necessary part of the business cycle?

NO: Recessions are bad for the economy and for society at large since they hit the most vulnerable sectors hardest

NO: Booms and busts are not good for the economy. Governments can avoid them with prompt action, such as encouraging spending and lowering interest rates at the first signs of slowdown.

Topic 3
ARE MONOPOLIES ALWAYS BAD?

YES
"DRUG MAKERS HIDING BEHIND FINANCIAL FIG LEAF"
FINALCALL.COM, FEBRUARY 7, 2002
RUSSELL MOKHIBER AND ROBERT WEISSMAN

NO
"THREATENING PHARMACEUTICAL INNOVATION"
COPLEY NEWS SERVICE, MAY 22, 2002
DOUG BANDOW

INTRODUCTION

A monopoly is a situation in which there is only one seller of a product or service in an economic market. This seller has complete control over the market price and dominates the production and distribution of a particular product or service. In order for a monopoly firm to retain its status, there must be barriers in place to prevent other companies from entering the market and competing. There are several types of potential barrier: (1) single ownership, in which a company has sole access to a key resource, such as a natural mineral deposit; (2) patent and copyright laws, which give one person or company exclusive rights to sell a product to the public; (3) setup costs, which make it prohibitively expensive for a new company to develop and produce a product—for example, the design and manufacture of automobiles; (4) marketing barriers, created when an existing company is closely identified with a specific product through advertising; (5) natural monopolies. A natural monopoly arises

when "economies of scale" result in just one firm producing in the marketplace—economies of scale mean that after initial setup costs, the greater the number of units produced, the cheaper the average cost of each unit becomes. Therefore a large, established firm can charge cheaper prices than a new firm just entering the market. A natural monopoly might also arise from a situation in which it is more practical for a single company to provide a product or service. For example, it would be impractical for more than one company to run water pipes under the ground to every tap in the country. Economists often categorize public utilities—water, electricity, gas, and telephone—and railroads as natural monopolies. Monopolies in these industries are encouraged by the government to achieve efficiency, but are also regulated to protect the public from possible abuses.

Many economists view monopolies as the opposite of a competitive market and consider them detrimental to the general public good. They argue that monopolies restrict output and raise prices, earning excessive profits that cannot be eroded by competing firms; that they are inefficient, producing less output than society desires; that they are under no obligation to choose the least costly method of production; and that they often waste their resources.

"If the market remains structured as it is currently, Microsoft will retain both the means and the incentive to do what it has done for years and restrict consumer choices, raise prices, and stifle innovation."
—STEPHEN HOUCK, GOVERNMENT LAWYER IN *U.S. V. MICROSOFT CORPORATION*, 1999

Government regulation and antitrust laws are in place to protect against monopolies. The three major antitrust laws are the Sherman Act (1890)—originally used to break up monopolies in the petroleum and tobacco industries—the Clayton Act (1914), and the Federal Trade Commission Act (1914). These measures prevent a single firm from taking over a market. They also prevent two or more firms from gaining monopoly power through merger or through collusion to fix prices or share markets exclusively between themselves. Government has

tried to take legal action to rein in highly dominant companies such as the software giant Microsoft. Lawyers acting for the government argued that such market domination is against the interests of competitors and consumers. Microsoft argued that its success is not in opposition to a competitive economy but is a result of it. Its market share has arisen as a result of entrepreneurship, and it should be allowed to enjoy the benefits.

The question of whether monopolies are a good or bad thing, and whether government intervention is fair, depends on a balance of interest between companies and consumers. Because different industries vary greatly, the issue is not always clear cut.

In the pharmaceutical industry monopolies are created through patents that grant companies the exclusive rights to produce and market a drug that they have developed for a certain period, normally 20 years. Yet the pharmaceutical industry is not subject to the same checks and balances as the public utilities—there are no regulatory price controls over the cost of drugs. Because of the nature of the product, as something that promotes good health and prevents disease and suffering, there are ethical questions over and above the usual issues of the general public good.

The following two articles examine the debate further and focus on monopolies in the pharmaceutical industry. In the first article Russell Mokhiber and Robert Weissman argue that U.S. drug companies work against the consumer interest. In the second article Doug Bandow asserts that the drug companies are crucial for the effective development and funding of new treatments and cures.

DRUG MAKERS HIDING BEHIND FINANCIAL FIG LEAF
Russell Mokhiber and Robert Weissman

Russell Mokhiber
is editor of the
weekly Corporate
Crime Reporter, and
Robert Weissman
is editor of the
Multinational
Monitor.

"Big Pharma"
means big
pharmaceutical
companies. A
generic drug is a
copy of another
drug, containing
the same active
ingredients. Generic
copies may be sold
after the patent on
a branded drug has
expired. Generic
drugs are generally
sold under their
chemical name
rather than under a
brand name.

The Tufts Center
for the Study of
Drug Development
was founded
in 1976 to
develop strategic
information to help
drug developers,
regulators, and
policymakers.
The study referred
to is How New
Drugs Move
through the
Development and
Approval Process
(2001). Go to
http://csdd.
tufts.edu/ for more
information.

YES

Drug prices in the United States are out of control, and rising. The reason is that the United States permits pharmaceuticals to be marketed by unregulated monopolies: Patent protection gives the drug companies monopoly control over their products. These companies face neither direct competition, nor price controls.

But what is the reason for the government grant of these patent monopolies (which often extend long beyond the official 20 years, thanks to a variety of Big Pharma "evergreening" tactics to block or delay the introduction of generic competition)?

Research and development costs

Leaving aside the raw political power of the pharmaceutical industry and its allies, the policy rationale for patent monopolies is the cost of drug development. According to the drug companies, the cost of researching and developing a new drug is $800 million.

The myth of astronomical drug development costs is the fig leaf behind which Big Pharma and its paid associates (inside and outside of government) hide to escape criticism for price gouging. If this myth were peeled away, Big Pharma would stand exposed. And the prospect of a more rational system of drug development and pricing would rise dramatically.

This matter could be resolved, simply, if the drug companies were to open their books and reveal their actual investments in research and development. Instead, they implausibly claim that this information would give away trade secrets and must remain proprietary.

The industry claim of $800 million costs per drug relies on a study from an industry-funded research center at Tufts University in Boston.

Tufts researchers supposedly had access to industry data to come up with their figure, but no one else is able to see the underlying data.

So if you choose to believe in this number, it is simply a matter of faith.

COMMENTARY: Drug pricing

In recent years the high prices of drugs and the large profits of pharmaceutical companies have been harshly criticized not only within the United States but also internationally. The situation in developing countries such as South Africa and Brazil has highlighted the often conflicting interests of large drugs companies and the people who need their products. The issue first came to widespread public attention in 1998, when 42 international drugs companies began court action against the South African government in *The Pharmaceutical Manufacturers' Association (PMA) v. The South African Government*. They brought this case after the South African government introduced Amendment 15 (1997) to the country's Medicines and Related Substances Control Act, thereby allowing cheap imports and the production of cheap generic forms of patented drugs.

A landmark case in making drugs affordable

The South African government had introduced the amendment to tackle the AIDS epidemic in its country. According to statistics compiled by the World Health Organization and the AIDS Foundation of South Africa, an estimated 4.7 million South Africans are infected with AIDS. Many of the sufferers are among the world's poorest people, and neither they nor their government can afford to buy adequate quantities of patented AIDS drugs. However, some countries—notably India, Thailand, and Brazil—have thriving generics industries, producing copies of branded drugs at a fraction of the cost. In the South African court case large drugs companies, such as GlaxoSmithKline, Merck & Co, and Bristol-Myers Squibb, argued that these generic products would lead to an unacceptable breach of their intellectual property rights, and that their resulting loss of profit would prevent them from developing new drugs. After three years of court action and a high-profile campaign by humanitarian groups, such as Oxfam and Médecins sans Frontières, the drugs companies withdrew their suit in April 2001.

Disagreement continues on the pricing of drugs

Although this retreat was a major step forward for developing nations, the issue of drug pricing remains unresolved. In 2002 negotiators at the World Trade Organization (WTO) tried to get agreement from the organization's 144 members for a two-tier system of drug pricing. Under this proposal poor countries would buy drugs from Western pharmaceutical companies at cost price, while the rest of the world would pay full price. The measure is aimed specifically at sub-Saharan Africa in order to prevent widespread and devastating diseases such as malaria and tuberculosis, and to treat AIDS. By February 2003, 143 countries had agreed to the measure, but the United States blocked the proposal. The issue appears likely to dominate talks on global trade and subsequent WTO meetings.

To get closer to the actual figures for the cost of drug development and company per drug expenditures on R&D [research and development], you have to peel away the assumptions and built-in biases of the Tufts industry study.

Explaining the costs

Approximately half of the Tufts-industry estimates are attributed to financing costs, known as opportunity cost of capital. Money invested in drug R&D could have been invested in treasury bonds. While the bonds would start returning revenues right away, R&D returns are not realized for years, until a drug is discovered, developed, approved and put on the market. So in the Tufts-industry study, a "cost" of development is the forsworn income during the period of development.

This is all true, as far as it goes, but it is not how people normally think about "cost." As James Love of the Consumer Project on Technology says, it is the equivalent of saying the cost of a car is not the sticker price, but the sticker price plus interest payments on a car loan.

Exacerbating the problem, the researchers may pick an unreasonably high interest rate. They may also set the period for drug development as too long—in the Tufts-industry model, relatively small delays in getting the drug to market leads to big increases in the overall cost.

Different types of drugs

The Tufts-industry estimate is for the cost of new chemical entities for which the industry was wholly responsible—that is, where there was no substantial public contribution to R&D.

It turns out, however, that the vast majority of new drugs Big Pharma brings to market do not involve new chemical compounds. A May 2002 study by the National Institute for Health Care Management (NIHCM) Foundation found that two-thirds of the prescription drugs approved by the FDA between 1989 and 2000 were modified versions of existing medicines or identical to drugs already on the market (and only about 15 percent were both new and deemed by the FDA to provide significant improvement over existing medicines).

Pharma denies it, but there is every reason to believe these less novel products are far cheaper to bring to market.

Then there's the not insignificant fact that the case of drugs brought to market without government support is the exception, not the norm.

The Consumer Project on Technology (CPTech) is a grant-funded, nonprofit organization founded in 1995. Currently CPTech is focusing on intellectual property rights and health care, electronic commerce, and competition policy.

Do you think that pharmaceutical companies should be allowed to charge full prices for drugs that are copies or slight modifications of existing drugs?

The Food and Drug Administration (FDA) is the government organization that regulates the new drugs that are allowed onto the market.

The federal government supports an enormous amount of research, and funds the earliest and riskiest portions of the R&D process: basic research and the earlier phases of clinical trials.

Finally, the Tufts-industry figures seem to wildly inflate the cost of clinical testing. Looking at company filings with the IRS [Internal Revenue Service] for tax credits on research for "orphan drugs" (drugs which treat small populations), however, the Consumer Project on Technology found that—adjusted for risk—drug companies report expenditures of only $7.9 million on clinical trials, less than 1 percent of the overall estimate.

Even if the costs for this category of drugs are below average, as the industry claims—even if they were, implausibly, a tenth of the average—this would still suggest a much lower total development cost than the Tufts-industry estimate. Any honest examination of available evidence on the costs of drug development suggests the United States—and most of the rest of the world, which thanks to the U.S./industry strong-arming tactics in international trade negotiations, now maintains or soon will adopt U.S.-style patent rules—is massively overcompensating Big Pharma for its work in bringing drugs to market.

Time for action

With the U.S. healthcare system bursting at the seams, seniors draining their bank accounts to buy drugs, and millions of people around the world going without medicines, the time has come for fundamental reform. Meaningful reform might include ending the industry's patent extension tricks, licensing drugs developed with public monies on a non-exclusive basis to permit price reducing competition (or at least permitting competition where prices are excessive), and considering rollbacks to the 20-year patent term and the adoption of price controls. But even these measures may be inadequate. Why couldn't the government simply take over the job of drug development, and then let private companies manufacture and distribute medicines in a competitive environment—doing away with patent monopolies on drugs altogether?

The government helps fund research and development through the National Institutes for Health, an agency of the Department of Health and Human Services.

The author is referring to World Trade Organization (WTO) rules on patents, which are based on the U.S. system of 20-year patent protection. Before the creation of the WTO in 1995 few countries in the developing world had intellectual property laws.

President George W. Bush addressed the cost of health care in his State of the Union address on January 28, 2003. Go to http://www.whitehouse.gov/news/releases/2003/01/20030128-21.html for more information.

In some countries such as Canada, the United Kingdom, and France drug prices are regulated by the government. Can you think of any reasons why the authors' suggested solution might not be workable?

THREATENING PHARMACEUTICAL INNOVATION
Doug Bandow

Doug Bandow is a senior fellow of the Cato Institute, a nonprofit public policy research foundation based in Washington, D.C. He worked in the Reagan administration as special assistant to the president from 1981 to 1982 and has written widely on economics and foreign policy.

NO

America's economic prosperity is built upon productivity and innovation, yet the entrepreneurial process is under constant attack. Sometimes the assault is direct, as in the case of Microsoft. More often it is indirect, as in the case of the pharmaceutical industry.

Federal and state officials are seeking to control prices, limit sales, destroy industry marketing networks and undercut patent rights. These efforts could hobble an industry that today dominates the globe while providing manifold health benefits through new drug discoveries.

Pharmaceutical innovation depends on the patents, which allow companies to profit from their research. Otherwise the industry would not spend more than $30 billion a year to develop new products.

Indeed, industry R&D averages 20 percent of sales, five times the American average. The industry figures that it spends an average of nearly $900 million per drug.

The Drug Price Competition and Patent Term Restoration Act, commonly known as the Hatch–Waxman Act (1984), extended patent terms for innovative drugs. It also reduced the testing requirements for approval of generic drugs, allowing them to enter the market—and so cut into the sales of brand-name drugs—more quickly. Go to http://www.cbo.gov/showdoc.cfm?index=655&sequence=2 for more information.

Balancing financial risks

Even such a significant investment doesn't guarantee results. Of every 5,000 to 10,000 substances reviewed, only one ultimately makes it onto the market. Just a third of them actually make money. These few must pay for everything— research, administration and costly "dry holes."

No wonder then, that doctors support pharmaceutical patents. In a recent survey, 98 percent of physicians said that continued drug development is important or somewhat important for patient care.

Unfortunately, however, drugs do not just appear. Three-fourths of doctors opined that patent rights were very important as an incentive for drug production; 23 percent said that they were somewhat important.

Nevertheless, patents do not run forever, creating room for a vibrant generic industry. In 1984, Congress approved legislation relieving the regulatory burden on generics, which have gone from one-fifth to half of the market. This has tempered drug prices and restrained pharmaceutical costs.

COMMENTARY: Research and development

Research and development (R&D) lie at the heart of the pharmaceutical industry, holding the key to the invention of new drugs and treatments that promote good health, relieve suffering, and treat disease. They are also among the main costs incurred by drugs companies—although some economists, pressure groups, and commentators dispute the extent of these costs. Since R&D is one of the highest costs involved in bringing a new drug to the market, the way that it determines price is a key issue.

Timescales and risks

Research and development for a successful new drug take a long time, usually around 12 years, and the failure rate is high. A 1993 report by the Congressional Office of Technology Assessment, *Pharmaceutical R&D: Costs, Risks, and Rewards*, stated: "For every 10,000 new medicines created in the lab, a thousand make it to animal tests, 10 end up being promising enough to test in human beings, and one or two will make it to market." Companies have to satisfy the Food and Drug Administration that products are both safe and effective before they are allowed on the market.

Who pays for research and development?

Pharmaceutical companies fund a large proportion of R&D of new products. The top 10 drug companies are reported to spend an average of 20 percent of their revenue in this area. However, the government also contributes both directly and indirectly to development costs. The National Institutes for Health (NIH), an agency of the Department of Health and Human Services and one of the world's leading medical research centers, conducts and supports much of the early work involved in developing new drugs. Similarly, tax advantages mean that the money companies spend on R&D and marketing can be offset against tax.

Time for change?

In order to reduce the price consumers pay for new drugs, many critics argue that the way R&D is funded and protected by patents should be reviewed. An increasing number of commentators inside the health-care industry would like to see the government impose price regulations on pharmaceutical companies, as it does on public utilities. In response to industry claims that such moves would stifle innovation, they argue that existing profit margins are too high, and companies could afford to reduce their profits. They also suggest that the government could provide increased resources and incentives, as it has already done with the Orphan Drugs Act (1983). This act offers support to firms to help develop treatments for rare diseases or conditions that would otherwise generate low returns for drugs companies due to the small market.

Yet patent battles have become common. The FDA's unnecessarily lengthy approval process undercuts the value of patents, causing Congress to allow for their extension if, for instance, a manufacturer adds a new chemical to the drug or develops a new use for the drug.

At the same time, a variety of interests often strongly resist patent extensions. The Federal Trade Commission just settled a case with Biovail Corp. involving its attempt to maintain the patent on the blood pressure medicine Tiazac. Controversy also has dogged AstraZeneca's effort to extend the patent life for Prilosec, which combats heartburn, Myers Squibb's Glucopohage, which treats diabetes, and Schering-Plough's Claritin, which mitigates allergies.

Protecting the rights of the drug companies

Whatever the specifics of individual cases, there is nothing wrong in principle with research firms attempting to extend their patents within the law. After all, the companies were created to make money; if they didn't, they wouldn't invest in R&D. The very purpose of patents is to provide a temporary monopoly to allow companies to enjoy the fruit of their labor.

Some legislators would change the law—Sens. Charles Schumer (D-N.Y.) and John McCain (R-Ariz.) want to close the "loopholes" that allow patent extensions. Pharmacist Lee Vermeulen of the University of Wisconsin suggests that the Food and Drug Administration block medicines which don't offer a significant advance over existing products: "We can't afford this kind of nonsense from the industry."

Health insurers are working to move patented products into the over-the-counter market. Some industry critics hope to discourage use of newer, patented drugs developed to replace older, off-patent medicines by banning consumer advertising, for instance. Medical reporter M. Alexander Otto, writing in the *Washington Post*, even complained that Schering-Plough had priced its antihistamine Clarinex lower than the drug it superseded, Claritin.

Any attempt to limit patent protection creates risks, however. Pharmaceuticals are well worth the cost: not only do they extend and improve the quality of life, but they reduce other medical expenditures, particularly for hospitalization and surgery.

No surprise, then, more than two-thirds of doctors worry that weakening patent protection will reduce research on rarer conditions and actually raise consumer prices, by forcing recovery of costs in a shorter period of

Go to http://corporate.findlaw.com/industry/drugs/index.html to learn more about these cases.

Is there anything wrong in principle with drug companies attempting to extend their patents? Are there any moral considerations?

The strengthening of patent protection through the Orphan Drug Act has resulted in the production of more than 200 new drugs for rare diseases since the act was introduced in 1983. Very few drugs of this type were produced before the legislation. Rare "orphan" diseases are those that affect fewer than 200,000 Americans and include sickle cell anemia, Tay-Sachs disease, and hemophilia.

time. A majority also fear that the result will be fewer generics, since the latter ultimately derive from brand drug development.

Advertising informs consumers, alerting some people to conditions and cures of which they were unaware; even doctors have trouble keeping up with the flood of medical advances. Moreover, physicians remain the gatekeeper, reviewing the appropriateness of a particular treatment.

Is advertising the best way to inform the public about new drugs?

Even "me-too" drugs often offer important advantages for some people. Doctors prescribing and patients taking newer products, not special interests lobbying politicians, should determine the relative advantages of, say, Schering-Plough's Clarinex over Claritin, or AstraZeneca's Nexium over Prilosec. They should decide whether any improvements are worth the added costs.

Is it practical for doctors and patients to select which products to use? Does it take too much effort to keep up with developments?

Generics have become a critical component of the drug market. But without patents, there would be no brand name medicines to copy. In attempting to lower health-care costs, we must not kill the pharmaceutical Golden Goose.

Summary

Russell Mokhiber and Robert Weissman argue that the price of drugs is increasing steeply. They are skeptical about claims that pharmaceutical companies could not afford to carry out research and development if they lost their patents or faced competition that forced them to reduce prices. The article also challenges the claim that it costs $800 million to develop a new drug and suggests that, although this figure is frequently quoted, it has never been convincingly substantiated by an independent authority. The authors are critical of the fact that part of this figure is made up of the loss of interest that would have been earned if the money had been left in the bank. The article then quotes research that shows that two-thirds of medicines prescribed over a 12-year period were no more than modified versions of drugs that were already on the market. The article concludes with a call for drug development to be administered by the government.

Doug Bandow claims that such a move would reduce productivity and stifle innovation. He states that pharmaceutical companies will carry out the requisite research and development—the cost of which the author puts even higher, at $900 million per drug—only if they can obtain patents that will protect their new products for long enough to let them turn their investments into profits. It criticizes the Food and Drug Administration (FDA) for taking too long to approve new drugs and the Federal Trade Commission (FTC) for opposing applications by manufacturers to extend their patents. In the author's view both policies will discourage research by companies, which, after all, exist to make profits and could not go on without them.

FURTHER INFORMATION:

Books:

Geisst, Charles R., *Monopolies in America: Empire Builders and Their Enemies from Jay Gould to Bill Gates*. New York: Oxford University Press, 1997.

Haas-Wilson, Deborah, *Managed Care and Monopoly Power: The Antitrust Challenge*. Cambridge, MA: Harvard University Press, 2003.

Useful websites:

www.capitalism.org/faq/monopolies.htm
Frequently asked questions about monopolies.
Evaluation of monopolies in the pharmaceutical industry.
www.stthom.edu/cbes/oje/articles/white.html
Detailed analysis of competition, price fairness, and regulation in the pharmaceutical industry.
www.guardian.co.uk/microsoft/0,2759,178712,00.html
Articles on Microsoft trial and related websites.

The following debates in the Pro/Con series may also be of interest:

In this volume:

Topic 1 Is a free market the best way to organize world trade?

Topic 8 Do transnational corporations have more influence on the world economy than national governments?

In *U.S. Foreign Policy*:

Topic 5 Does big business have too much influence on foreign policy?

ARE MONOPOLIES ALWAYS BAD?

YES: In many cases it would make no financial sense for more than one firm to provide services to every home

YES: Competition among companies helps keep the market innovative and keeps prices down. This benefits the consumer.

ECONOMY OF SCALE
Can one large company provide a better service than several smaller ones?

COMPETITION
Is competition always a good thing?

NO: Small companies are usually more flexible and provide better services than vast conglomerates

NO: In many markets competition means lots of different manufacturers making products that are substantially the same as all the others

ARE MONOPOLIES ALWAYS BAD? KEY POINTS

YES: Some of the services provided by government-monitored monopolies would be cut if they were in unregulated, private hands because they are unprofitable

YES: Governments can act to prevent overcharging and other abuses

CHECKS AND BALANCES
Can monopolies work if they are strictly regulated?

NO: External monitors can easily be misled into thinking that a service cannot be improved because there is nothing to compare it with

NO: Drugs firms are granted patents but make no effort to supply their products more cheaply to poor people

HOW TO WRITE A RESEARCH PAPER

"My aim is to put down on paper what I see and what I feel in the best and simplest way."

—ERNEST HEMINGWAY (1899–1961)

At some point in your academic career you will have to write a research paper. To do this to the best of your ability, it is important to prepare well and to follow set procedures. If you read and do the following, it will help you achieve the best possible grade. It is important to remain calm and focused from the beginning stages right through to when you hand your paper in to your teacher. These procedures can be applied to any assignment you have at school, college, or later in life.

Getting started

In order to write a good paper, it is important to be properly prepared. Make sure that you completely understand your assignment: Read the teacher's instructions thoroughly. If you are unsure about anything, ask before you begin. Be certain that you know what kind of paper you have been asked to write, and bear in mind its purpose at all times: Is it a report? Should it be scholarly? Is it informal? Can you assume that the readers have knowledge of the subject?

Choosing a subject

Your teacher may give you a list of questions from which to select your research topic, or you may be asked to choose something yourself from the curriculum. Try to find something that interests you. The more enthusiastic you are about the subject, the more willing you will be to research it thoroughly. It is important to limit your subject and to choose something manageable. If the topic is 20th-century U.S. history, jot down a list of issues that are of interest. You may find that the topics on your list relate to a particular year or decade, or are focused on U.S. relations with one country, for example. Try to turn the headings on your list into questions—if you are looking at U.S.–Middle Eastern relations, you could ask, "Was the Persian Gulf War about oil?" Avoid subjects that are too technical or specialized or about something that you do not fully understand. Visit the library and surf the Internet to find out how much research information is available. The more reliable information you can find, the easier it will be to research and write your paper.

Researching

For general information use dictionaries, almanacs, and encyclopedias. Most are available in print and electronic formats. Search engines such as www.google.com and www.yahoo.com are useful starting points, but pay attention to domain names. Web addresses ending in *.edu* usually denote an educational institution, those ending in *.gov* a government site, or *.org* a nonprofit organization. Some government sites may have a particular political bias; and while many .*com* sites are excellent, be aware that some are purely commercial, and the information they give may need to be checked against a reliable source. The Internet is not the only source available, and many primary source collections are not online. Go to a good, local school, or college library to find information. Specialized magazines and newspapers are also a good source of knowledge. Take notes, print or photocopy any information that you think is relevant, and remember it is essential to record things accurately; that will help prevent plagiarism. You must cite your sources correctly, including the title, author, publisher, URL, and the location where you found the material. While you are researching, keep your list of questions in mind. Ask yourself if you are compiling information that supports or opposes any of the questions.

Finding your thesis

Once you have chosen your subject, in a sentence note your thesis statement or the main point of your research paper. Most of your essay will consist of argument and evidence to support this statement. Sometimes the thesis is clear from the research material you have obtained; sometimes it emerges slowly when you bring your notes and evidence together into a convincing argument. Organizing your notes will help you spot if there are holes in your research and if you need to go back to the library, to certain books, or the Internet. Try to determine if there are any gaps in your research as quickly as possible.

Making an outline and organizing your notes

A good outline is key to a good research paper. The outline helps you think through your argument carefully and to organize it clearly before you begin writing. The outline should show you if your points flow logically and will enable you to arrange your notes in such a way as to support your argument.

Essay structure

Your essay must be organized and well structured. The introduction should state the thesis of your paper clearly and explain briefly what you are going to discuss. The main body of your paper should present the arguments to support your thesis in a logical sequence. A poorly defended argument will not get you an A. The conclusion should restate your thesis, summarize your arguments, and generally explain how you reached your conclusion.

Revising and proofreading the paper

You may have to write several drafts before you get it right. It is useful to reread your instructions to ensure that you have met the requirements. Remember the purpose of the paper, and rearrange your ideas if necessary. Do not be afraid to edit out irrelevant information; if it does not support your thesis, it will only detract from your main argument. Read your essay carefully to check for spelling or grammatical errors. Be clear and concise. Present your paper neatly, since that will make a difference. Ask yourself: Is this the best I can do?

Topic 4
DO UNIONS ADVERSELY AFFECT ECONOMIC GROWTH?

YES
"UNION TACTICS COST JOBS"
*WASHINGTON TIME*S, MARCH 13, 2003
STEPHEN MOORE

NO
"LABOR UNIONS GOOD FOR ECONOMIES AND EQUITY, SAYS WORLD BANK"
US.ONE.WORLD.NET
JIM LOBE

INTRODUCTION

A union is a group of workers who form an organization to negotiate on their behalf for favorable salaries, benefits such as pensions and health insurance, and flexibility for work and family needs. This is collective bargaining, so called because it differs from the individual bargaining for terms and conditions that a nonunion employee must do with his or her employer. Unions have historically helped secure safety in the workplace, combat discrimination, encourage worker education, and allow workers and employers to negotiate as equals. Unions have also provided a check against employers' power; they have campaigned for laws ending child labor, establishing eight-hour workdays, protecting workers' safety, creating Social Security and unemployment insurance benefits, and setting minimum wage requirements.

Critics of unions have long argued, however, that by protecting weak or lazy workers along with the strong, they promote inefficiency. Unions are also often accused of resisting technological improvements because they cost jobs. Critics claim that unions in expanding industries tend to become complacent about their prosperity and unreasonable in their demands. When negotiating with employers, the ultimate bargaining tool is the threat to withdraw their members' labor—a strike. Since that could have a major effect on a company's profits, employers must weigh carefully whether they will lose more by agreeing to union demands or by holding out against terms they consider unreasonable. Critics argue that unions' demands have sometimes weakened the companies that employ them, put pressure on business, and hindered the economic growth of the country as a whole: There is anecdotal evidence that unions do put undue pressure on corporations in the United States, leading to the loss of jobs.

The Wagner Act of 1935 established relatively favorable legal conditions under which unions could operate by protecting workers from "unfair practices" such as discriminating against union members. It was amended in 1947 by the Taft–Hartley Act. By requiring union leaders to affirm that they were not communists, the act marginalized radicals in the union movement, but was also used as a weapon against many noncommunists whose effectiveness as organizers made them a target for employers.

"With all their faults, trade unions have done more for humanity than any other organization of men that ever existed."

—CLARENCE DARROW,

LAWYER AND WRITER (1909)

Taft–Hartley also restricted the ability of unions to organize in new areas (their representation was weak in the South and West). Despite this act, union membership continued to grow because of industrial expansion in the Northeast. The proportion of U.S. workers in unions reached its highest, more than 30 percent, in the early 1950s, while the highest total number of union members (22.5 million) was reached in 1975, since when it has declined continuously.

Since the 1970s employers have made it increasingly difficult for unions to organize by classifying many jobs as "supervisory," thus barring holders from union membership. Complaints about employers' "unfair practices" also rose sevenfold between 1955 and 1980. Another reason for union decline was that new employees, often women and teenagers, had little loyalty to traditional unions. The final, and possibly the most important, reason was that unions achieved wages substantially above those paid to nonunion workers. This meant that companies with union workers were forced to cut jobs.

Since the mid-1990s the situation has changed again. The rate of membership decline has slowed due to expansion in the public sector, and overall membership was the same in 2002 as it was in 1997, according to the AFL–CIO (American Federation of Labor–Congress of Industrial Organizations). Roughly 13 million American workers are currently members of unions, or 13.2 percent of the total working population.

With the end of Soviet communism and the subsequent acceleration of globalization unions and labor standards have moved onto the international agenda. Advocates of unions claim that strong unions ensure a better-paid workforce, meaning a stronger economy (since workers are also consumers) and a stronger, less volatile political and social system, thus creating a better investment climate.

The following two articles examine the debate further. In the first, journalist Stephen Moore cites examples of situations in which he claims unions are dragging their employers down. Conversely, the second article, by Jim Lobe for OneWorld U.S., looks at a World Bank study that defends union activity on the grounds that it promotes both greater social equality and growth for national economies.

UNION TACTICS COST JOBS
Stephen Moore

The latest statistics released this month from the U.S. Department of Labor indicate 2002 was another dismal year for labor unions. Private sector unions lost more than 400,000 jobs. Only the public sector gained union jobs. At no time in the last 50 years have unions represented a smaller percentage of the American work force than today.

To understand the sad demise of the unions, consider the case of the unions' spat with United and American Airlines. United and American both lost roughly $3 billion last year, or almost $5 million a day. Both these once great and profitable airlines are perilously close to being grounded permanently—as were Eastern and TWA in the 1990s. One factor behind the sudden fall of these airlines is extravagant unionized salaries that have risen to in some cases 50 percent above the industry average.

Destructive impulse

The machinists, pilots and flight attendant unions have refused to budge in renegotiating contracts with these companies that are bleeding cash. Meanwhile, discount airlines that are much less hamstrung by unions, like JetBlue and Southwest, are whipping United in every category of service and efficiency.

One can only wonder whether the union bosses fighting United and American have lost all sense of economic reality. With salaries that can exceed $100,000 per worker, if labor costs are not cut in the next several months, there will be no jobs at all for the union to fight for. Federal officials cited out-of-control salaries as a primary cause for turning down United's recent $1.5 billion bailout request.

The purpose of unions is to negotiate favorable salaries for their workers—but certainly not at the expense of extinguishing jobs. The union movement in America is losing hundreds of thousands of card-carrying members every year precisely because new 21st-century industries refuse to deal with militant unions.

The airlines case is not the only one where unions have engaged in self-destructive behavior of late. Last year, Transit

Other factors that have been blamed for the loss of revenue have included a reduction in air travel due to war and fear of terrorism, the downturn in the economy, and the 2003 SARS outbreak (see Volume 17, New Science, pages 72–73).

In April 2003 agreements were reached by both United and American with unions representing pilots, flight attendants, and ground crew. In American's case the deal was almost lost when it emerged that the company had failed to disclose that it was protecting the pension and bonus privileges of its top 45 executives. American's chairman had to resign in a bid to defuse the row. See www.bizjournals. com/dallas/ stories/ 200/04/21/ daily25.html for further details.

COMMENTARY: U.S. labor unions

Labor unions have four main activities: to recruit new members, to represent their members in negotiations with their employers when discussing pay and conditions, to organize strikes when necessary in support of their members' demands, and to lobby for or support politicians who favor labor unions. U.S. labor unions have traditionally been far less radical and politicized than their European counterparts: U.S. unions tend to concentrate more on their members' terms and conditions.

Early unions

The first major labor group to form in the United States was the American Federation of Labor (AFL), which was started in 1886 by Samuel Gompers (1850–1924). Samuel Gompers had come to the United States from London, England, as a boy. He worked as an apprentice cigarmaker before becoming leader of the national Cigar Makers Union. His aim was to help workers like himself. The AFL represented only skilled workers, and its aim was "To protect the skilled labor of America from being reduced to beggary and to sustain the standard of American workmanship and skill."

The most significant breakthrough in workers' right came in 1914 with the Clayton Act. This law legalized strikes, boycotts, and peaceful picketing, as well as limiting the used of injunctions in industrial disputes. For the first time it made legal the concept that "the labor of a human being is not a commodity or article of commerce."

AFL–CIO

The next major development happened in 1935, when the first industrial unions, under the Committee for Industrial Organizations (CIO), were founded. This organization represented all workers, both skilled and unskilled, in entire industries. At first, the AFL and CIO were very antagonistic toward each other, but in 1955 the two labor groups merged to become the AFL–CIO, the main labor organization in the United States.

Unions today

Since the 1970s there has been steady decline in the numbers of union members and union influence. As traditional industries have shrunk, the economy has become less reliant on industrial jobs. Instead, there has been a shift toward high-technology and service industries. Americans today are more likely to be well-educated, professional white-collar workers.

In 2002 it was estimated that about 14.7 percent of the total male workforce were union members and 11.6 percent of the total female workforce. The largest union is the Teamsters. Initially the Teamsters represented truck drivers and workers in related industries, but today it also represents labor in clerical, high-technology, and service industries.

Ronald Reagan (1911–) is the only U.S. president to have led a union: The Screen Actors Guild.

workers went on strike demanding massive pay increases from an all-but-bankrupt municipal agency.

The transit workers already receive salaries 30 percent to 40 percent above comparable skilled private sector jobs.

The dockworker work stoppage in California this past October involved union complaints against the evils of technological progress. ...

Most recently, the Communications Workers of America launched a $2 million ad campaign against Verizon, the Baby Bell of the Northeast. As even the most casual investor knows, the last three years have been brutally unkind to the telecom industry. In 2000, the telecom sector contracted by 28 percent and bled almost $1.7 trillion in lost share values. More than half-a-million telecom workers have lost their jobs.

The CWA strategy of blasting Verizon for laying off 3,500 workers makes as much sense as Kobe Bryant and Allen Iverson running TV ads encouraging fans not to go to any more NBA games.

A more realistic approach

Union membership as a share of the work force has fallen by half over the past 30 years or so, according to the Public Service Research Foundation. Today only roughly 1 in 6 workers is a dues-paying union member and the percentage of private sector union workers is much lower than that. Only public sector unionism is growing. Pollster Scott Rasmussen has pointed out that on Election Day, 3 times as many voters were stockowners than union members. These workers understand that their 401(k) plans and their individual retirement account nest eggs depend on the profitability of American industry.

As a United Airlines frequent flyer traveler, I sure hope the unions come to their senses and allow new management to make the reforms necessary to cut costs. There is no law of economics that says airlines have to lose money. Southwest has proven that.

Saving United and American airlines will save union jobs. But only when union officials realize that in this industry, as with telecom, and so many others, when they destroy the companies that hire their workers, they destroy themselves.

The dispute between the Pacific Maritime Association and the International Longshore and Warehouse Union began with a lockout after allegations of a work "slowdown," which the ILWU said was in response to safety fears. The PMA countered that safety was only an issue because the ILWU insisted on tracking and marking containers by hand to preserve jobs instead of automating the process, as has been done in more modern ports. The two sides reached a tentative agreement on November 1, 2002.

Another reason that has been cited for the fall in union membership is that the Taft–Hartley Act of 1947 prohibits supervisors from joining unions. That makes it possible for employers to classify white-collar jobs as supervisory, preventing holders from joining a union.

LABOR UNIONS GOOD FOR ECONOMIES AND EQUITY, SAYS WORLD BANK
Jim Lobe

NO

Washington: In a major policy statement, the World Bank said Wednesday that labor unions are good both for promoting greater equity within societies and for national economies.

In a report based on more than a thousand studies of the effects of labor unions and collective bargaining on the performance of national economies, the Bank found that workers who belong to trade unions earn higher wages, work fewer hours, receive more training, and have longer job tenure on average, than their non-unionized counterparts.

What are some of the advantages for an economy as a whole if workers are well paid and have longer job tenure? What are the disadvantages?

Unionization and income inequality

High rates of unionization also lead to lower inequality of earnings, especially for women and minority groups, and can improve economic performance in the form of lower unemployment and inflation, higher productivity, and speedier adjustments to economic shocks, according to the report, "Unions and Collective Bargaining: Economic Effects in a Global Environment."

Go to web.worldbank.org to see the World Bank's own summary of the report.

Good industrial relations between labor and capital can lead to a more stable and productive economy, according to Mamphela Ramphele, the World Bank's managing director, who introduced the report at the Bank's headquarters in Washington, D.C. Wednesday afternoon. "Coordination among social partners can promote better investment climates while also fostering a fairer distribution of output," she said.

The report, which resulted in part from a dialogue over recent years between the International Labour Organization (ILO) in Geneva, the Brussels-based International Confederation of Free Trade Unions (ICFTU) and the Bank, comes amid ongoing debate about the impact of globalization, or the increasing integration of national economies around the world, on social welfare and solidarity.

"Labor standards are now a prominent item on the international agenda and are likely to stay there for a long time to come," said Zafiris Tzannatos, the report's lead author.

Polish union leader and later president of Poland (1990–1995), Lech Wałęsa, after his negotiations with the government in the Lenin Shipyard, Gdansk, August 27, 1980. The talks gave workers in Poland the right to form free trade unions outside government supervision.

"[They] can no longer be the concern of just individual governments but also of the entire international community."

Skeptics

Globalization skeptics have expressed concern that countries that adopt lower labor standards and ban independent labor

COMMENTARY: The case of Poland

Since Poland, along with other European satellites of the Soviet Union, called themselves "workers' states," and unions represent workers, communist governments could not afford to be seen to disallow unions. Governments in such countries therefore created compliant, party-run unions that could be relied on to agree to whatever terms were offered by government, and whose real job was to manage the workers and contain any dissatisfaction.

This situation was maintained in Poland until the late 1970s. In the summer of 1980 sudden price hikes of basic foodstuffs in Poland led to an unofficial strike—a courageous and provocative act that could have led to the strikers being branded "anticommunists"—at the shipyards in Gdansk. To simple demands for an increase in pay the strikers, led by the electrician Lech Wałęsa, soon added broader political aims, including the right to form unions independent of government control, the right to strike legally, an end to censorship, and the release of people imprisoned for political "crimes." The groundswell of popular support caught the government off guard, and seeking to contain the movement, it agreed to these concessions in August 1980. This led to the formation the following month of Solidarność ("Solidarity"), the first free trade union in Poland in four decades. By the middle of the following year Solidarność and its offshoot, the farmers' union Wiejska Solidarność ("Rural Solidarity"), had some 10 million members—a quarter of the population. Moderates, led by Wałęsa, wanted to restrict the movement to what they considered achievable aims, working within the communist system, while radicals wanted to use Solidarność as a means of destabilizing the government and challenging the entire structure of the state.

While Wałęsa and Solidarność were denounced in the Soviet Union and Eastern Europe, they were lionized in the West for throwing off the shackles of repression, especially by governments on the right such as those of Britain and the United States. Martial law was imposed in Poland in December 1981, Solidarność was banned, and Wałęsa was jailed for nearly a year. President Ronald Reagan in an address to the nation condemned the Polish government saying, "They have answered the stirrings of liberty with brute force, mass arrests, and the setting up of concentration camps." Solidarność spent most of the 1980s as a quasi-underground organization, though Wałęsa, its public face, was awarded the Nobel Peace Prize in 1983. The Polish population returned to their traditional means of distributing information clandestinely, such as underground presses, illicit radio broadcasts, and reading out foreign newspapers in church. Only in the late 1980s, after the Gorbachev reforms in the Soviet Union, was it finally possible to liberalize Eastern Europe, and Solidarność reemerged as a political force in the free elections of 1989. Its work as a reform movement done, it has since refocused on the normal concerns of a labor union.

unions gain [an] unfair advantage in attracting foreign investment over those with higher standards and strong unions. Some have charged that the Bank itself, in urging reforms in poor countries that are designed to attract foreign investment, has actually contributed to this process and weakened union activities in many countries.

For instance, World Bank policies in the past have been blamed for the increased use of children to work in the garment industry in countries such as Bangladesh and Honduras as a means of reducing labor costs.

The Bank has long had [an] agnostic attitude toward labor unions and their impact on national economies, but the new report is likely to make it seem more supportive, particularly in light of its self-described mission to reduce poverty.

"The need for workers, employers and governments to find solutions that cut poverty through both growth and better distribution of income is becoming increasingly urgent in an era of globalization," according to Robert Holzmann, the Bank's director of social protection....

Unions better for workers?

The report found that union members and other workers covered by collective bargaining agreements in both industrialized and developing countries tend to get significantly higher average wages than those who are not affiliated with a union. It also found that union membership reduces wage differences between skilled and unskilled workers and between men and women.

Coordination of bargaining involves groups of employers on one side and groups of unions on the other, all bargaining in a single process to achieve a result that can be applied across an industry rather than to one isolated employer. The unions involved vary according to the industry.

Moreover, countries with highly-coordinated collective bargaining tend to be associated with lower and less persistent unemployment, lower earning inequality, and fewer and shorter strikes than uncoordinated ones. In contrast, fragmented unionism and many different union confederations within a national economy or sector are often associated with higher inflation and jobless rates, according to the report. Such positive assessments were greeted with enthusiasm by ICFTU's General Secretary Guy Ryder who called on the Bank "to translate these important findings into policy, which may involve a significant shift in ... organizational culture."

"In contrast to the worker-friendly statements at the global level," he said, "country-level Bank staff still routinely advise governments to, in effect, violate the core labor standards by making access to unionization ... more difficult."

Summary

As major international organizations such as the World Bank shift their policies in support of unions, private sector union membership declines in the United States. Some studies, including one cited here, marshal evidence to support and oppose the proposition that unions hinder economic growth and stability. While the World Bank's study, which takes data from more than 1,000 earlier studies, supports the argument that unions contribute to stability and growth, critics point to cases in which unions have increased pressure on corporations through wage demands, leading to job losses.

The first selection, a piece by Stephen Moore in the *Washington Times*, provides evidence from recent labor disputes in the United States that unions hinder growth and in some cases risk bringing harm to the very workers they are supposed to protect. He cites examples from the airline industry, transit workers in an unnamed municipality, and longshoremen at West Coast ports. In all of these cases unions have taken what the author considers an irresponsible position, holding their employers—and the economy—to ransom. The second selection is a report by Jim Lobe and details the World Bank's recent study indicating the positive role unions play in supporting economic stability and growth. They lead to better-paid workers, who in turn spend money and stimulate their economies as consumers. However, commentators say this new policy outlook by the leadership of the World Bank has yet to filter through to country-level bank staff, who still routinely advise governments to violate core labor standards in the pursuit of greater market "flexibility."

FURTHER INFORMATION:

 Books:

Bennett, James T., and Bruce E. Kaufmann, *The Future of Private Sector Unionism in the United States.* Armonk, NY: M.E. Sharpe, 2002.
Century Foundation Task Force on the Future of Unions, *What's Next for Organized Labor?* New York: Century Foundation Press, 1999.
Lichtenstein, Nelson, *State of the Union: A Century of American Labor.* Princeton, NJ: Princeton University Press, 2002.

 Useful websites:

www.cfier.org/
The Center for Collaborative Solutions, which provides a nonadversarial way of settling industrial disputes.
www.pscw.uva.nl/sociosite/TOPICS/indrel.html
Resource page with links on industrial relations topics.

www.etuc.org/ETUI/Publications/Transfer/intro301.PDF
Paper on "Trade Unions and Labour Relations in the United States."

> ### The following debates in the Pro/Con series may also be of interest:
>
> In this volume:
>
> Topic 9 Would banning imported goods made by children help stop child labor?
>
> Topic 15 Has NAFTA cost the United States jobs?

DO UNIONS ADVERSELY AFFECT ECONOMIC GROWTH?

YES: Unions help keep inefficient and lazy workers in employment, which is bad for the economy

YES: Unions have become so powerful that they can bring whole industries to a standstill if they do not agree with pay or work conditions

INEFFICIENCY
Do unions help protect inefficient workers?

STRIKES
Do unions have unfair strike power?

NO: Unions serve to protect workers' rights, and happy workers are more productive

NO: Strike action is one of the few ways workers can influence their employers; it is only taken with the support of the majority of a union's members

DO UNIONS ADVERSELY AFFECT ECONOMIC GROWTH?
KEY POINTS

YES: Since capital can now be moved around the world without restriction, it is even more important that some organizations represent the interests of workers, who would otherwise be exploited

YES: Without unions companies would pursue a "divide and rule" policy, particularly with unskilled workers, paying them as little as possible

BALANCE OF POWER
Are unions necessary as a check on the power of corporations?

NO: Corporations have an interest in treating their workers well, so they can be relied on to look after them

NO: Underpaid workers would soon move to other jobs, so companies will pay them a fair wage in order to keep them

59

PART 2
GLOBALIZATION AND ITS EFFECTS

In his book *Globalization and its Discontents* (2002), author Joseph Stiglitz defined globalization as the "closer integration of the countries and peoples of the world … brought about by the enormous reduction of costs of transportation and communication and the breaking down of artificial barriers to the flows of goods, services, capital, knowledge, and (to a lesser extent) people across borders." A looser definition describes the operation of economic and cultural forces across national boundaries, particularly with regard to the influence of industrialized, western nations on developing countries.

Many economists and politicians believe that globalization is not only inevitable but also beneficial. It brings increased trade and employment opportunities, they argue, and encourages the growth of the global economy. Globalization also has many critics, however. They believe that the process is exploitative, and inevitably benefits western governments and corporations more than those in developing countries. The free trade values that globalization both promotes and depends on, they claim, do nothing to protect the vulnerable domestic economies of developing nations from competition from more established

western economies. Globalization has provoked violent protest, as seen in the riots that have accompanied World Trade Organization (WTO) talks from the United States to Italy and Mexico.

The developing world

One of the most controversial aspects of globalization is its effect on the developing world. Western firms sometimes move their operations to developing countries, where there are typically fewer legal constraints, and where labor and materials are often much cheaper than in the west. Although critics argue that these practices are exploitative, some advocates counter that an increased involvement in trade inevitably benefits a whole economy.

A World Bank report entitled *Globalization and Poverty—Turning the Corner* observed of China and India, two countries that had experienced globalization: "When these two countries rose out of the list of the 20 poorest countries in the 1980s, they took a large share of the world's population out of extreme poverty. Around 2.2 billion people in these two countries have, on average, seen their material standards of living rise remarkably over the past two decades."

The report went on to say, however, that many other states were excluded from globalization by factors such as internal conflict, bad governance, antibusiness policies, and a lack of involvement in international trade. These nations—often relatively new and unstable—tended to become poorer as parts of the developing world experienced economic growth. Topic 5 examines the effect that globalization has had on the economic development of developing countries.

International organizations

Critics of globalization believe that some of the problems of poor nations are a product of the failure of the

able to export goods into lucrative western markets.

Similar criticisms have been levied at the IMF, established in 1946. The IMF is funded by its 182 member nations and lends money to countries in financial distress. Although rich countries pay or loan more money toward IMF membership than poor nations, they also have higher borrowing privileges and more voting rights, both of which critics condemn as unfair to poor nations. Topic 6 looks at whether the WTO needs reforming; Topic 7 asks if IMF financial assistance policies do more harm than good.

"The NGOs that protested in Seattle did have a valid point about the WTO: its rules pay no attention whatsoever to important issues like the protection of the environment or labor standards. But the solution ... is not to destroy the WTO."

—GEORGE SOROS, FINANCIER, IN A SPEECH TO

THE STATE OF THE WORLD FORUM (2001)

---

international organizations established to help them. Much of the criticism is directed at organizations such as the WTO, the International Monetary Fund (IMF), and the World Bank. The WTO was established in 1995, and evolved out of the General Agreement on Tariffs and Trade (GATT). The aim of both organizations was to reduce trade barriers between nations. Some critics argue that this serves the interests of rich western countries like the United States by opening new markets to western imports at a time when a developing country is unlikely to be

The final topic in this section looks at the power of transnational corporations (TNCs) on the world economy. Such corporations have widespread influence. They can ignore traditional national boundaries and shift operations and money to whichever country offers the best advantages in resources, labor, tax breaks, and so on. Critics argue that TNCs' activities are exploitative and undercut local economies. Topic 8 asks if multinational concerns have become more powerful than governments, whose laws they can easily avoid or disobey.

Topic 5

HAS GLOBALIZATION HINDERED THE ECONOMIC GROWTH OF DEVELOPING COUNTRIES?

YES

"GLOBAL TRADE IS AGAINST DEVELOPING NATIONS—KENNETH KAUNDA"
THE POST (LUSAKA), NOVEMBER 26, 2002
BRIGHTON PHIRI

NO

"ICC BRIEF ON GLOBALIZATION"
NOVEMBER 22, 2000
INTERNATIONAL CHAMBER OF COMMERCE

INTRODUCTION

For most economists "globalization" means liberalization—the opening up of world markets to international trade and competition so that goods, services, and capital can flow freely between countries. The promotion of international free trade has been a fundamental principle of economic policy since the end of World War II (1939-1945) and is regarded by many economists as the foundation for a stable and expanding world economy. Supporters of free trade believe that it allows nations to specialize in those goods and services they are best at producing and to exchange them for products where they have less of an advantage; in this way economic efficiency is achieved, meaning that consumers can get the best goods and services at the lowest possible prices.

However, many people question whether that is how globalization really works. An issue of particular concern is whether globalization benefits poor nations to the same degree that it does rich countries. Although Africa, South and Central America, parts of Asia, and Eastern Europe have seen some growth since the 1960s, there has been little or no improvement in living standards across much of sub-Saharan Africa.

Since the debt crisis of the 1980s the World Bank and the International Monetary Fund (IMF) have required that developing countries adopt certain strict economic policies, known as Structural Adjustment Programs (SAPs), in exchange for loans and debt relief. Many people believe these two institutions to be the main architects of globalization. SAPs involve the country concerned having to adopt market disciplines—opening up its borders to foreign investment and trade, becoming more export-oriented, encouraging free enterprise, increasing interest rates, and making cuts in public spending.

Supporters of SAPs say they are intended to create economic growth, which is an essential part of addressing poverty. To achieve this aim, firms and industries must become more efficient, more competitive, and sell more both locally and overseas.

"The poor have sometimes objected to being governed badly; the rich have always objected to being governed at all."
—G.K. CHESTERTON, BRITISH AUTHOR (1908)

However, figures suggest that there has been a net outflow of wealth from the developing world since the 1980s; it has paid out around five times more capital to the industrialized nations of the West than it has received. Supporters of globalization argue that these are short-term setbacks as different economies are brought together in the international marketplace. They also point out that the World Bank and IMF have adjusted their lending programs to take into account the special needs of developing countries.

Those who argue that globalization has not brought benefits to the world's poor also point to issues such as unfair trading conditions and exploitation of cheap labor. Large corporations often locate in developing countries to take advantage of cheap raw materials and labor. Poor nations complain that free trade forces them to export simple commodities such as sugar or copper, which have low profit margins, rather than helping them develop industries that add value to those commodities.

Meanwhile, many tariffs against cheap manufactured and other goods from the developing world remain in place in the United States, Europe, and elsewhere, where powerful vested interests prevent poorer nations from taking full advantage of international markets.

In addition, those who are against globalization point to the inability of small domestic enterprises to compete with established transnational corporations (TNCs) either in terms of the skills and education of their workers or in their access to technology, finance, and investment.

Those who argue that globalization has promoted economic growth in the developing world, on the other hand, say that evidence suggests a strong correlation between openness to trade and economic growth. Nations that have opened their borders to trade and foreign investment have been forced to become more competitive and have benefited in the long run.

In the first of the following articles, Brighton Phiri presents the viewpoint of Kenneth Kaunda, the politician who led Zambia to independence in 1964 and served as the nation's president until 1991. She reports Kaunda's belief that global trade does not benefit developing countries. The second article is a press release from the International Chamber of Commerce, a world federation of business firms and people. It presents the view that globalization is broadly beneficial for developed and developing nations.

GLOBAL TRADE IS AGAINST DEVELOPING NATIONS—KENNETH KAUNDA
Brighton Phiri

YES

Global economic and trade conditions are definitely against developing countries, Zambia's first Republican president Dr. Kenneth Kaunda has said. Speaking at the Business Forum of the University of South Florida, Tampa City, U.S.A., Dr. Kaunda … said with unfair conditions it was not possible for Africa to compete successfully in the global economy. "What we purchase from the industrial world, we pay through the nose for. The commodities and products we produce and sell are made to be sold at give-away prices," Dr. Kaunda said. "It means we must keep on sweating and extracting very hard because the prices are poor."

"When buyers and investors get our raw materials, they make money for themselves and leave Africa with almost nothing. Protectionism against us is rife." Dr. Kaunda said developing countries' economic woes were worsened by the International Monetary Fund (IMF) conditions. He said African leaders were concerned that the advances they made on people's access to basic needs, just after independence, were regressing.

A step backward

"Almost every leader … has complained about the economic policy conditions of IMF and creditor governments," Dr. Kaunda said. However, Dr. Kaunda expressed his happiness with current World Bank president Dr Wolfensohn, and the new IMF managing director's leaders, saying they seem to be listening to the voices of the many thousands of protesters and demonstrators.

He said globalisation was good if it was considered as a process of the human family working across artificial barriers. "However, the reality is that so far, for Africa, what is being called globalisation has been unfair on us," he said.

Dr. Kaunda complained that Africa had been put on the margins because, like during times of slavery and colonisation, its economies were being made to serve the interests of the industrial world. He said the industrial world could not prosper at the expense of other parts of the world.

Ghana is a large producer of cocoa beans, for example, and Zambia is a major producer of copper, yet Ghana does not have a chocolate making industry, and Zambia does not have a significant copper products industry.

To find out more about IMF policies, see Topic 7 Are International Monetary Fund financial assistance policies harmful?

In June 1995 James D. Wolfensohn became president of the World Bank, an international organization affiliated with the United Nations, with headquarters in Washington, D.C. As the main creditor of the bank, the United States has chosen its directors since the bank was founded in 1944.

COMMENTARY: Regionalism—a way ahead?

One possible way for countries to try to improve their chances in the global market is a regional approach: joining with neighboring countries in a grouping whose members abolish trade restrictions with the aim of increasing the volume and value of their trade. The North American Free Trade Agreement (NAFTA, founded in 1993, encompassing Canada, the United States, and Mexico—see *Topic 15 Has NAFTA cost the United States jobs?*) established one such grouping. Member states may go a step further and set up a single, joint currency, eliminating exchange-rate fluctuations and therefore cutting the costs of trade. A dozen of the European Union's 15 members, for example, have adopted a single currency, the euro.

Customs and monetary unions are also found in the developing world: Two major ones in Africa are the West African Economic and Monetary Union (UEMOA, founded in 1994 and comprising Benin, Burkina Faso, Guinea Bissau, Ivory Coast, Mali, Niger, Senegal, and Togo) and the Central African Economic and Monetary Community (CEMAC, also founded in 1994 and comprising Cameroon, the Central African Republic, Chad, the Republic of Congo, Equatorial Guinea, and Gabon).

Africa has seen several such groupings in the past, many with overlapping memberships, and each promising to increase trade and prosperity for their members. Few have achieved any success (apart from some increase in trade for some individual countries), and none has been able to have any effect on Africa's steadily diminishing share of world trade. In recent years the World Bank has announced a new Regional Integration Assistance Strategy for both UEMOA (2001) and CEMAC (2003). It aims to improve on past efforts by funding the development of basic infrastructure, such as dock facilities and roads, as well as streamlining customs procedures, to have a real effect on the speed with which goods can be moved around and producers can be paid. Time will tell whether "greater openness to the rest of the world and a more favorable business climate" (as the bank's press release described the strategy's aims) will also enable the recipient countries to, in Kenneth Kaunda's words, "do economic activities in an environmentally and socially sustainable way."

"To advance, we must avoid Africa being enslaved again," Dr. Kaunda said. "The human family can only advance collectively if there are fair relations for all its members."

Dr. Kaunda said in order for Africa to be a strong and fair part of the world, it needed fair trade. He said Africa needed to be allowed to implement policies which were relevant to its needs. Dr. Kaunda said many policies being forced on Africa by the financial institutions were not sustainable for the continent and the world.

An example of such unsustainable policies is the introduction of fees for basic health services. Experts believe that fees discourage people from seeking medical care.

Kenneth Kaunda, president of Zambia from 1964 to 1991, photographed in 1977. Following a fall in the world copper price in 1975—a commodity on which Zambia relied for its export earnings—the country became massively indebted to the International Monetary Fund. IMF policies to stabilize the economy resulted in huge increases in food prices, leading to riots. As a result of internal opposition, Kaunda broke with the IMF in May 1987.

"We need to trade as you would trade with your brother and sister," Dr. Kaunda said. "Of course, as others, we need good technology. This is technology which is good, safe, relevant, and not dirty." Dr. Kaunda said Africa still held eco-systems which were vital for the world. "We must therefore, be able to do economic activities in an environmentally and socially sustainable way," he said.

Dr. Kaunda said the New Partnership for Africa's Development (NEPAD) and Africa's partners had big challenges of dealing with Africa's past disadvantages. He called for the removal of systems and practices that slowed down Africa's advances for a stable place in the world economy. "We must make sure that new finance and investment is not dependent upon conditionalities which, as in the past, create instability and problems that live on for long and are still with us today," Dr. Kaunda said.

"We must ensure that economic activities do not create gender imbalances as the IMF programmes have done." Dr. Kaunda said as the world implemented NEPAD, there was need to consider Africa's experiences that should include the previous economic plans. Dr. Kaunda said civil wars and their causes needed to be dealt with if Africa was to advance economically and in peace.

Peace equals progress

He said bad economies could lead to armed conflict and civil wars just as civil wars led to bad economies. Dr. Kaunda cited southern Africa's fight against Apartheid and racism as among the wars that left southern African countries' economies shattered through bombings, economic sanctions, and loss of human life. He said southern African countries were also forced into debt because of the struggle….

"We lost economic opportunities. Yet we have not had sufficient practical international support for the rehabilitation of our economies because of the impact of the repression and war-machinery of apartheid and racism," he said. Dr. Kaunda said all economic policies should take into account the impact of HIV/AIDS.

"Let us have fair trade. Let us have fair economic conditions. Allow us the space to create appropriate policies. When you invest in Africa or do business with us, please think of the environment and workers," Dr. Kaunda said.

"Please think of practices that will not worsen the HIV/AIDS situation in Africa. In short I am asking for ethical business. We are all members of our one world. We are all our brother and sister's keepers. Let us advance together."

NEPAD, founded in Lusaka in July 2001, is "a commitment by African leaders to get rid of poverty and to place the African continent on a path of lasting growth and development." See www.nepad.org for more information.

IMF policies that cut spending on social programs have a much greater effect on women than on men because in developing countries roles at home and work tend to be more rigidly defined than in the West. This leads to the "gender imbalances" that Kaunda refers to.

In 2002 about 40 million people worldwide were infected with HIV/AIDS. Some 70 percent of them were in sub-Saharan Africa. The economic impact of AIDS includes caring for orphans, victims being unable to work, and the cost of the drugs required for treatment.

ICC BRIEF ON GLOBALIZATION
International Chamber of Commerce

NO

 ### EXECUTIVE SUMMARY
1. Introduction

Globalization is about worldwide economic activity—about open markets, competition and the free flow of goods, services, capital and knowledge. Consumers are its principal beneficiary. Its benefits in terms of faster growth, quicker access to new technology, cheaper imports and greater competition are available for all. Globalization has made the world economy more efficient and has created hundreds of millions of jobs, mainly, but not only, in developing countries. It generates an upward spiral of jobs and prosperity for countries that embrace the process, although the advantages will not reach everybody at the same time.

Do technology and economics make globalization inevitable? Or has it been created by bodies such as the World Trade Organization?

2. Globalization and national sovereignty

Governments which seek to opt out of the globalization process are at liberty to do so, though there will be a cost. They may choose the extent to which they wish to participate or to stay out. Globalization is a process, not a programme driven by any country or group of countries. The sovereignty of nations is shared, not abandoned. But the degree of sovereignty-sharing involved is far less than that required, say, of members of the European single currency or of the NATO alliance.

Objectors to globalization claim that any rules favor developed nations over developing ones. Is that inevitable?

3. Globalization and global rules

Globalization requires a framework of rules as the foundation of a sound global economic order. Examples are rules to secure market access for foreign goods and services and to protect intellectual property rights and foreign investment. While more reliance on free enterprise, open markets and more competition reduces the need for detailed government regulation, governments must still provide the political and economic stability domestic entrepreneurs and foreign investors look for. An international rules-based structure is required to provide the stability, transparency and predictability business needs to operate at global level. ...

4. Globalization and the gap between rich and poor

Globalization has helped raise the living standards of the world's poorest people. The proportion of the world population living in absolute poverty is lower than 10 years ago. Moreover, new research suggests that, when income data are adjusted to reflect purchasing power, income inequality between rich and poor countries is diminishing. Globalization cannot be seen as a one-size-fits-all cure for poverty. But it is part of a broader mix of solutions for poverty eradication involving the international community and the self-help potential of the poor countries themselves.

The proportion of the world's population living in absolute poverty (living on less than $1 a day) has fallen from about 24 percent in 1987 to 20 percent in 2001. However, population growth means the number of people living in absolute poverty has remained constant at about 1.2 billion.

5. Globalization and information technologies

Information technologies are a key driver of globalization, opening up huge potential for greater efficiency through e-commerce, the internet and the instantaneous delivery of information anywhere in the world, at any time. They also provide greater access to information and knowledge, the raw materials of innovation, and spread the free flow of information from all sources which authoritarian regimes cannot stop even if they wanted to. Technology and innovation cut costs to the direct benefit of consumers.

To what extent is it true that the Internet allows people access to information even if their governments disapprove?

6. Globalization, multinationals, smaller firms, and consumers

Globalization rewards firms that are innovative and competitive, whether multinational or smaller enterprises. As global companies enter local markets, local companies enter global ones. The resulting competition increases product quality, widens the range of available goods and keeps prices low. Consumers everywhere are the big winners from the globalization process.

7. Globalization and financial stability

Via the integration of currency, bond and stock markets, globalization brings about a more productive allocation of savings and investment resources. Capital mobility and the communications revolution mean that technology and production can be readily transferred to locations where the comparative advantages are greatest. But increased capital mobility brings risks, especially in regions without a long-standing tradition of banking supervision. When governments get into financial difficulties, the problems are generally of their own making. But international monitoring and action is also needed to help prevent crises or limit their impact. What

"Capital mobility" means companies can stop production in one country and transfer it to another where the costs are lower—but workers do not usually have the same mobility to move to where jobs are most easily found. Does that matter?

open markets do is to make sure that when mistakes are made, they are punished sooner rather than later.

An environmental issue not mentioned by the author in this article is that companies whose operations produce pollution can move to countries with lower environmental standards to avoid the costs of cleaning up. What do you think would be an effective way to tackle this problem?

8. Globalization and the environment
Environmental protection can be pursued at global, regional, national and local levels, and efforts should be targeted at the level most appropriate to the problem. Where there are international impacts, international cooperation, information sharing, and technology innovation—each of which is enhanced by the process of globalization—can significantly accelerate efforts to find solutions. More fundamentally, globalization fosters economic growth, which in turn generates and distributes additional resources for environmental protection. Increased trade and investment also promote opportunities to exchange more environmentally-efficient technologies, share good practices, and contribute to environmental capacity-building, particularly in developing countries.

9. Globalization and cultural diversity
Globalization actually creates more diversity, not less. While it integrates markets, making products and services universally available, it also increases consumer choice. Technology enables global products to be customized to meet local, or even individual, consumer tastes. The information revolution has ended the monopoly on the flow of ideas and information. The result is that many people now have more cultural freedom than before.

The WTO meeting in Seattle in December 1999 was attended by large-scale, sometimes violent demonstrations against WTO policies by a variety of environmental and development groups.

10. Globalization and the WTO
The WTO has become the most prominent symbol of globalization and the complex changes that are driving the world economy. As such it has become the target for all opponents of globalization, as events in Seattle in December 1999 showed clearly. Despite the criticism, the WTO is a powerful example of a rules-based international system to promote more open trade and investment worldwide.

11. Globalization and labour standards
Globalization is creating jobs and bringing more prosperity to developing countries which have joined the process. While labour standards in these countries are still lower than in industrialized nations, they are rising. There is considerable evidence that multinationals investing outside their home country or region pay higher wages than local firms, create new jobs at a faster rate, and spend much more on R&D.

While wage differentials will continue between rich and poor countries, they will reflect factors like the level of qualification of workers and their relative productivity. This is hardly the "race to the bottom" the critics of globalization claim to observe.

12. Globalization and human rights

Advanced industrialized economies like the United States and the European Union have been inserting human rights clauses into their trade and cooperation agreements with partner countries in recent years. Trade concessions are suspended for countries breaching these clauses. Democracy and respect for human rights are part of the political stability and confidence-building that form a necessary precondition for local entrepreneurship and for attracting foreign direct investment. The communications revolution that is going hand in hand with globalization is also facilitating efforts to better protect human rights.

13. Globalization and the poorest nations

Globalization has stimulated entrepreneurship and empowered people and countries in a position to participate in the process. This is not the case for the poorest nations. They need technical and financial assistance to acquire the tools to join the process of globalization. This requires a major joint effort on their part and on the part of the international community. They must adopt policies aimed at providing better government, reinforcing macroeconomic stability, liberalizing their economies while creating fair tax structures. The international community needs to act to reduce the debt burden of the poorest countries and to improve market access for their exports. Crucial to enabling the benefits of globalization to spread … is the maintenance of peaceful conditions between and within sovereign states.

14. Globalization and employment

At world level, globalization creates jobs—hundreds of millions of them—not unemployment. These are mainly in the developing countries, but they are only marginally at the expense of jobs in advanced countries. In fact, fewer than five percent of the EU [European Union] workforce are in direct competition with workers in low-wage countries. Europe's unemployment is largely structural and predates globalization. Sharing the gains from globalization means that workers and firms in advanced countries need to be more adaptable to improve competitiveness, skills, and productivity.

A "race to the bottom" refers to the competition between companies based on lowering their costs rather than improving the quality of their product. This includes relocating to countries with lower wage levels.

For many countries, paying back interest and capital on loans taken out by previous governments many years ago is proving an unsustainable burden, which G8 leaders promised to write off in 1999. See www.guardian.co.uk/debt/Story/0,2763,869371,00.html for an explanation of why this has been only partly achieved.

Summary

In the first of the two articles Brighton Phiri reports on a speech made by Dr. Kenneth Kaunda, former president of Zambia, in which he claims that unfair trade conditions make it impossible for the poorest developing countries, such as those in Africa, to compete in terms of international trade. According to Kaunda, globalization has merely resulted in developing countries having to sell raw materials and commodities on global markets at ever-lower prices, making it virtually impossible for exporters to make a profit. Meanwhile, protectionism by the west against exports from the less developed countries continues. Kaunda also makes the point that economic policies and conditions imposed by the International Monetary Fund (IMF) are not sustainable; such conditions make it impossible for African governments to protect workers' rights or the environment.

Conversely, the International Chamber of Commerce (ICC) brief takes a different view. Here the author believes that globalization has "made the world economy more efficient and has created hundreds of millions of jobs"—most of them in developing countries. It has helped promote technology and innovation worldwide, and has rewarded firms that are innovative and competitive regardless of their size. As such, globalization has helped raise standards of living the world over and, the author claims, has helped diminish income inequality between rich and poor. Nonetheless, the ICC brief recognizes the need for technical and financial assistance if the world's poorest nations (such as those on the African continent) are to participate fully in, and benefit from, the process of globalization.

0FURTHER INFORMATION:

Books:

Cavanagh, John, et al., *Alternatives to Economic Globalization*. San Francisco, CA: Berrett-Koehler, 2002.
Marber, Peter, *Money Changes Everything: How Global Prosperity Is Reshaping Our Needs, Values, and Lifestyles*. Upper Saddle River, NJ: Prentice Hall, 2003.
Stiglitz, Joseph E., *Globalization and Its Discontents*. New York: W.W. Norton & Co., 2002.

Useful websites:

www.baobabconnections.org/
Monthly online magazine about globalization issues.
web.worldbank.org/WBSITE/EXTERNAL/EXTABOUTUS/EXT ARCHIVES/0,,pagePK:38167~theSitePK:29506,00.html
World Bank's archives include a chronology since 1944.
www.guardian.co.uk/debt/0,2759,178197,00.html
The Guardian newspaper's resource page on debt relief.

The following debates in the Pro/Con series may also be of interest:

In this volume:

Topic 1 Is a free market the best way to organize world trade?

Topic 6 Does the WTO need reforming?

Topic 8 Do transnational companies have more influence on the world economy than national governments?

HAS GLOBALIZATION HINDERED THE ECONOMIC GROWTH OF DEVELOPING COUNTRIES?

YES: Globalization has just made rich countries richer while the poor have been left standing

DIVIDE
Has globalization created a bigger divide between rich and poor nations?

NO: Globalization has opened up new markets for industries in developing countries

YES: Protectionism makes it impossible for developing nations to trade effectively and efficiently

PROTECTIONISM
Have developing countries suffered from unfair tariffs?

NO: Protectionist policies help regulate and balance national and international needs

HAS GLOBALIZATION HINDERED THE ECONOMIC GROWTH OF DEVELOPING COUNTRIES?

KEY POINTS

YES: All globalization has done is make it easier for transnational companies to produce their goods in developing nations, at exploitative wages and in bad conditions

YES: Companies in developing nations cannot compete with foreign companies operating in their countries that have tax breaks and possibly better pay

EXPLOITATION
Has globalization taken jobs away from domestic industries?

NO: International goods are too expensive by comparison, and so people buy local products, thus generating demand and more jobs

NO: Developing countries can specialize in making goods that they are best at, leading to more jobs, not fewer

Topic 6
DOES THE WORLD TRADE ORGANIZATION NEED REFORMING?

YES

FROM "RETHINKING LIBERALISATION AND REFORMING THE WTO"
WORLD ECONOMIC FORUM, DAVOS, SWITZERLAND, JANUARY 28, 2000
MARTIN KHOR

NO

"THE WORLD TRADE ORGANIZATION WORKS FOR YOU"
HTTP://WWW.USTR.GOV/HTML/WTO4YOU.HTML
CHARLENE BARSHEFSKY

INTRODUCTION

The World Trade Organization (WTO) was established on January 1, 1995, when it replaced the General Agreement on Tariffs and Trade (GATT) as the main administrative body of international commerce. The WTO is empowered by a multilateral agreement of December 1993 to mediate trade disputes between its member states. In addition, the organization has worldwide responsibilities for tackling environmental issues, for maintaining and where necessary improving labor standards and conditions, and for dealing with problems arising from foreign investment.

The WTO is a member-driven organization funded by its membership. As of April 2003 it had 146 members who represent more than 90 percent of world trade. Its senior decision-making body—the Ministerial Conference—meets at least every 2 years, and members reach decisions by consensus. The WTO Secretariat is based in Geneva, Switzerland, and has a staff of around 550 people who come from 60 different nationalities. It is headed by a director-general who is elected by the members every 3 years. The secretariat has no decision-making powers.

Most governments and companies, especially in the West, regard the WTO favorably. In their view its arrival has leveled the playing field for world trade by removing trade barriers such as import tariffs—taxes that make foreign goods more expensive and therefore discourage people from buying them. When governments trade openly under the same rules, it makes trade easier, more efficient, and truly global. Many believe that the free trade policies promoted by the WTO are preferable to protectionism, which shields domestic industries from foreign competition. But there are others who say that under the WTO global inequality has grown. Within the WTO there are deep divisions between developed and developing nations. Increasingly the WTO has become the focus—some would say the scapegoat—for antiglobalization protest.

To its supporters the WTO operates in a democratic manner, helping trade flow smoothly, settling trade disputes, and organizing trade negotiations. They believe that WTO trade agreements have led to economic growth, stability, and prosperity. WTO agreements establish the rules for trade, reduce tariffs, limit the use of subsidies, promote the sustainable use of natural resources, and reduce unfair obstacles to trade such as customs procedures.

"The battles are not only on the streets; they are in closed rooms with heavy political pressure. It is business as usual in the WTO."
—BARRY COATES, DIRECTOR, WORLD DEVELOPMENT MOVEMENT (1999)

Critics paint a less positive picture. They argue that far from creating a new equality, the growth of unrestricted world trade has favored North America and Europe more than the developing world. Supporters respond that the WTO protects the weak as well as the strong countries. The World Bank has forecast that developing countries will grow at twice the rate of developed countries in the next decade, so that inequalities are likely to be reduced.

Critics also point to the WTO's lack of democracy and the way it favors businesses rather than individuals. They say that although the interests of companies are well protected, little concern is given to others affected by corporate decisions, such as employees and local communities. Meanwhile, supporters insist that the WTO is one of the few remaining hopes for multilateral cooperation.

Concerns about WTO policies reached a peak during its summit in Seattle, Washington, in 1999, when negotiations on new trading rules foundered on objections to proposals favored by the United States. Developing nations claimed that by insisting that labor standards in poor countries should be made to conform to those of the developed world, the United States was gaining an unfair trading advantage. Poorer nations also said that they were not properly involved in the negotiating process. Such views were echoed by rioting protesters outside the meeting.

It is widely agreed that the WTO has overseen a shift in power from nation states to commercial corporations. Some reformers say that the WTO should now take on more of the historic responsibilities of the national governments, protecting citizens from exploitation by foreign powers, and ensuring public health.

In the first of the following articles Martin Khor, director of Third World Network, argues that to restore its credibility, the WTO should be reformed to deal solely with trade issues. The second article, by Charlene Barshefsky, the United States Trade Representative, contends that the WTO does more than promote world trade—it also fosters democratic values.

RETHINKING LIBERALISATION AND REFORMING THE WTO
Martin Khor

YES

The failure of Seattle

The spectacular failure of the WTO Seattle meeting had its roots in both the system of decision-making and the substance of the negotiations. In the many months of the preparatory phase, developing countries generally were more concerned about their non-benefits from the WTO Agreements and about the need to correct the problems of implementation. Most of them were not in the frame of mind to consider or welcome the new issues being pushed by developed countries. The latter on the other hand were aggressively promoting several new issues, such as investment, transparency in government procurement, competition, a new round of industrial tariff cuts, and finally labour and environmental standards. At Seattle, the U.S. push for labour standards led by President Clinton confirmed the worst fears of developing countries that the WTO was sought to be tilted even more against them by the big powers.

The clash of interests over substance was worsened greatly by the utter disrespect for democratic participation of the majority of Members and the great lack of transparency in the multitude of talks held in small groups that the majority had no access to. This was compounded by several manipulative tactics, including the non-incorporation of the views expressed by many Members in the negotiating drafts. It became clear that an attempt was being made to railroad developing countries into agreeing to proposals and texts they had not agreed to, had opposed or had not even seen at all. In the end many developing country delegations made it clear, including through open statements and media conferences, that they would not join in a "consensus" of any Declaration in which they had no or little part in formulating. The talks had to be abandoned without the issuing of any Declaration or even a short statement by Ministers.

The tasks ahead include the need to address both substance and process. The grievances and complaints of developing countries—that they have not benefitted from the Uruguay Round, and that the problems of implementation of these Agreements have to be rectified—must urgently and seriously be tackled. The process of decision-making and negotiations in the WTO has to be democratised and made transparent. "Green Room" meetings should be discontinued. Every Member, however small, must have the right to know what negotiations are taking place, and to take part in them. Until the reforms to the system and to the substance of the WTO take place, the organisation's credibility will remain low. And for the reforms to take place, there should be a stop to the pressures being exerted by some of the developed countries to inject yet more new issues into the WTO....

> The Uruguay Round is the name given to the international series of GATT talks between 1986 and 1994 that led to the creation of the WTO on January 1, 1995. For more information on the founding and aims of the WTO see pages 86–87.

Why the WTO should not take on new issues

A major reason for the failure at Seattle was the reluctance and refusal of many developing countries for allowing the WTO to be given the mandate to take on more new issues for negotiating new agreements, which had been proposed by some of the developed countries. Saying no to the proposed new issues makes much sense.

If the WTO is to improve its already poor credibility, it should focus in the next few years on reviewing problems of implementing the Agreements and make the necessary changes in the agreements. These will be enormous tasks. They will not be properly carried out if there is a proliferation of new issues in a new Round. The extremely limited human, technical and financial resources of developing countries and their diplomats and policy makers would be diverted away from the review process to defending their interests in the negotiations on new issues. The limited time of the WTO would also be mainly engaged in the new issues.

> Khor argues that the limited resources of developing countries puts them at a disadvantage in WTO negotiations. Do you agree?

There will be little time for examining, reviewing and improving the existing agreements, and the problems arising from their implementation will increase through time and accumulate, and manifest themselves in social and economic dislocation and political instability in many countries.

If this is not enough, most of the proposed new issues would also have the most serious consequences for the South's future development. Issues such as investment rules, competition policy and government procurement do not belong in the WTO (which is supposed to be a trade organisation) in the first place. They are sought to be placed there by the developed countries to take advantage of the enforcement capability (the dispute settlement system) of the WTO, so that disciplines can be effectively put on developing

> If the WTO is a trade organization, why does it cause such controversy?

Protection is the regulating of imports and exports to shield domestic industries from foreign competition. Protectionist devices include trade bans and imposing duties on imported goods, making them more expensive than domestic products.

countries to open their economies to the goods, services. and companies of the developed countries. Other issues relate to labour, social, and environment standards. These too should not enter the WTO as issues to be negotiated into new agreements. If they do so, then these issues are likely to be made use of by developed countries as protectionist devices against the products and services of developing countries.

Should the developed countries continue to push and pressure for these new issues, then the WTO will continue to be split, and moreover other pressing issues such as the problems resulting from the existing Agreements would not be tackled. Developing countries should therefore not accept and developed countries should refrain from the injection of these new areas into the WTO.

Conclusions

The multilateral trade system faces a crisis and a crossroads. To resolve the crisis of identity and credibility, the following should be considered:

"Liberalization," or free trade, is the absence of governmental interference in international trade. For more information on this concept see Topic 1 Is a free market the best way to organize world trade?

1. Review the record of liberalisation and take a more realistic approach. This requires a slowdown or stop to pressures being put on developing countries for further liberalisation. …

2. Reassert the objective of the trade system as primarily the development of developing countries which form the majority of the membership. Liberalisation or "free trade" should not be the operational aim. The goal should be development." …

Is development one of the main goals of the WTO, or is it free trade? Go to www.wto.org for details of the organization's objectives.

3. The problems of implementation of the Uruguay Round agreements should be given the top priority at the WTO. There is a danger that after the Seattle failure, these problems will again be sidelined as the focus is given to the problem of participation and transparency. It must be recognised that the main cause of the Seattle failure was the disillusionment of many developing countries with the inequities of the rules and the negative effects these would have on their economies and societies.

To restore credibility to the trading system in the eyes of developing countries, the following should be done:
a. Developed countries should take measures to greatly increase market access for developing countries' products, such as in agriculture, textiles and industrial products (where

there are now high tariffs); moreover they should stop taking protectionist measures such as anti-dumping measures;

b. In the many areas where developing countries face problems in implementing their obligations (such as in TRIMS, TRIPS, agriculture), a review and change of the existing rules should be done on an urgent basis. For a start, the sets of proposals put forward by developing countries during the preparations for Seattle … should be treated with urgency by the WTO General Council. A mechanism should be set up to consider these proposals and to rectify the problems (including through amending the agreements) as soon as possible;

c. In the meanwhile, where the transition period for developing countries has expired (for example, in TRIPS and TRIMS), an extension should be given at least until the review process is completed. There should also be a moratorium on bringing dispute cases against developing countries on issues where the reviews are taking place.

4. Serious consideration should also be given to trimming the WTO so that it can carry out its tasks of regulating trade relations for the benefit especially of developing countries. In areas where it has accumulated a mandate that is inappropriate, steps should be considered to hive off these aspects.…

5. There should not be pressures to introduce new issues such as investment, competition, procurement, labour and environmental standards as these would overload the system further and lead to tremendous systemic stress and great tensions and divisions in the organisation.

6. The system and culture of decision making in the WTO must undergo serious reform. This cannot be done in a rush but has to be considered carefully, in a process in which all Members have full participation rights. The exclusive Green Room meetings (which do not have the mandate of the full Membership, and which are not officially announced, nor are the results of the meetings made generally known) should be discontinued. Manipulative methods (such as at Seattle where chairpersons of groups declared there was a consensus view when there was none …) should stop. At meetings where issues are discussed and drafts are made and negotiated, there should be transparency and participation, where each Member is given the right to be present and to make proposals.

"Dumping" is the term given to the practice of selling goods, usually exports in international trade, at less than normal price. Antidumping measures include increasing import duties.

TRIPS stands for Agreement on Trade Related Aspects of Intellectual Property Rights. It places copyrights, patents, and trademarks, for example, under international WTO rules. TRIMS is an abbreviation of Agreement on Trade Related Investment and applies to any measure that discriminates against foreigners or foreign products.

The so-called "green room" meetings are unofficial and exclusive meetings in which a group of countries is invited to participate by the director general or the chairman. A green room is also a room in a theater or concert hall where performers can relax before or after appearances.

THE WORLD TRADE ORGANIZATION WORKS FOR YOU
Charlene Barshefsky

NO

Giving positive examples is a good way to try to quickly gain the reader's approval of your argument.

X Good-paying American jobs, higher living standards, and the continued growth of the U.S. economy depend on our ability to sell the goods and services we produce to consumers everywhere. The World Trade Organization (WTO), founded in 1995, helps the United States achieve this goal.

The United States and the WTO

The United States was a leading force in establishing the WTO, which is an international institution in which we negotiate agreements to reduce barriers to trade with 134 other members, allowing American businesses, farmers and working people to find new opportunities, create new jobs, and raise family living standards. The WTO is also a forum for countries to enforce trade agreements and continue negotiations toward expanding world trade opportunities.

The author argues that the United States' membership in the WTO helps its workers compete internationally on a more equal basis. Do you think that U.S. workers are unfairly treated because of the free market?

Our country entered agreements in the WTO to ensure that American workers, the most productive in the world, can compete on a level playing field. Since the United States is among the world's most open markets, the Agreements in the WTO help open foreign markets on more reciprocal terms. Under WTO rules, foreign nations assure us greater access to their markets, and are constrained from giving their workers and firms unfair advantages through subsidies and protectionist domestic policies. At the same time, WTO rules recognize and respect governments' right to maintain high standards for the environment, labor, health, and safety.

Are the WTO agreements only favorable to the United States?

The Agreements are thus designed to help American families by opening foreign markets to our products, lowering the prices of business inputs and of everyday goods we purchase in grocery and department stores, and establishing fair trade rules that safeguard American companies and workers. Finally, membership in the WTO helps to advance democratic values abroad, such as freer markets, more open societies, transparency and the rule of law in commercial transactions, and peaceful settlement of disputes.

Do you agree with the author that the WTO leads to democracy? Would developing countries share this view?

COMMENTARY: The battle of Seattle

The third Ministerial Conference of the World Trade Organization was held in Seattle, Washington, from November 30 to December, 3, 1999. Delegates representing 135 countries assembled to discuss issues including agriculture, the environment, market access, antidumping legislation, and labor standards. The talks were extended for hours in the hope that agreement on some issues could be achieved; but eventually the agenda was abandoned, and the talks ended because no consensus could be reached.

The protesters

While the meetings were taking place, an estimated 60,000 people took to the streets of Seattle to protest against the World Trade Organization. The protesters represented a wide spectrum of causes and comprised environmentalists, students, trade unionists, Christians, anarchists, and activists in one of the biggest civil disturbances over political issues since the era of the Vietnam War. The protesters argued that free trade is not fair trade and claimed that the WTO has too much power to promote globalization at the expense of democracy. They argued that the WTO agreements can overrule laws of member nations that protect the environment, health, and human rights. The protesters were united against the WTO in their deep concern about the globalization of the economy under the domination of a few transnational corporate giants.

Violence and rioting

The Seattle authorities expected organized protest during the ministerial meetings but were not prepared for the scale of the demonstration on November 30. Smaller, peaceful protests had taken place on November 29, but the following day the mass of protesters delayed the WTO opening ceremony. The demonstrations erupted into violence and rioting on several occasions, and many properties were attacked and looted. President Clinton ordered that the protesters be controlled or that the WTO meeting would be canceled. A state of emergency was declared, bus service was suspended, and a curfew was enforced in downtown Seattle. The National Guard and Washington State Patrol were called to maintain order. On December 1 around 500 people were arrested amid allegations of police brutality and protester criminality and intimidation. The closing ceremonies were held on December 3, and order was gradually restored to the city.

Many people believe that the problems in Seattle could have been avoided with better planning and preparation by the authorities. The demonstrations raised important issues and highlighted the growing concerns about the WTO and what it represents. However, neither the organizers nor the participants put forward a real alternative to transnational corporations or capitalist governments.

Trade benefits America's workers and families

The trade gains that the United States has won through the WTO Agreements and other trade policies have been a major contributing factor to our thriving economy. Studies estimate that the effect of full implementation of the WTO Agreements will be to boost U.S. GDP by $125–250 billion per year (in 1998 dollars). We have a great stake in further expanding opportunities for U.S. companies and workers in manufacturing, agriculture, and services industries through the WTO.

GDP is an abbreviation of gross domestic product. It refers to the value of domestic productivity excluding the value of net income earned abroad.

Did you know?

- Promoting U.S. exports and jobs

- WTO rules lower trade barriers abroad and help us export more of our goods and services to other countries.

- On average, every billion dollars of goods and services exports results in thousands of jobs here at home.

Many people find the debate about globalization more emotional than logical. Do you think that statistics are an effective response?

- Between 1994 and 1998, 1.3 million new jobs supported by exports of goods and services have been created in the United States. Over the same period, total U.S. employment increased by 11.7 million jobs, and the unemployment rate declined from 6.1% to 4.5%.

- Jobs supported by goods exports pay 13-16% above the average wage.

- Today, industrial production in the United States is over 34% higher than it was in 1992. This compares to a 3.5% increase in Germany and a .5% decline in Japan. Between 1992 and 1998, manufacturing productivity was up nearly 4% per year, and manufacturing jobs increased by over half a million.

Are U.S. interests always the most important way to judge a particular question?

- Benefitting from new opportunities created by WTO rules, over one-third of U.S. agricultural production was exported in 1998, with a value of $52 billion.

- The services sector including retailing, transport, construction, insurance, finance, accounting, advertising, computer services, tourism, engineering, and environmental services accounts for over 60 percent of the U.S. economy, and 80 percent of our jobs.

- Helped by WTO services rules, the United States leads the world in trade in services with over $264 billion in exports annually. It is the fastest growing sector in our economy and provides the greatest number of new jobs.

- Raising living standards for all Americans

- The creation of higher-paying jobs supported by trade raises living standards for tens of thousands of American households.

See also
Topic 1 Is a free
market the best
way to organize
world trade?
and Topic 14
Is protectionism
good for
U.S. business?

- Trade barriers, by making goods and services more expensive, cost you money at the store. In 1990, prior to the WTO, private sector studies estimated that trade protection cost U.S. consumers approximately $70 billion per year. Our commitment to open markets has led to more affordable prices and a greater variety of the things that we purchase everyday, in the grocery shopping cart and for household goods, such as clothes, autos, toys, and consumer electronics. The standard of living improves for all Americans, but particularly for low-income families, since lower prices mean that your paycheck goes further in the marketplace.

- The WTO Agreements result in lower prices for business and consumer products. By the time that the Agreements are fully implemented in 2005, the annual effect will be equivalent to an increase of $1500–$3000 in purchasing power for the average American family of four.

Summary

At the beginning of the first article Martin Khor suggests that in the failure of the 1999 WTO meeting in Seattle, the industrialized nations reaped what they had sowed in the previous round of talks, which concluded in Montevideo, Uruguay, in 1994. The developing nations felt that they had seen no benefits in the intervening period, and so they rejected President Bill Clinton's proposal for an international labor standard. The author's view is that the WTO, as presently constituted, has two fatal flaws: It is undemocratic, attaching undue weight to the opinions of most powerful nations, and it involves itself in matters that should not concern it. He recommends that the WTO be reformed and thereafter restrict itself to trade issues. It should also stop trying to impose liberalism on undeveloped countries—the fact that free trade works in the West does not prove that it can increase productivity or improve social conditions in every country.

The second article lists some of the benefits that the WTO has brought to the U.S. economy. One of the greatest of them is that the abolition of trade restrictions has helped make the domestic markets of member nations as open as the domestic market of the United States. U.S. exports have thus reached vast new markets, enabling local consumers to buy top-quality goods and increasing the prosperity of the manufacturing nation. The advantages of the WTO are not just economic, the author argues—the organization's insistence that member nations protect the environment and maintain high standards of labor, health, and safety encourages developing countries to improve their openness in political matters—and move toward democracy.

FURTHER INFORMATION:

Books:

Hoekman, Bernard, and Will Martin (eds.), *Developing Countries and the WTO: A Pro-Active Agenda*. Malden, MA: Blackwell, 2001.
Irwin, Douglas A., *Free Trade under Fire*. Princeton, NJ, Princeton University Press, 2002.
Kiggundu, Moses N., *Managing Globalization in Developing Countries and Transition Economies: Building Capacities for a Changing World*. Westport, CT: Praeger, 2002.
Milner, Chris, and Robert Reed, *Trade Liberalization, Competition, and the WTO*. Cheltenham, UK: Edward Elgar, 2002.
Shrybman, Steven, *The World Trade Organization: A Citizen's Guide*. Toronto, Canada: James Lorimer, 2002.
Stiglitz, Joseph E., *Globalization and Its Discontents*. New York: W.W. Norton & Co., 2002.

Useful websites:

www.wto.org
Official site of the World Trade Organization.
www.ifg.org
Site for the International Forum on Globalization, a non-government organization critical of the WTO.

> **The following debates in the Pro/Con series may also be of interest:**
>
> In this volume:
> Topic 1 Is a free market the best way to organize world trade?
> Part 2: Globalization and its effects

DOES THE WORLD TRADE ORGANIZATION NEED REFORMING?

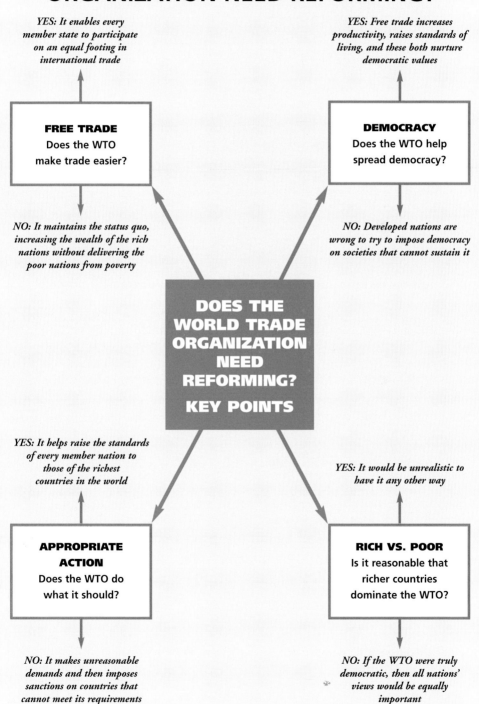

YES: It enables every member state to participate on an equal footing in international trade

YES: Free trade increases productivity, raises standards of living, and these both nurture democratic values

FREE TRADE
Does the WTO make trade easier?

DEMOCRACY
Does the WTO help spread democracy?

NO: It maintains the status quo, increasing the wealth of the rich nations without delivering the poor nations from poverty

NO: Developed nations are wrong to try to impose democracy on societies that cannot sustain it

DOES THE WORLD TRADE ORGANIZATION NEED REFORMING?

KEY POINTS

YES: It helps raise the standards of every member nation to those of the richest countries in the world

YES: It would be unrealistic to have it any other way

APPROPRIATE ACTION
Does the WTO do what it should?

RICH VS. POOR
Is it reasonable that richer countries dominate the WTO?

NO: It makes unreasonable demands and then imposes sanctions on countries that cannot meet its requirements

NO: If the WTO were truly democratic, then all nations' views would be equally important

THE WORLD TRADE ORGANIZATION (WTO)

"The WTO is no would-be tyrant. It is democratic to a fault, and has few powers of its own."
—*THE ECONOMIST*, SEPTEMBER 29, 2001

The World Trade Organization (WTO) was formed on January 1, 1995, as the international organization to govern world trade. According to its literature, the WTO's "main function is to ensure that trade flows as smoothly, predictably and freely as possible." Since the late 1990s the WTO has become the focus of antiglobalization protesters who claim the organization is antidemocratic and unfair to poorer countries. Some critics call for the abolition of the WTO, while others insist reform is necessary. Supporters contend that it is a credible and necessary institution that contributes to world prosperity.

Background

The WTO was established to replace the General Agreement on Tariffs and Trade (GATT), which went into effect in 1948. GATT was both a set of rules and the name of the organization set up to administer the rules. After the end of World War II (1939–1945) there was a new spirit of international economic cooperation. Twenty-three countries, led by the United States, aimed to reduce customs tariffs (taxes on imports) and set up an open trading system that would benefit all countries. They instituted the GATT document, which was based on the fundamental principle of nondiscrimination with regard to the treatment of trade in goods among countries. In other words, each member country was required to treat all its trading partners in the same way. The WTO continues to uphold the principles included in GATT; but whereas GATT dealt only with trade in goods, the WTO also covers services and intellectual property.

Structure of the WTO

The WTO is based in Geneva, Switzerland. As of April 2003, it had 146 members and around 30 observer governments, most of which had applied for membership in the organization.

The highest-level group within the WTO is the Ministerial Conference, which meets every two years. The Ministerial Conference is made up of a political representative from each member country—in the case of the United States the Trade Representative. The conference looks at work in progress and decides the agenda for future programs. The second level within the WTO is the General Council, which oversees the day-to-day working of the organization and also monitors the national trade policies of member countries and settles trade disputes. The General Council meets several times a year in Geneva, and each member country sends a representative, usually of ambassador rank. The WTO secretariat in Geneva provides technical support to the organization, but has no decision-making power—the member countries themselves determine the rules of the WTO by negotiation and consensus.

Advantages of the WTO

Supporters of the WTO say that the economic benefits it brings are indisputable. The organization acts as a forum in which its member countries negotiate trade agreements. According to WTO advocates, these trade agreements have contributed to prosperity and stability by lowering trade barriers and creating predictable trading conditions through requiring signatories to honor their commitments. In the case of the United States WTO agreements have helped companies export more goods and services. American businesses and working people have found new opportunities and jobs as a result, and living standards have been raised.

WTO proponents also argue that the organization has reduced the likelihood of trade-related conflicts—both by enabling trade to operate smoothly, thus preventing international friction, and by providing the machinery for settling disputes among members should they arise. Furthermore, supporters assert, the WTO simplifies world trade by enabling members to negotiate with all other members at one time. It also provides a measure of equality—all members, regardless of size and wealth, must obey WTO rules.

Disadvantages of the WTO

Critics of the WTO insist that while the wealthy nations of North America and Europe have gotten richer, the poor of the world have gotten poorer as a result of free trade. They argue that the lowering of trade barriers in developing countries leads to floods of imports that the people can ill afford, the profits on which go to foreign companies and not into the local economy. Critics also contend that free trade encourages the exploitation of the labor force in poorer countries—for example, by forcing those countries to accept lower pay and working conditions to attract foreign companies to build factories. Environmentalists have also criticized the WTO for not being strict enough on issues of food safety and animal welfare.

Discontent with WTO policies came to a head at the Ministerial Conference in Seattle in late 1999. On the streets activists protested vigorously. In the conference there was disagreement between members about the proposed new trading rules. Third World countries argued that a suggestion to incorporate a certain level of labor standards into WTO rules was not a humanitarian move but a protectionist one—it would give richer countries an excuse not to import from countries unable to meet those standards. Debate over the benefits and achievements of the WTO seems likely to continue well into the 21st century.

Topic 7
ARE INTERNATIONAL MONETARY FUND FINANCIAL ASSISTANCE POLICIES HARMFUL?

YES
"THE IMF STRIKES OUT ON BRAZIL"
HERITAGE FOUNDATION MEMORANDUM 569, FEBRUARY 4, 1999
BRETT D. SCHAEFER AND JOHN P. SWEENEY

NO
"DEBT RELIEF FOR POOR COUNTRIES, (HIPC): PROGRESS THROUGH MARCH 2003"
IMF FACTSHEET, APRIL 2003
INTERNATIONAL MONETARY FUND

INTRODUCTION

The United States and its wartime allies conceived the International Monetary Fund (IMF) toward the end of World War II (1939-1945) at the Bretton Woods Conference (July 1-22, 1944), held to discuss financial arrangements for the postwar world after the expected defeat of Japan and Germany. They believed that an interdependent global political economy would be essential for preserving international peace and prosperity, especially after the interwar experience of depression, which resulted in grave political turmoil and, ultimately, the most devastating war in history. The IMF, founded in 1946, and the World Bank, instituted a year earlier, were the organizations created to achieve this vision. Both institutions are based in Washington, D.C. They have become immensely influential, but have also attracted criticism. In recent years there has

been a growing debate about whether the IMF's financial assistance policies do promote the economic well-being of the countries they are intended to help.

According to Article I of its founding charter, the IMF is responsible for promoting international monetary cooperation; facilitating the expansion and balanced growth of international trade; promoting the stability of exchange rates (the rate used by one nation to exchange its currency for another's); assisting member states in maintaining stability in their financial inflows and outflows (their balance of payments); and making its resources available, under adequate safeguards, to members experiencing balance-of-payments difficulties. In general, the IMF is responsible for promoting financial stability, international trade, and economic growth. The IMF uses a variety of means to help member nations pursue economic policies necessary for maintaining a reliable supply of foreign exchange and relatively stable exchange rates. These measures include technical assistance and training, and a variety of credit and loan programs.

> *"I think there is a broad sentiment among both the left and the right that the IMF may be doing more harm than good."*
> —JOSEPH STIGLITZ,
> ECONOMIST, JUNE 2002

The effectiveness of these policies has been questioned by some observers and economists, notably by Joseph Stiglitz, a former chief economist and vice president at the World Bank from 1997 to 2001 and winner of the Nobel Prize for Economic Science in 2001. Critics such as Stiglitz ask who benefits most from IMF policy: poor debtor nations or wealthy creditor nations, since it is the rich nations that exercise most control in the IMF. The IMF is structured to reflect the national income—and financial input—of its members, making the United States, Japan, France, the United Kingdom, and Germany the most influential nations. Critics believe that the interests of the banking and corporate elite are often placed before those of workers and the poor. One example they give is the austerity measures that the IMF obliges countries receiving financial assistance to adopt. These measures generally revolve around the adoption of strict financial policies, including tax increases and reductions in government spending. The poorest members of society are often affected most by the increased tax burden and the reduction in spending on welfare and education. Critics of IMF loan and credit programs also believe that they are short-term measures that hinder long-term development objectives, and that they burden nations with debt when these countries should be focusing on the development of new trade and industry.

Supporters of the IMF see the organization's financial assistance policies as an important stabilizing influence on the world economy. They recognize that there may be shortcomings involved in some assistance programs, but argue that they are dealing with countries at crisis point, whose economies are about to collapse, and that some suffering is inevitable in any rescue package. They also explain that the IMF has a range of financial relief measures to suit different circumstances, and that it has modified its policies to try to help the most vulnerable members of society through programs such as the Heavily Indebted Poor Countries (HIPC) initiative, begun in 1996 and designed to reduce the debt of the world's poorest countries to sustainable levels.

The articles that follow present different sides to the question of whether IMF policies are harmful. Brett D. Schaefer and John P. Sweeney argue that they are detrimental to poor nations and refer to the example of Brazil in support of their case. Set against this, an official IMF policy statement about the HIPC asserts that the organization's policies are both responsive and effective.

THE IMF STRIKES OUT ON BRAZIL
Brett D. Schaefer and John P. Sweeney

YES

Brett D. Schaefer is a fellow in international regulatory affairs at the Heritage Foundation, a research and educational institute. John P. Sweeney was policy analyst for Latin America at the foundation. Go to http://www. heritage.org/about/ to find out more about the organization.

The financial crisis that crippled Brazil in January despite a preemptive international bailout last November further discredits the lending policies of the U.S. Department of the Treasury and the International Monetary Fund (IMF)—policies supporters claimed would solve the global financial crisis. Brazil's inability to avoid devaluating its currency on January 13 confirms lessons the global community should have learned in Asia and Russia last year: The IMF's lending policies harm, rather than help, economies; keep them from instituting sound financial policies on their own; and undermine support for free trade. Instead of continuing support for IMF bailout packages, the Clinton Administration should pursue solutions that specifically address the financial problems in each country.

A record of failure.

U.S. tax payers underwrote the loans because the IMF gets its funds from subscriptions and resources provided by member nations. As the wealthiest member of the IMF, the United States contributes most to its funds.

Following the Asian financial crisis that began in Thailand in July 1997, the IMF orchestrated a succession of bailouts—with President Bill Clinton's enthusiastic support—that totaled over $175 billion in emergency loans to Thailand, South Korea, Indonesia, Russia, and Brazil. U.S. taxpayers underwrote these loans with tens of billions of dollars. The IMF and the Clinton Administration argued that these packages would strengthen the economies of the afflicted countries, prevent their citizens from suffering undue economic hardship, and prevent the spread of the financial crisis to other countries.

The IMF and the Administration were wrong on all counts, however. The global financial crisis continued to expand following the bailouts, undermining world trade and economic growth. Every country under the IMF's financial "guidance" suffered severe economic contraction and plunged hundreds of millions of people back into poverty in a domino effect that threatens economic growth even in the United States.

The use of the emotional term "victim" shows how strongly the authors feel about the damaging effects of IMF policies.

The IMF's latest victim is Brazil. After the successive failures of IMF loans to arrest financial crises in Asia and Russia, President Clinton proposed in October 1998 the creation of a "new mechanism" to prevent future crises. This new IMF

Michel Camdessus, who as managing director of the International Monetary Fund from 1987 to 2000 oversaw the $41.5 billion loan given to the Brazilian government in November 1998.

mechanism is to provide billions of dollars in loans to a troubled country before the onset of a crisis. This mechanism represents a significant departure from previous policy because no evidence of a crisis would need to be demonstrated in order to obtain IMF loans; merely the possibility of a crisis would be sufficient.

Brazil is Latin America's largest economy and the eighth largest in the world. It became the first beneficiary of the new mechanism in a $41.5 billion rescue package in

Austerity programs are a method favored by the IMF of reducing and controlling debt, and stabilizing struggling national economies. Supporters argue that they reduce government spending and encourage more responsible and sustainable economic policies. However, some critics argue that they have the opposite effect and actually contract the economies they are intended to help, inhibiting the growth of new business, industry, and trade, which are necessary to boost the domestic economy in the long term, among other things.

Do you think the fact that IMF financial relief affected political reform has serious implications?

Brazil has a large public sector workforce, which has had generous pension provision in return for low contributions. As the number of retired public sector workers has increased, additional stress has been placed on the system. Pension reforms began in 1998.

November. According to U.S. Secretary of the Treasury Robert Rubin, the package would "guard against financial market contagion" by convincing investors Brazil had more than enough resources to defend its currency—the real—indefinitely. In return, Brazil's government, under President Fernando Henrique Cardoso, agreed to enact a three-year, $84 billion austerity program that included tax increases, government spending cuts, and a firm commitment to preserve the stability of the real.

The new preventive package for Brazil failed to "prevent" a crisis. After receiving over $9 billion of the $41.5 billion, Brazil announced on January 13, 1999, that it would allow the real to trade within a larger band (representing, effectively, a devaluation). On January 15, Brazil abandoned all pretense of supporting the real and allowed the currency to float. During January, the real lost more than 40 percent of its value against the U.S. dollar, and investors took more than $8 billion out of the country. This failure occurred for several reasons:

- The initial $9 billion IMF disbursement alleviated the urgency in Brazil to enact reforms.

- Brazil's National Congress and state governors enjoy an extraordinary degree of autonomy in dispensing patronage and contracting debt. President Cardoso's promised reforms attacked this system of constitutionally protected political patronage and privilege.

- Faced with strong political opposition and an IMF package that made his reforms appear less urgent, President Cardoso failed to exercise leadership and force his reforms through an unwilling legislature.

- When Governor Itamar Franco of Minas Gerais declared a 90-day moratorium on paying his state's $15.4 billion debt in early January, investors quickly lost confidence in Brazil's ability to meet its obligations.

In the wake of the real's collapse, Brazil's government is rushing to enact the reforms President Cardoso pledged nearly three months ago. Both houses of the National Congress passed a bill to reform the social security and pension fund systems for public workers, which together account for about half of the government's $64 billion budget deficit (over 8 percent of gross domestic product). Cardoso also proffered to the state governors a plan to restructure their debts—estimated to be more than $85 billion of the $270 billion in total domestic debt—to the federal government if they agreed to downsize their bureaucracies, cut spending, and privatize water and sewage services. Most state governments are controlled by opposition political parties, however, and they do not appear disposed to accept fiscal reforms that threaten their clout.

Implications for the two Americas

The crisis in Brazil will hurt the United States, too. More than 2,000 U.S. multinational corporations conduct business in Brazil, with combined direct investment totaling over $30 billion; U.S. banks have some $28 billion at risk. Although Brazil accounts for only 3 percent of total U.S. exports ($16 billion in 1998), over 200,000 jobs inside the United States are at stake. The impact on the United States will worsen if the Brazilian crisis ripples across Latin America. The region's economic growth—forecast at less than 2 percent for 1999—is likely to slow even further. Other countries may devalue their currencies to compete with exports from Brazil. Interest rates, unemployment, and poverty are likely to rise in the region this year, leading many Latin Americans to question the free-market policies that have been blamed—incorrectly—for the crisis.

Conclusion

The record shows that IMF lending practices impose undue hardships on consumers and workers in developing countries. They destroy developing economies, waste U.S. tax dollars, and hurt the economic and security interests of the United States. Instead of relying on an IMF bureaucracy that lacks transparency and accountability, the Clinton Administration should restore the primacy of free trade in U.S. foreign policy: It should reinvigorate the effort to create a Free Trade Area of the Americas in Latin America and promote currency stability through currency boards or adoption of the U.S. dollar. This would lower the risk of financial crises in the future and mitigate the severity of any such crises that may occur; it also would promote economic growth throughout the hemisphere.

The privatization of national and state-owned services is encouraged by IMF policy as a means of raising funds. Can you think of any negative effects that such action might have?

The authors point out that Brazil's failing economy has international consequences and will adversely affect the United States. Do you think the situation would be any different without IMF financial assistance policies in Brazil?

Here the authors are referring to the Free Trade Area of the Americas (FTAA), a proposed measure that would expand the existing North American Free Trade Agreement (NAFTA) to every country in Central America, South America, and the Caribbean, except Cuba. Negotiations began after the launch of NAFTA in 1994 and are set to be completed in 2005. Go to http://www.ftaa-alca.org/View_e.asp to find out more.

DEBT RELIEF FOR POOR COUNTRIES, (HIPC): PROGRESS THROUGH MARCH 2003
International Monetary Fund

NO

The IMF and the World Bank have approved debt-reduction packages for 26 countries, 22 of them in Africa, under the enhanced Initiative for the Heavily-Indebted Poor Countries (HIPC). These packages will provide nominal debt service relief of about $41 billion ($25 billion in net present value terms). Taken together with other traditional debt relief mechanisms and additional voluntary bilateral debt forgiveness, these countries will see their debts fall, on average in net present value terms, by about two thirds.

Debt service is the interest payable on the sum of money loaned.

Traditional debt relief mechanisms include extending the period over which loans are repayable or taking out new loans to pay off existing debts. Bilateral debt forgiveness is when one country releases another from its obligation to repay a debt.

GDP, or Gross Domestic Product, is the measure of the total value of goods and services produced by a particular economy over a specified period, usually a year.

Can you think of other ways that IMF policies could reduce poverty and stimulate the economies of countries in which it has programs?

The international community has put substantial effort, not to mention financial resources, into debt reduction for poor countries. While many of the HIPC debt relief packages were approved less than two years ago, the HIPC Initiative is already bringing real benefits to poor countries. For the 26 countries that have benefited, we can say that debt service falling due:

• Will fall by about half in relation to exports or GDP [Gross Domestic Product] between 1998–1999 and 2001–2005;

• Will decline from 24 percent to about 11 percent of government revenue by 2005

For debt reduction to have a tangible impact on poverty, the additional resources need to be targeted at the poor. Before the HIPC Initiative, eligible countries were on average spending slightly more on debt service than on health and education combined. For the first 26 countries that have qualified for HIPC relief, this is no longer the case: all of them are now spending more on social services than debt service, on average almost four times as much; and all have shown a marked increase in the share of health and education in their budgets under their recent IMF-supported programs.

COMMENTARY: The HIPC initiative

The IMF and World Bank launched the Initiative for Heavily Indebted Poor Countries (HIPC) in September 1996 to provide special assistance to poor countries with exceptionally high debts that cannot be managed or repaid through standard systems of debt relief. The program was conceived to address the situation in a number of countries, particularly in Africa, where the amount owed in foreign debt far exceeds national income, and where continued external assistance remains necessary. The long-term goal of the program is to make debt repayments manageable, to help make economies sustainable, and to reduce poverty. The latter marks a change in emphasis in IMF and World Bank policy as a response to increasing criticism in the 1980s that its debt relief programs were too narrowly focused on recovering debt and often had the effect of increasing poverty and unemployment and reducing spending on health care and education in poor countries. The IMF and World Bank classify 41 countries as HIPCs. Of them 31 have applied for the HIPC initiative, and 26 have been accepted.

How the HIPC initiative works

The HIPC initiative has two phases. The first is a three-year qualifying phase, in which a country has to adopt a Poverty Reduction Strategy in consultation with the IMF and World Bank to reduce its debt burden and to tackle poverty. A "decision point" follows at which the IMF assesses whether the country qualifies for assistance under the HIPC initiative. Eligibility is assessed by comparing a country's debt burden to its export earnings; if its annual debt repayments are one and a half times or more than its annual export earnings, then the country is eligible, since the IMF considers this level of debt unsustainable. Selected countries then follow a second phase of structural reform and debt repayment with the objective of achieving a sustainable economy. There is no time limit on how long this process takes. Instead, key reforms and targets agreed at the decision point have to be achieved. The "completion point" is then reached, at which the IMF gives final assistance, including debt relief of up to 80 percent.

Campaign groups such as Stop the Debt and Oxfam argue that the IMF threshold for sustainable debt is too high and also that the organization's forecasts for export growth in HIPCs are overly optimistic. For example, a collapse in the price of coffee on the world market has caused the economy of Uganda, the first country to complete the HIPC initiative, to fall back below a sustainable level of debt. Campaign groups argue that complete debt cancellation is the most constructive way forward. They urge rich creditor nations and companies to forgo the money they are owed so that poor countries can concentrate their existing resources on tackling poverty, social welfare, and humanitarian crises such as famine and epidemics, thereby also reducing the dependence of these countries on external aid.

HIPCs: debt service and social expenditure

The table below was compiled by the IMF to show how the HIPC initiative is reducing debt repayments and increasing spending on social welfare in the 26 countries participating in the program. It shows the amount of debt service (interest payments on debts) already made or due and the amount of expenditure on social services. These amounts are expressed in millions of U.S. dollars. Most of the countries reached their decision points—at which they were judged eligible for the initiative—at the end of 2000 or later, so the full impact of IMF debt relief and structural reform programs does not appear until after 2001. The table also shows the amounts spent on debt service as a percentage of the countries' exports and of their fiscal revenues (income from taxation). The last row shows money spent on social welfare as a percentage of that spent on debt service.

	1999	2000	2001	2002	2003
Debt service paid ($ million)	3,118	3,009	2,225	2,251	
Debt service due after HIPC relief ($ million)					2,297
Social expenditure ($ million)	5,825	5,777	6,970	8,437	9,317
Debt service/exports (percent)	15	14	10	10	9
Debt service/fiscal revenue (percent)	21	21	15	15	13
Social expenditure/debt service (percent)	187	192	313	374	406

This information is available on the IMF's website. Go to http://www.imf.org/external/country/index.htm to find out more.

These countries are seeing clear gains, and the IMF has released the … data on debt service and social spending for all to see. These gains did not come automatically. It has taken time and effort to ensure that money is redirected to aid the poor in ways that most reduce poverty. Some of the HIPCs have uneven policy records, especially when it comes to governance. Often, this is because of serious problems that governments confront, including in many cases civil conflict, making it more difficult to qualify for the HIPC Initiative. Securing poverty reduction through debt relief in these countries will require creative solutions as well as unswerving efforts to use money as effectively as possible.

These countries face difficult problems. In war-ravaged Rwanda and Ethiopia, pressing reconstruction needs may mean large new loans at the same time that old debt is being reduced. Liberia and Sudan, both afflicted by civil conflict, have arrears on their debts that—if peace were restored and the countries set on a reconstruction path—would be too large to write off from the HIPC Initiative's current funding. And all of the HIPCs face the challenge of turning poverty reduction strategies into results, and ensuring that debt does not again become a barrier to social progress. These are not easy problems, and the IMF and World Bank are looking for solutions, with poverty reduction as the central focus.

Can more be done for poor countries? Debt relief under the HIPC Initiative will remove a critical obstacle to poverty reduction and growth from the path of poor countries, but it is no panacea. Without renewed growth, these countries could once again fall into a debt trap. We are working with the countries to lay the foundations for sustained growth through good policies. The HIV/AIDS crisis afflicting many poor countries is taking an enormous human toll. As it rips at the fabric of these societies, it makes such growth an even more difficult—though no less needed—undertaking.

More outside help is also essential. IMF Managing Director Horst Köhler, and World Bank President James Wolfensohn, have called in no uncertain terms for rich countries to meet the UN target for development assistance of 0.7 percent of GNP. Even more important, by removing trade barriers, the rich could also help to provide a livelihood for millions in the poorest countries while benefiting themselves.

Do you think that creditor nations and organizations should cancel the debts of such severely debt-ridden countries? Or might such action encourage poor countries to be irresponsible with loans and their own economies?

Is renewed growth an overoptimistic goal? Are some countries always going to be poorer than others because of a lack of resources?

Summary

The two articles present opposing points of view on the question of whether IMF financial assistance policies are harmful. Brett D. Schaefer and John P. Sweeney criticize these policies as worse than useless because they actually do significant harm to the economies of those countries they are intended to benefit. The authors are especially concerned about the austerity measures that are attached to such policies as a condition of aid, measures that make worse the severity of conditions faced by the most needy in the recipient countries. What's more, such measures are mandated by "an IMF bureaucracy that lacks transparency and accountability," meaning that they are imposed by international officials who devise these measures behind-closed doors with no incentive—such as democratic elections—to worry about their human consequences. In its policy statement about the Heavily Indebted Poor Countries initiative the IMF concedes that the organization's policies have not been successful in every case. But according to the IMF, this is not because of the policies themselves but rather because of serious problems that many governments confront, such as civil strife and the HIV/AIDS crisis. It also stresses the initiative's emphasis on spending on social welfare to alleviate poverty. The IMF therefore calls for a renewed commitment from rich countries to support policies that have, on the whole, had a very positive impact on helping put poor countries on the path to economic prosperity.

FURTHER INFORMATION:

Books:

Stiglitz, Joseph E., *Globalization and Its Discontents*. New York: W.W. Norton and Company, 2002.
Vreeland, James Raymond, *The IMF and Economic Development*. West Nyack, NY: Cambridge University Press, 2003.
Tirole, Jean. *Financial Crises, Liquidity, and the International Monetary System*. Princeton NJ: Princeton University Press, 2002.

Useful websites:

http://www.imf.org/
International Monetary Fund website.
http://www.globalpolicy.org/socecon/bwi-wto/imf/faq.htm
Straightforward information answering frequently asked questions on the IMF compiled by *Financial Times* staff.
http://www.globalpolicy.org/socecon/bwiwto/wbank/stigindx.htm
Articles outlining criticisms of the IMF.

http://www.globalpolicy.org/socecon/ffd/debtind.htm
Links to articles on international debt relief.

The following debates in the Pro/Con series may also be of interest:

In this volume:

Topic 5 Has globalization hindered the economic growth of developing nations?

Topic 6 Does the World Trade Organization need reforming?

The World Trade Organization, pages 86–87

ARE INTERNATIONAL MONETARY FUND FINANCIAL ASSISTANCE POLICIES HARMFUL?

YES: IMF programs focus on credit and loan programs when they should be concentrating on generating new trade and industry

YES: Austerity measures accompanying IMF debt relief programs cause economies to contract and suppress the development of new businesses and industry

DEBT
Do IMF financial assistance policies burden countries with debt?

RESTRICTING DEVELOPMENT
Do IMF policies limit the development of poor countries?

NO: They provide structured loans with workable interest rates and repayment periods to enable countries in need of economic assistance to carry on functioning

NO: They provide workable frameworks and support to countries at crisis point, helping get their economies back on track and encouraging social and economic development

ARE IMF FINANCIAL ASSISTANCE POLICIES HARMFUL?

KEY POINTS

YES: Rich nations—particularly the United States—have more influence on IMF policy than poor nations because representation at the institution directly reflects national income

YES: The IMF imposes its own values and systems on poor countries. Additionally, its decision making is conducted behind closed doors.

BENEFICIARIES
Do IMF policies serve the interests of rich nations rather than poor countries?

ACCOUNTABILITY
Does the IMF act arrogantly and fail to make its dealings transparent?

NO: The system of representation is fair; as the economies of poor countries become stronger, their influence on policy will increase

NO: The IMF is seeking to work with poor countries and is providing more information on its activities through media such as its website

Topic 8

DO TRANSNATIONAL CORPORATIONS HAVE MORE INFLUENCE ON THE WORLD ECONOMY THAN NATIONAL GOVERNMENTS?

YES

FROM "MEGA-MERGERS, MEGA-INFLUENCE"
NEW YORK TIMES, OCTOBER 26, 1999
JEFFREY GARTEN

NO

"COUNTRIES STILL RULE THE WORLD"
FINANCIAL TIMES, FEBRUARY 6, 2002
MARTIN WOLF

INTRODUCTION

Transnational corporations (TNCs) are firms that own and operate production units in more than one country. Economists have noted the rise of TNCs over the past 30 years in terms of both their size and numbers. In 1970 about 7,000 such businesses were operating internationally; by 1999 the figure had risen to more than 60,000. Many of these corporations today control assets that far exceed those of many countries. For example, in 2001 Wal-Mart had a revenue of $219 billion; this was about the same as the GDP (Gross Domestic Product) of Sweden in that year. General Motors, meanwhile, made some $177 billion in the same year, more than the GDP of Denmark.

Some people argue that not only are TNCs wealthier than many countries, but that they can exert greater economic and political influence than the governments of certain countries. However, other observers point out that TNCs are subject to the controls of national governments both directly and through the guidelines of international organizations.

A national government conducts the policies and affairs of a country; it has sovereignty (supreme authority) over its citizens and its territory, including the power to enact laws and to levy taxes. Much of today's international trade abides by the rules and agreements drawn up by the World Trade Organization (WTO). By 2000 WTO membership stood at some 135 nations. The heads of these states meet regularly to make decisions about the global economy; members have agreed essentially to recognize WTO rulings as having the power of national law. Other influential economic organizations include the World Bank and the International Monetary Fund, as well as the European Union; they, too, are bodies whose memberships are made up of individual nation states.

Corporations come under the sovereignty of the country in which they operate, so must comply with that country's laws, policies, and regulations. In addition TNCs are ruled by the treaty agreements that emerge from meetings of the WTO and the other government-controlled economic institutions.

"Did you ever expect a corporation to have a conscience when it has no soul to be damned and no body to be kicked?"
—EDWARD, 1ST BARON THURLOW
(1731–1806), ENGLISH JURIST

Commentators who believe that national sovereignty is not under threat from the rise of TNCs maintain that regardless of its wealth and size, a transnational cannot be compared to a country. A national government can still regulate, legislate, or override any corporation should its interests appear to be under threat.

What is more, not only does the United States maintain control of corporations located within its geographical boundaries, it also asserts jurisdictional control over the activities of U.S. corporations overseas. If a firm commits an act that renders it liable to

criminal or civil action by a U.S. authority, it can be prosecuted even though the act may not be a crime in the country in which it is operating.

Other people, however, believe that the size and wealth of transnationals can make them more influential than national governments. In 1998 official lobbyist expenditure by corporations in the United States was well over a billion dollars, while during the 1998-1999 political campaign contributions only came to over half a billion dollars. Lobbying firms include such TNCs as AT&T, Monsanto, IBM, and Enron. Critics argue that this kind of money exerts a powerful influence on politicians. Such lobbying promotes the passage of legislation that is beneficial to particular industries. Some people believe that much of the economic and foreign policy of George W. Bush, who became president in 2001, can be explained in terms of his links to the oil industry.

Transnationals may also be seen to exert a direct influence on the world economy because of their ability to pull out of certain markets. Some countries are reliant on TNCs in terms of jobs, investment capital, foreign exchange, and so on. The threat to withdraw from a country could lead to its government offering incentives such as generous tax breaks, direct capital investment, and flexible labor laws.

In the first of the two articles that follow, Jeffrey Garten argues that transnationals exert a major influence on trade and foreign policy, an influence that is often greater than that of some countries. Martin Wolf contends that such a view is misguided and based on incorrect figures. He argues that the economic power of corporations is actually in decline.

MEGA-MERGERS, MEGA-INFLUENCE
Jeffrey Garten

In business a merger is a fusion of two or more firms to increase profits or to diversify production. Horizontal mergers combine firms that produce the same product or service. A fear with these so-called mega-mergers is that the merged company might gain control of an entire industry, eliminate competition, and raise prices.

Garten was writing in October 1999. On November 30, 1999, the merger between Exxon and Mobil was completed to form the Exxon Mobil Corporation. The proposed merger between MCI Worldcom and Sprint (the second and third largest long distance carriers) was blocked by the Justice Department because of fears that the merger would be anticompetitive and would stifle long distance and Internet traffic. On April 26, 2000, the Justice Department approved the merger between Viacom and CBS, which now trades simply as Viacom.

YES

New Haven—Congress is about to eliminate the legal walls that separate commercial banks, brokerage firms, and insurance companies—opening the doors to a new wave of mega-mergers. Critics worry that huge banks will dampen competition and pay less attention to the average customer. But by itself, sheer size—whether in finance or in other industries—should not be a concern. The real problem could be the unchecked political influence of the new global goliaths.

Corporate giants

In just the past few years corporate giants have emerged across all industries. Citibank and Travelers, Bank of America and Nationsbank, and Deutsche Bank and Bankers Trust are among the major mergers that have reshaped banking. In other industries, Daimler-Benz has linked up with Chrysler; AT&T with Mediaone; British Petroleum with Amoco.... Still awaiting regulatory approval are some of the biggest combinations of all, including those between Exxon and Mobil, MCI Worldcom and Sprint, and Viacom and CBS.

We are likely to see much more of this. For starters, deregulation in Europe, Japan and countries like Brazil and South Korea is leading to many more possibilities for large acquisitions. In the past, a similar wave of mergers would have produced an outcry over mass layoffs, but with unemployment at 30-year lows, few today are complaining. Nor are many alleging today that competition is being eliminated. Because the markets are global, no company is reaching the size and scale that should cause concern about monopolies. If executives can manage these large entities effectively, Americans—in their roles as consumers, investors and even employees—ought to benefit from these new, competitive companies, receiving more and better goods and services at a lower cost.

The big problem is not with how these businesses are affecting competition, but with the inability of our political system to respond to potential problems resulting from economic globalization. Business leaders understandably operate on a global stage, while government leaders act in a

Do transnational corporations have more influence on the world economy than national governments?

Advertising for the 2002 Soccer World Cup. Coca-Cola was one of 15 international companies that were "official partners" of the event, reflecting the importance of TNCs as sponsors.

COMMENTARY: TNCs and development

The presence and activities of transnational corporations (TNCs) in the developing world have been the subject of much controversy. Most commercial enterprises exist to pursue their own corporate objectives, such as gaining market share and increasing profits, and some observers believe that such aims clash with the host country's economic and social development. TNCs and governments often have diverging views on some fundamental issues, such as human rights and wage rates.

Damage to developing countries

According to a study of the top 200 TNCs in December 2000 by the Institute for Policy Studies, the economic power of those firms is enormous compared to that of the poorest people in the world. The combined sales of the top 200 TNCs is 18 times larger than the combined annual income of the 1.2 billion people (24 percent of the total world population) living in "severe" poverty (defined by the World Bank as those who survive on less than $1 a day). Critics of TNCs such as Corporate Watch claim that they can cause a great deal of harm in the developing world. They cite incidents of incorrect or illegal behavior, such as the alleged exploitation of workers by TNCs such as Nike and McDonalds, which have been accused of employing children and paying extremely low wages. TNCs have also been accused of ignoring environmental and health and safety standards, bribery, corruption, causing homelessness, and mistreatment of their workforce.

Positive contribution to development

Advocates claim, however, that TNCs can give developing countries access to modern technological and management know-how, such as research and development, marketing, and finance, and can supply investment, employment, education, and training. TNCs claim that they are not all driven by greed and that they do make a positive contribution to the developing world. Global Business Coalition (GBC) on HIV/AIDS, founded in 1997, is an alliance of 80 international businesses, including Coca-Cola and Citibank, dedicated to increasing the number of companies committed to fighting HIV/AIDS. GBC believes that the business sector can help by implementing prevention and care programs for their employees (often the only program available), and by using marketing, lobbying, and communications skills to assist global HIV/AIDS programs.

way that fails to recognize the new global economy. Members of Congress spend infinitely more time dispensing pork in their hometowns than they do worrying about the stability of the global financial system or the strengthening of the World Trade Organization. Their narrow perspective on globalization is reflected in their eagerness to slice the budgets of the Securities and Exchange Commission and the Justice Department's antitrust division, the two institutions that have some ability to watch over global companies.

Too big to fail

To put it another way, the seesaw of private and public power is seriously unbalanced. Here is some of the fallout. Mega-banks like Citigroup or the new Bank of America have become too big to fail. Were they to falter, they could take the entire global financial system down with them. Many mega-companies could be beyond the law, too. Their deep pockets can buy teams of lawyers that can stymie prosecutors for years. And if they lose in court, they can afford to pay huge fines without damaging their operations.

Moreover, no one should be surprised that mega-companies navigate our scandalously porous campaign financing system to influence tax policy, environmental standards, Social Security financing, and other issues of national policy. Yes, companies have always lobbied, but these huge corporations often have more pull. Because there are fewer of them, their influence can be more focused, and in some cases, the country may be highly dependent on their survival.

For example, corporate giants can have enormous leverage when they focus on America's foreign and trade policy. Defense contractors like Lockheed Martin, itself a result of a merger of two big firms, were able to exert extraordinarily powerful force to influence legislation that approved enlarging NATO, a move that opened up new markets for American weapons sales to Poland and the Czech Republic.

Companies like Boeing, which not long ago acquired McDonnell Douglas, have expanded their already formidable influence on trade policy toward countries like China. Boeing is now the only American commercial aircraft manufacturer. Corporations like Exxon-Mobil will negotiate with oil-producing countries almost as equals, conducting the most powerful private diplomacy since the 19th century, when the British East India Company wielded near-sovereign influence in Asia.

But sooner or later … the United States will have to confront one of the great challenges of our times: How does a sovereign nation govern itself effectively when politics are national and business is global? When the answers start coming, they could be as radical and as prolonged as the backlash against unbridled corporate power that took place during the first 40 years of this century.

The task of the Antitrust Division is to promote and protect the competitive process through the enforcement of antitrust laws. Those laws apply to almost all industries, and they prohibit a variety of practices, including price fixing and predatory acts designed to achieve or maintain monopoly power. Go to www.usdoj.gov/atr for more information on the Antitrust Division.

The British East India Company was founded by a royal charter under Queen Elizabeth I in 1600 to trade with Asia. By the mid-19th century the company's rule extended across most of India, Burma, Singapore, and Hong Kong, and one-fifth of the world's population was under its authority. The company was deprived of its trade monopoly in 1813 by an act of Parliament and lost its administrative functions to the British government in 1858. It was dissolved in 1874.

COUNTRIES STILL RULE THE WORLD
Martin Wolf

NO

X Of the largest economies in the world, 51 are corporations; only 49 are countries. Critics of "corporate globalisation," some of whom protested against the annual meeting of the World Economic Forum in New York, rely on this supposed fact to justify their view that governments lie prostrate before unbridled corporate power.

Paranoid delusion

Theirs is a paranoid delusion. The calculations on the relative size of corporations on which so many critics of globalisation depend come from the left-of-centre Institute for Policy Studies in Washington, D.C. [*Top 200: The Rise of Corporate Global Power*, December 2000]. But they rest on an elementary howler. The authors, Sarah Anderson and John Cavanagh, compute the size of corporations by sales but that of national economies by gross domestic product.

Yet GDP is a measure of value added, not sales. If one were to compute total sales in a country one would end up with a number far bigger than GDP. One would also be double-, triple- or quadruple-counting.

To take one example, Bethlehem Steel sells steel wire to Bridgestone, Bridgestone sells tyres to Ford and Ford sells cars to consumers. If national income statisticians added the sales of Bethlehem Steel, Bridgestone and Ford, the steel would appear three times: it would be triple-counted. Instead, they sum the value added by each company, which is the difference between their value of sales and the cost of inputs bought from outside the company.

Empirical claims demolished

This example comes from a paper by Paul De Grauwe of the University of Leuven and Filip Camerman of the Belgian Senate, in which the empirical claims of the corporate critics are demolished [*How Big Are the Big Multinational Companies?*]. What, the authors ask, happens if corporations, too, are measured by value added, as national economies are? The answer is that they tend to shrink by between 70 and 80 percent. In 2000, sales by General Motors were 185 billion dollars but value added was 42 billion dollars; sales by Ford were 170 billion dollars but value added was 47 billion dollars; and sales by Royal Dutch/Shell were 149 billion dollars but value added was only 36 billion dollars.

The critics argued that in 1999, 14 of the 50 largest economies and 51 of the 100 largest were companies. In fact, only two of the top 50 economies, measured by value added, and 37 of the top 100 were corporations. For the critics, General Motors is bigger than Denmark and Wal-Mart is bigger than Poland. Properly measured, Denmark's economy is more than three times bigger than GM. Even impoverished Bangladesh has a bigger economy than that of GM.

Does the debate have any purpose if both sides use different sets of statistics? Is it even possible to decide who is right?

Countries vs. companies

But the flaw in such claims is not just factual but also conceptual, since countries and companies are radically different. A country has coercive control over its people and its territory. Even the weakest state can force millions of people to do things most of them would far rather not do: pay taxes, for example, or do military service. Companies are quite another matter. They are civilian organisations that must win the resources they need in free markets. They rely not on coercion but on competitiveness.

Does anybody doubt that the US legal system could break up Microsoft if it wanted to do so? Or that Microsoft would itself disappear if it ceased making products its customers wanted? Even the property rights of companies depend on the coercive power of states. In the 1970s, for example, the strongest oil companies were unable to resist nationalisation of their assets by some weak developing countries.

Some of these points can be illustrated empirically. Since companies must compete, they can fail. They do. Some countries perform better than others. But the ups and downs of corporate life are far more dramatic. Between 1980 and 2000, 20 companies had dropped out of Fortune's list of the top 50 companies and five out of the top 10. The economic power of corporations—their command over the markets in which they operate—is limited.

Fortune, a business and financial news magazine, compiles various lists of the United States' largest corporations and leading business people.

Corporations on the decline

There is also evidence of a decline in the economic power of corporations. One indicator of power is market concentration, on the—admittedly questionable—assumption that this indicates the potential for monopoly profits. Yet there is no evidence of a general increase in concentration. In some important sectors—telecommunications, for example—concentration has certainly declined.

COMMENTARY: The Enron case

Enron was originally a natural gas pipeline company. It was formed in 1985 by the merger of Houston Natural Gas and InterNorth, although the corporation did not take the name Enron until 1986. The company grew quickly, branching out into the electricity and water industries and in particular into energy trading. By 2001 Enron was one of the largest companies in the United States.

Enron falls

In August 2001, however, Enron's chief executive suddenly resigned, triggering concern about the company and a fall in its stock price. Then in November 2001 Enron revealed that its earnings from 1997 to 2000 were almost $600 million short of the figures it had originally reported. The company had created partnerships in which it had hidden its debts, so that the company appeared more profitable than it was. Enron's new stock value hit rock bottom, dipping below $1 a share (Enron was worth more than $90 a share in the summer of 2000), and in December the energy giant filed for bankruptcy. Executives who knew the true situation at Enron sold their stock before the crash took place and made a profit; shareholders who did not know what was going on lost their investments. Many employees lost their jobs, and to make matters worse, Enron retirees saw their pensions shrink because the company had invested much of the retirement fund in its own stock. The collapse prompted numerous investigations, not only into Enron but also the company's accountants, Arthur Andersen, who were found guilty in June 2002 of obstructing justice by destroying documents relating to Enron.

Political fallout

Over the years Enron had donated millions of dollars to both Democrat and Republican funds, including a large contribution to George W. Bush's 2000 drive for the presidency. The extent of this outlay raised concerns that Enron may have gained political leverage. Accusers point to the way in 2000 the company managed to avoid federal investigation in its dealings in energy derivatives (a type of financial product). Suspicion also remained about whether Enron influenced U.S. energy policy, and in 2001 the General Accounting Office, Congress's investigative agency, launched an inquiry into discussions between Enron and the energy task force headed by Vice President Dick Cheney. In March 2002 President Bush signed into law the Bipartisan Campaign Reform Act, which outlawed "soft money," the sometimes huge donations made by corporations technically for nonfederal political use. In March 2003 the law's constitutionality was challenged in a federal court; it received a mixed decision, which was due to be reviewed by the Supreme Court later in the year.

More fundamentally, the analytical assumptions of the critics are wrong-headed. Globalisation means an increase in competition and a reduction in monopoly power. Just ask GM or Ford what Toyota means for them.

Wrong numbers, incorrect understanding of trends and, above all, a misleading analytical framework—the critics are guilty of all these. But the worst of these is the last. By comparing the ability of companies to grow by satisfying customers, paying employees and rewarding investors with the ability of governments to exert coercive power, they are guilty of, at best, confusion and, at worst, deliberate misrepresentation. Companies are not comparable with states. Even if they were far bigger, they would still not be.

Does this mean there is nothing to the critique of corporate power? Not quite. Two points are correct. First, open borders increase the choices open to citizens, particularly to owners of mobile factors of production. This limits the coercive power of states. To critics, this represents an erosion of democracy. To supporters, it represents an increase in individual freedom. Both are correct, in their own terms, though the impact is not of corporations but of markets.

Influence of corporations

The second and more directly relevant point is that corporations do influence political decisions through lobbying and election contributions—as the Enron case demonstrates. For reasons explained by the late Mancur Olsen, famous for his influential analysis of the logic of collective action, concentrated interests generate unbalanced political outcomes. Yet corporations are not unchallenged masters of the universe. What changed in the 1980s and 1990s was not corporate power itself but what governments thought would work.

The change we have seen over the past 20 years should not be called "corporate globalisation." It is market-driven globalisation unleashed, consciously and voluntarily, by governments. Corporations are neither as big nor as powerful as critics claim. The firmly held belief in the opposite position is another urban myth.

For more information on transnational corporations and global economics see Volume 3, Economics, Multinational corporations and their role in world economics, pages 196–197.

How important is the sheer size of a company in its influence?

Summary

Writing in 1999, Jeffrey Garten argues that modern transnational corporations do indeed have more influence on the world economy than national governments. His worries do not lie so much with the ever-increasing size of these companies, the result of deregulation and major mergers the world over. Rather, he believes that people should be concerned about their political power. Business leaders are used to operating in today's increasingly globalized world; politicians, on the other hand, maintain a narrow, almost parochial perspective, which results in an inadequate understanding of corporate power. Modern corporate giants have enormous influence over tax policy, environmental standards, Social Security financing, and foreign and trade policy, and they use this influence to lobby for legislation that will be to their advantage. Garten thinks corporate power has reached near-sovereign levels in sectors such as oil and defense.

Martin Wolf argues that views such as Garten's are based on incorrect statistics and insufficient understanding of economic trends. First, Wolf contends that calculations that compare a firm's sales with a country's gross domestic product (GDP) are wrong; the two figures are not comparable, and the results overestimate the wealth of transnational corporations. Wolf also argues that countries and companies are radically different entities. A country has coercive control over its people and territory, while a company is a civilian organization: Companies rely on competitiveness rather than coercion to succeed. Corporations can, and do, fail, while countries rarely do. Finally, national governments always retain sovereign power over firms operating within their territories and thus control the growth of transnationals.

FURTHER INFORMATION:

Books:

Barnet, Richard J., and John Cavanagh, *Global Dreams: Imperial Corporations and the New World Order*. New York: Simon and Schuster, 1994.

Dahms, Harry F., *Transformations of Capitalism: Economy, Society, and the State in Modern Times*. New York: New York University Press, 2000.

Fatemi, Khasrow (ed.), *The New World Order: Internationalism, Regionalism, and the Multinational Corporations*. Oxford: Pergamon, 2000.

Ietto-Gillies, Grazia, *Transnational Corporations: Fragmentation amidst Integration*. New York: Routledge, 2002.

Montgomery, John D., and Nathan Glazer (eds.), *Sovereignty under Challenge: How Governments Respond*. New Brunswick, NJ: Transaction Publishers, 2002.

Useful websites:

www.corpwatch.org
Provides comprehensive information and analysis on the social and economic impact of transnational corporations.

http://www.transnationale.org/anglais/
International site that provides in-depth information on more than 1,000 companies around the world.

The following debates in the Pro/Con series may also be of interest:

In this volume:
Part 2: Globalization and its effects

DO TRANSNATIONAL CORPORATIONS HAVE MORE INFLUENCE ON THE WORLD ECONOMY THAN NATIONAL GOVERNMENTS?

YES: Governments have traded power for the revenue and business opportunities that transnationals bring to their economies

YES: TNCs are ultimately subject to the laws of the countries in which they operate

ACCOUNTABILITY
Is the influence of TNCs on the world economy limited by governments?

MONEY
Have governments allowed transnationals to accumulate power in exchange for money?

NO: Because TNCs operate in many countries, they can effectively escape legislation in all but the most regulated

NO: Governments are part of a larger international community; all transnationals are subject to international regulations and laws

DO TRANSNATIONAL CORPORATIONS HAVE MORE INFLUENCE ON THE WORLD ECONOMY THAN NATIONAL GOVERNMENTS?

KEY POINTS

YES: TNCs focus on a global outlook, whereas countries concentrate on national interests

YES: The economic power of TNCs is so great that they effectively shape government policy

OUTLOOK
Are TNCs more influential because they focus on a global rather than a national outlook?

POWER
Is the type of influence TNCs exert comparable to that of governments?

NO: National governments exercise power on an international level through organizations such as the WTO, which have authority over TNCs

NO: Unlike governments, TNCs are civilian organizations that exert influence through competitiveness and profit rather than the coercion of national laws and enforcement agencies

PART 3

CORPORATIONS AND THE LAW IN THE GLOBAL ECONOMY

In the closing decades of the 20th century the international community began to pay closer attention to the ways in which businesses operated. Problems caused by manufacturing, such as pollution and other environmental damage, became increasingly visible. Illegal accounting practices were exposed by events such as the spectacular collapse of the giant U.S. corporation Enron at the start of the 21st century. In response, many people began to push for governments to make corporations accountable for their business practices.

At the same time, however, globalization—the operation of companies in numerous countries— has not only opened trade barriers but has also made it more difficult to introduce and regulate effective legislation to control business activities. Transnational corporations (TNCs), for example, that object to the legal restraints in one country can easily relocate to another. Critics argue that pressure from TNCs weakens existing labor and environmental laws that already favor international business over the rights of local workers. Other commentators argue, however, that globalization has in fact made corporations more accountable for their

business practices. They point to the increased awareness of and spotlight on business practices led by antiglobalization campaigners, and to the establishment of organizations such as the Program on Corporations, Law and Democracy. Set up in 1994, the program campaigns to make people aware of the dangers of big business and its effects on the economy and culture in which they live.

Myth or reality

Between the 1970s and 1999 the number of transnational corporations grew from just over 7,000 to 60,000. Many of these corporations today control assets that far exceed the GDP of many countries. Such power, some commentators argue, inevitably leads to abuse. It is thus important that international legislation is introduced and enforced to protect the rights of other nations, particularly those lacking the economic or political might to adequately defend themselves.

There are many examples of the abuses committed by TNCs. For example, a British Broadcasting Corporation (BBC) report alleged that there were carcinogens— cancer-causing chemicals—in sludge generated by a Coca-Cola bottling plant in Kerala state, in southwest India. The sludge was distributed to local farmers as fertilizer, allowing carcinogens to filter into the water supply. Local people also protested that the plant's operations had resulted in an acute shortage of drinking water.

After an inquiry the Kerala state government has threatened to close the plant. Such episodes have convinced commentators that legislation is essential in ensuring the maintenance of ethical business practice.

break the cycle of poverty in which children find themselves caught. Other critics claim that establishing a global minimum wage would reduce the need for child labor, because adults would earn enough to support their family. Topics 9 and 10 examine whether banning goods made by child labor would stop the problem and ask if an international minimum wage is feasible.

A particularly controversial issue in any discussion of corporate responsibility is the arms trade. Do arms companies have as much right as other

---

"Socially responsible business practices strengthen corporate accountability, respecting ethical values and in the interests of all stakeholders. Responsible business practices respect and preserve the natural environment. Helping to improve the quality and opportunities of life, they empower people and invest in communities where a business operates."

—BUSINESS FOR SOCIAL RESPONSIBILITY

Corporate responsibility

TNCs are often accused of having exploitative labor policies, in the form of poor wages, bad working conditions, long hours, or using child labor to produce their goods. Some critics argue that nations should ban imports made by child labor or impose sanctions on countries that allow the practice. But others counter that poor families in countries such as Thailand and India often need the income earned by children. They claim that outlawing child labor could worsen the lives of the very people it is intended to help. Human rights organizations argue that investment in education would help

manufacturers to sell their products in a free market? Or should they be punished for supplying arms to nations that support terrorism. Topic 11 examines this issue further.

Copyright and the Internet

Corporations argue that legislation has to work both ways and that they must also be protected against business abuses. One particular area of concern is copyright infringement. Topic 12 examines the effect of the Internet on copyright enforcement, especially since firms claim that peer-to-peer networks have cost them billions of dollars in lost revenue every year.

Topic 9

WOULD BANNING IMPORTED GOODS MADE BY CHILDREN HELP STOP CHILD LABOR?

YES
"MEASURE TO BAN IMPORT ITEMS MADE BY CHILDREN IN BONDAGE"
NEW YORK TIMES, OCTOBER 1, 1997
STEVEN GREENHOUSE

NO
"CHILD LABOR"
ISSUE BRIEFS
WWW.HERITAGE.ORG

INTRODUCTION

"Child labor" generally refers to work that harms or exploits children in some physical, mental, moral, or cultural way. The children's charity UNICEF defines child labor as "employing children below 15 years old in factories and industries where they are not directly under the supervision of their parents." Statistics on the numbers of children working vary, but the International Labor Organization (ILO) estimates that there are at least 250 million children between the ages of 5 and 14 working in developing countries.

Until the late 20th century child labor was not recognized as a global issue. Although most developed countries have child labor legislation that restricts or prohibits minors from working in hazardous conditions—such as the 1938 U.S. Fair Labor Standards Acts—and international codes exist such as the UN Convention on the Rights of the

Child, some critics argue that the international community is not doing enough to stop the problem. They say that sanctions against companies or countries that permit child labor would help solve the problem by forcing them to ban the practice. Others state that although child labor needs to be eradicated, sanctions would simply increase poverty—the main reason why child labor exists—in these regions.

For many centuries it was acceptable for children to work. In the West children were viewed as little adults, subject to the same demands as adults, and frequently working for very long hours in very poor conditions. In the 19th century, however, matters began to change as laws were introduced to protect workers from exploitation. Gradually, the number of hours children could work decreased as children were taken out of the workplace and put into schools. But the problem has still not vanished. Even in western democracies children continue to work, particularly in agrarian communities where labor laws do not protect them.

"As many as 50 to 60 million children between the ages of 5 and 11 are engaged in hazardous work.... All are deprived of childhood, solely for someone else's gain."

—SENATOR TOM HARKIN, CHILD LABOR COALITION CONFERENCE, JUNE 2000

According to the U.S. Department of Labor's International Labor Affairs Bureau (ILAB), most child labor is in agriculture, service industries, and small workshops. Children are exposed to a variety of health-endangering materials, such as harmful pesticides in farming and carcinogenic substances like asbestos, mercury, and benzene in the mining, construction, and manufacturing industries. ILAB states that "one of the most basic strategies for addressing the exploitation of child labor is the enactment and enforcement of child labor laws." Many critics argue that sanctions would be effective in ensuring such enforcement.

Many people believe that trade sanctions have successfully brought about much needed change in the world. They cite the case of South Africa, for example, and claim that sanctions helped end apartheid there.

Supporters of sanctions believe that they are especially effective when offending countries or industries are reluctant to take decisive action. Trade sanctions can involve boycotting employers or governments that allow the use of child labor, denying aid to countries or industries using child labor, or banning the importation of goods produced by the use of child labor. However, ensuring that employers and countries do not use child labor—even when they claim that they do not—means that they need to be adequately and independently monitored. Sanctions supporters point to the ban on sporting goods produced using child labor during the 1990s as an example of the effectiveness of such an approach.

Some critics claim that sanctions are not the best way to eliminate child labor, especially since the ILO estimates that only around 5 percent of child labor works in export industries. They argue that family poverty often necessitates child labor and that sanctions would increase that poverty. Investment in development by the World Bank or UN-sponsored programs could raise the standard of living in these countries. Similarly, aid to create childcare facilities might help reduce dependence on child income. Meanwhile, some businesses have taken their own steps to address the issue by adopting codes of conduct for their overseas suppliers.

Other critics cite the significance of education in stopping child labor. They argue that greater investment in schools and teacher training in developing countries would greatly reduce the problem, leading to a better educated labor force in the future. The following two articles examine the debate further.

MEASURE TO BAN IMPORT ITEMS MADE BY CHILDREN IN BONDAGE
Steven Greenhouse

YES

"Indentured" child laborers are those who are obliged to work for a certain amount of time in order to pay off a debt; they also receive board and lodging.

Would you buy a product if you knew that child labor had been used to produce it?

Critics argue that if a child is the only member of a poor family who can find work, it is better than the family having no income at all. Do you agree?

As a result of a quiet maneuver by House and Senate conferees, Congress is expected to enact the nation's first ban on imports of goods made by forced or indentured child laborers, children who are sold into bondage by their parents and who must often work a decade or more to buy their freedom. The bill's sponsors say it will greatly affect the importing of rugs and carpets from Pakistan and India, where some children as young as 4 years old are sold into bondage. Human rights organizations estimate that South Asia has more than 15 million indentured child laborers.

"This is extremely important as a moral issue," said Representative Bernard Sanders, an independent from Vermont who introduced the legislation in the House. "Consumers in the United States of America shouldn't be purchasing goods made by children who are indentured servants and virtual slaves. We should not do business this way, and we should not be perpetuating this system."

Some experts on child labor question how effective the measure will be, suggesting that children will be exploited as long as poverty remains endemic worldwide.

The conference bill that includes this measure is expected to pass Congress quickly but Congress has not approved extra money to enforce the provision.

Children's rights groups estimate that the United States imports more than $100 million worth of goods each year—for the most part rugs and carpets—produced by bonded or indentured children. These groups also say that indentured child laborers are used to mine gems or to produce exported goods like leather goods and rattan baskets. Such labor, however, is also prevalent in brick and matchstick factories, which export little of their products.

Although Congress first passed laws restricting child labor in the United States early in this century, the provision in the conference bill would be [the] first law barring the import of any goods made with child labor.

"This is an incredible breakthrough," said Terry Collingsworth, general counsel of the International Labor

Would banning imported goods made by children help stop child labor?

A Palestinian child working in a shoe factory in Beit Hanoan in the Gaza Strip.

Rights Fund, a Washington-based group that has campaigned against child labor. "Now when we approach child-labor users in the carpet sector or other sectors, we have a tool. This will change the dynamics completely for us.

"Before, if you talked to someone in Pakistan who used bonded child labor, they'd say they didn't have to worry because there's no legal sanction in the United States," he said. "From the day this bill is signed, that will change."

Banning imports made by children

The bill, which is backed by the Clinton Administration, would not ban the importing of apparel or footwear made in factories that employ 13 and 14 year olds who are not indentured workers. But Senator Tom Harkin, an Iowa Democrat who also sponsored the provision, said he hoped that it would be a first step toward barring imports of all products made by children....

Mr. Sanders persuaded the House to insert the provision, on a voice vote, into the Treasury-Postal appropriations bill. He then joined with Senator Harkin to persuade House and Senate conferees on Monday evening to keep the provision in the bill, even though the Senate had not passed a similar provision. The appropriations bill is widely expected to be enacted in the next week.

Those campaigning against child labor predict that the United States Customs Service will receive help in cracking down on these imports: a steady stream of tips from child labor groups, here and abroad, that seek to hunt down employers who use forced child labor.

"This will empower nongovernmental organizations and child labor groups to investigate where children are being exploited," Senator Harkin said.

Federal officials say that before goods from a factory are barred from the United States, Customs investigators would visit the site to determine whether forced child labor was being used.

According to Human Rights Watch, desperately poor parents in India sometimes sell 5-year-olds into bondage for $50. The children often work for rug makers and are sometimes chained to their looms to prevent their escape.

In theory, these children are supposed to be able to pay off their debts in a few years, but their employers often pile on high interest and add to the debt whenever the children make mistakes in a task like tying knots in a rug. Many children remain in such bondage until they are 21.

This bill, which was passed in 1997, prohibited the Customs Service from allowing the importation of any product that is made by "forced or indentured child labor."

To read more about Senator Tom Harkin and his involvement in the child labor issue, see page 121.

A "voice vote" is a vote based on estimating the strength of "ayes" and "noes" called out rather than more formal forms of voting, such as counting ballots.

If child labor is a fact of life, would it not be better to try to regulate working conditions rather than impose bans that will not work?

Some experts on child labor say the bill fails to address the underlying cause of child labor: poverty in developing nations.

Elliot Schrage, a Columbia Business School professor who has helped coordinate an effort by the sports-equipment industry to stop the use of children in stitching soccer balls in Pakistan, said, "If Congress and the Administration really wants to end child labor in the developing world, they need to support efforts to educate children in poor communities, to provide their parents with meaningful jobs and to enforce laws that already exist in those countries that already prohibit forced labor."

…[R]ecently, Representative Sanders got rapid approval, without any debate, to insert the provision into the Treasury-Postal appropriations bill. His strategy, aides said, was to introduce the provision as an amendment when the House was trying to ram through the bill, which contained a cost-of-living raise for Congress that many House members were embarrassed about and wanted to dispose of quickly.

Since the Senate has not approved a similar child-labor provision, some House Republicans said they were ready to delete the amendment, voicing concern that it might be expensive for the Customs Service to enforce it. But Mr. Harkin, and Mr. Sanders, with the aid of the Child Labor Coalition, lined up the support of some important members of the conference committee, including Senator Ben Nighthorse Campbell, a Colorado Republican, and Representative Jim Kolbe, an Arizona Republican. The Administration helped by stating that the provision would cost little to enforce.

"This bill is a small step, but an important step," Senator Harkin said. "If we can show this works, the mechanism will be in place for a more comprehensive ban on imports made by child labor."

In 1930, Congress enacted a law that barred imports of goods made by forced, indentured convict labor conducted "under penal sanctions." That provision has been enforced only against goods involving adult labor; Federal officials said it did not apply to children because forced child laborers did not work under penal sanctions.

Opponents of child labor have often urged the Clinton Administration to stop the imports of some rugs and other goods made with forced child labor. But Customs officials have hesitated, saying they did not have the authority to do so. Administration officials said they backed the bill to end what they called an important oversight in the 1930 law.

Some experts argue that in certain countries, such as India, a lack of compulsory education is the main cause of child labor. They point out that other poor countries, such as China, have higher literacy rates and fewer child laborers. How might education help reduce child labor?

The Smoot–Hawley Tariff of 1930 was introduced to protect industry at a time of economic depression. The most significant part of the act was to raise import duties by an average of 60 percent. One section of the law prohibited the importation of goods produced by convict, forced, or indentured labor. It was partly directed at preventing the importation of goods from communist and fascist countries.

CHILD LABOR
www.heritage.org

NO

A number of policymakers have called for an import ban on products made in violation of another nation's child labor laws. While no American wants to see children exploited anywhere in the world, trade restrictions will hurt families in other countries by limiting their income and slowing their development.

Trade restrictions will further endanger, rather than protect, many children by driving child labor underground into even more unregulated jobs. An import ban will also hurt American families by raising prices and limiting consumer choices.

Should U.S. consumers be prepared to accept higher prices to combat child labor?

Unilateral policies

Discouraging child labor in other countries is near impossible to implement unilaterally. Child labor can be abolished only so far as societies are able, out of their own interest, to recognize and act on the need to limit the work of children. To achieve progress against child labor, developing countries have to address the root causes in the popular culture and institutions of their own societies. It is a complicated global problem that will not be solved by implementing U.S. trade restrictions.

Do you agree that it is up to developing countries to address the root causes of child labor in their own societies? What about the fact that many of the goods produced by child labor are exported to other countries such as the United States?

Poverty

Children work in other countries for a variety of reasons. The most important is poverty. Child labor often helps ensure the survival of their family and themselves. Children are often prompted to work by their parents. According to one study, parents represent 62 percent of the source of induction into employment. Though children are not well paid, they still serve as major contributors to family income in developing countries. To the extent a U.S. import ban is effective, it may have the unintended consequence of reducing already low family incomes and living standards. Moreover, an import ban will not address the root causes of child labor, poverty, the lack of schools, and traditional and cultural factors.

Some experts argue that certain cultures do not actively encourage social equality through national education. Do you think this hinders development?

Trying to eliminate child labor from other countries' export industries and occupations through import restrictions can result in the dismissal of working children. But they often just

COMMENTARY: Tom Harkin and child labor

Senator Tom Harkin has for a long time campaigned on domestic issues, such as health care, pensions, education, and children's rights. Harkin was born in Cumming, Iowa, in 1939 to a coal miner father and a Slovenian immigrant mother. After graduating from Iowa State University, he joined the Navy and served as a pilot from 1962 to 1967. In 1984 he was elected to the Senate, and he was again returned in 1990 and 1996, making him the first Iowa Democrat to earn a third senate term.

Child labor and the manufacture of sports equipment

Although child labor exists in the West, it is far more common in the developing world. Children in developing countries often work in cottage industries manufacturing sports equipment. In India, for example, the charity Christian Aid estimates that 25,000–30,000 children work in the sports equipment industry. These Indian children are forced to work to manufacture many different products, such as boxing gloves, shuttlecocks, volleyballs, and soccer balls. Although it is illegal in India for children to be employed in factories, the 1986 Child Labor Act allows for children to be used in cottage industries. Therefore this type of work is not strictly illegal under Indian law. The issue of child labor in the developing world and how people in the west were unknowingly buying sports goods made by children in poorer countries came to the public's attention in 1996, when *Life* magazine published an exposé on child labor and the manufacture of soccer balls. This led Tom Harkin and other politicians to take an active role in trying to stop the worst examples of child labor.

FIFA and the Code of Labor Practice

In 1998 Senator Harkin, along with Congress and international trade union organizations, first began to put pressure on FIFA (Fédération Internationale de Football Association), the governing body for soccer throughout the world, to adopt a code of practice that would prohibit the use of child labor and require decent working conditions and wages for adult workers in all FIFA-licensed production. Harkin was particularly concerned with child labor in Morocco, Pakistan, and India, where it was known that children were used to manufacture soccer balls that were then sold in the west. Consequently FIFA voluntarily agreed to adopt a code. However, in 2002 Harkin and other members of the House and Senate again called on FIFA to honor its code of conduct after it was revealed that there was evidence that there were routine violations of the code. They proposed imposing trade sanctions on sporting goods manufactured by child labor. In May 2002 the Senate approved an amendment to the trade bill, authored by Harkin, making the elimination of the worst kinds of child labor a priority in future trade negotiations.

Protesters in New York in 2001 demonstrating against Sean Puffy Combs' "Sean John" clothing line, which they claimed had been produced with the help of child labor and sweatshops.

transfer to other domestic jobs. This can further endanger, rather than protect, many children by driving child labor underground into even more unregulated economic sectors.

Unilaterally implementing an import ban runs the risk of starting a trade war that would hurt families around the world. Moreover, who would decide when child labor laws have been violated? How would it be enforced? Would this mean revoking the most favored trading status of countries such as China? What impact would the World Trade Organization have? Proposing an import ban may be good political rhetoric, but it is terrible trade policy.

China does not admit to having a problem with child labor. However, it has been estimated that as many as 5 million children may be working in factories in China.

Protectionism is not the answer

Threatening trade restrictions based on labor standards is not justified. The problem with such a stance is that not all forms of child labor are exploitive or cruel; the age deemed "child" labor is not clear and varies across countries; poor countries cannot necessarily afford such measures; and levels [of] poverty would increase. Furthermore, free trade is probably part of the solution to eradicating child labor. This is because free trade promotes development worldwide, and as countries develop, the incidence of child labor decreases substantially. Genuine human rights concerns are important, but protectionism is not the answer.

The author suggests that definitions are a problem in the fight against child labor. What definition could you come up with?

Summary

Child labor is an area of global concern. Most countries have child labor legislation in place, and international codes exist to try to eliminate the use of children in the workplace. While most people agree about the desirability of eradicating child labor, they disagree on the best method to use, and the idea of banning imports made by child labor has caused much debate.

In the first article journalist Steven Greenhouse, writing in *The New York Times*, looks at a bill proposed in 1997 by Congress to enact the United State's first ban on imports of goods made by forced or indentured child laborers. Greenhouse explains that supporters of the bill argue that it will help track down employers who use forced child labor. The article goes on to explain that although there is a law that bars imports made by forced, indentured adult labor, there has never been a bill to take into account child labor. This new bill goes a considerable way to addressing this oversight.

The second article, a labor information website brief on child labor, asserts that an import ban would endanger rather than protect most child labor by driving it underground into even more "unregulated" jobs. It would also, the authors of the brief argue, hurt U.S. families by raising prices and limiting consumer choice. The authors claim that poverty is the most important reason why children work in other countries and that an import ban would make the situation worse while not addressing the problem itself. A trade ban might also lead to a trade war, which would further hurt poor families.

FURTHER INFORMATION:

Books:

Hindman, Hugh D., *Child Labor: An American History*. New York: M.E. Sharpe, 2002.

Meltzer, Milton. *Cheap Raw Material*. New York: Viking Press, 1994.

Weiner, Myron. *The Child and the State in India*. New Jersey: Princeton University Press, 1990.

Useful websites:

us.ilo.org/ilokidsnew/ILOU/101.html
International Labor Organization facts on child labor.

www.childlaborphotoproject.org/childlabor.html
Child labor: frequently asked questions.

www.hrw.org/children/labor.htm
Human Rights Watch site on child labor.

harkin.senate.gov/news.cfm?id=183263
Senator Tom Harkin and World Cup child labor abuse.

www.dol.gov/ilab/media/reports/iclp/sweat5/execsum.htm
Department of Labor site.

The following debates in the Pro/Con series may also be of interest:

In this volume:

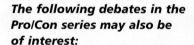

Part 1: Trade and the economy

Part 3: Corporations and the law in the global economy

Child labor, pages 126–127

In *Human Rights*:

Topic 12 Is the UN an effective advocate for children's rights?

WOULD BANNING IMPORTED GOODS MADE BY CHILDREN HELP STOP CHILD LABOR?

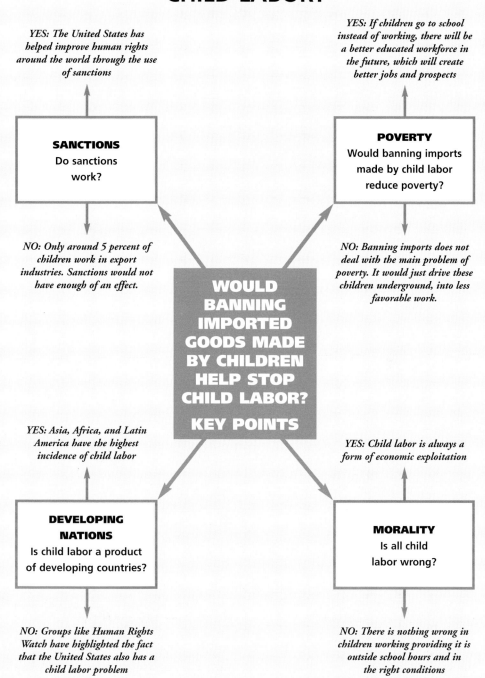

YES: The United States has helped improve human rights around the world through the use of sanctions

YES: If children go to school instead of working, there will be a better educated workforce in the future, which will create better jobs and prospects

SANCTIONS
Do sanctions work?

POVERTY
Would banning imports made by child labor reduce poverty?

NO: Only around 5 percent of children work in export industries. Sanctions would not have enough of an effect.

NO: Banning imports does not deal with the main problem of poverty. It would just drive these children underground, into less favorable work.

WOULD BANNING IMPORTED GOODS MADE BY CHILDREN HELP STOP CHILD LABOR?

KEY POINTS

YES: Asia, Africa, and Latin America have the highest incidence of child labor

YES: Child labor is always a form of economic exploitation

DEVELOPING NATIONS
Is child labor a product of developing countries?

MORALITY
Is all child labor wrong?

NO: Groups like Human Rights Watch have highlighted the fact that the United States also has a child labor problem

NO: There is nothing wrong in children working providing it is outside school hours and in the right conditions

CHILD LABOR

"One in six children aged five to seventeen—
246 million in all—are involved in forms of child labor that
should be abolished ... the causes are poverty, war,
natural disaster, disease (especially HIV/Aids)...."
—FELICITY LAWRENCE, *THE GUARDIAN* NEWSPAPER, JUNE 12, 2002

Toward the end of the 20th century many humanitarian organizations began to highlight the plight of working children, particularly in developing countries, claiming that most of them were exploited, working long hours for little pay, in often dangerous conditions. The United Nations (UN) has developed guidelines and legislation to tackle the problem, but child labor remains widespread. Many children in Asia, Africa, and Latin America work in agriculture, manufacturing, construction, mining, service industries, and domestic service.

The extent of the problem

Child labor remains a way of life in many developing countries, where families often rely on income from their children for their very survival. According to International Labor Organization (ILO) estimates, 61 percent of working children are concentrated in Asia, 32 percent in Africa, and 7 percent in Latin America. The World Bank estimates that there are 40 million child laborers in India, 12 million in Nigeria, and 7 million in Brazil. Yet the problem is also closer to home: Human rights organizations believe that more than 300,000 children, mostly from Latin America, are illegally employed in seasonal work on U.S. farms.

The age of working children ranges from four to eighteen, and the type of work in which they are engaged varies from hawking goods on streets to heavy manual labor in quarries and agriculture. The terms under which they work also vary, from assisting in family businesses or farms to being sold into bondage—when a family sells a child into enforced labor in return for a loan of money. Children often work 12-hour days in cramped, unsanitary conditions in which they are exposed to dangerous machinery, tools, and chemicals. Humanitarian organizations such as Human Rights Watch continue to research and publicize the extent of child exploitation. However, due to the often illicit nature of child labor, the common lack of infrastructure in the countries where it occurs, and the sometimes remote and inaccessible regions were it takes place, it is difficult to determine accurately the true extent of the problem.

A few of the most publicized cases in recent years include the use of child labor in sweatshops to make consumer products such as clothing and sports items for export to developed countries; the use of child labor on Ecuadorean banana plantations, where children aged as young as eight are exposed to toxic chemicals as they work beneath fungicide-spraying airplanes; and the use of bonded labor in India and Pakistan, particularly in the rugmaking trade.

International policy and guidelines

In association with humanitarian organizations and nongovernment organizations, three UN agencies have played a key role in formulating policy to alleviate the problems of child labor: the UN Commission on Human Rights, the UN Children's Fund (UNESCO), and the International Labor Organization (ILO). Building on three earlier declarations on the rights of the child (1928, 1948, and 1959), the UN approved the Convention on the Rights of the Child in 1989. Whereas the earlier declarations were statements of moral and ethical intent, the convention has the weight of international law. Article 32 addresses child labor, stating that governments signing the document "recognize the right of the child to be protected from economic exploitation and from performing any work that is likely to be hazardous or to interfere with the child's education, or to be harmful to the child's health or physical, mental, spiritual, moral or social development." The convention has been ratified by all members of the United Nations, except the United States and Somalia. In 1999 the ILO approved the ILO Convention for the Prohibition and Immediate Action for the Elimination of the Worst Forms of Child Labor, which has so far been ratified by 132 nations. It defines the worst forms of child labor as "all forms of slavery or practices similar to slavery, such as the sale and trafficking of children, debt bondage and serfdom and forced or compulsory labor," as well as the use of children in armed conflict, prostitution, and illegal activities—"work which, by its nature or the circumstances in which it is carried out, is likely to harm the health, safety, or morals of children."

Complexities and solutions

The international community is seeking to address the worst and most exploitative forms of child labor, while also recognizing that children will continue to work in poor countries for many years to come. The UN acknowledges that the type of work undertaken by children varies and in some cases can promote their sense of well-being and that of their family. In common with many humanitarian organizations and aid agencies it acknowledges that child labor is primarily a consequence of poverty, the lack of adequate welfare provision, and ingrained cultural practices. Developing countries need improved education and health care to break the cycle of poverty and to encourage a healthier, better educated workforce able to command higher wages and thereby remove the need for children to work.

Enforcing compliance to international guidelines is difficult for the same reasons as those already outlined for monitoring the extent of child labor. While some people advocate sanctions as an effective means to make governments accountable, such actions can have negative results, pushing children into even worse forms of work and greater poverty. Many people favor constructive intervention, such as conditions accompanying aid packages stipulating that the recipient country will restructure its welfare provision.

Topic 10
SHOULD MULTINATIONALS BE FORCED TO PAY LOCAL WORKERS A RECOGNIZED MINIMUM WAGE?

YES
"TO HEAD OFF MASS MIGRATIONS, SET A GLOBAL MINIMUM WAGE"
INTERNATIONAL HERALD TRIBUNE, JANUARY 23, 2002
MICHAEL ARDON

NO
"THE MINIMUM WAGE—GOOD INTENTIONS, BAD RESULTS"
WWW.LIBERTYHAVEN.COM
ROGER KOOPMAN

INTRODUCTION

Although wage regulation was introduced elsewhere in the late 19th and early 20th centuries—notably in Australia, New Zealand, and Great Britain—the United States has the oldest national minimum wage system in the industrialized world. It dates back to 1938, when a federal minimum wage of 25 cents per hour was set by the Fair Labor Standards Act, passed as part of the "New Deal" of President Franklin D. Roosevelt (1933-1945). That figure has risen over the years to the present rate of $5.15 per hour, introduced in 1997.

Today many countries have laws in place to enforce a national minimum wage. However, many developing countries do not. According to the United Nations, "over half of the world's six billion people [are] living lives of substantial deprivation, living on incomes that amount to $2 dollars a day or less." Therefore, some experts argue that the trend toward economic globalization means that there is a case for introducing a recognized minimum wage on an international basis. But would such a minimum wage benefit the workers of developing countries? Or would it put global business profitability and employment at risk?

Globalization has gone hand in hand with an increase in the influence of multinational companies on the world economy. Multinationals have been accused of exploiting the workers in some developing countries by paying very low wages and accepting low labor standards. Critics point to a phenomenon called the "race to the bottom," under which workers are forced to accept ever lower wages because of competition from countries where labor is cheaper. For workers in many developing countries the U.S. hourly minimum wage is a lot more than they can earn in a day. Critics of globalization view what they see as the growing inequality across the globe as morally unjustifiable and advocate an international minimum wage as a means of closing the gap between the "haves" and the "have-nots."

"It is not easy for men to rise whose qualities are thwarted by poverty."

—JUVENAL (55–127),

ROMAN POET

Paradoxically, however, the adoption of an international minimum wage might benefit workers in developed economies more than those it was primarily intended to help. Some commentators blame globalization for job losses in the industrialized world as companies move production to less-developed countries to save on labor costs. An international minimum wage would, some claim, help safeguard jobs in developed countries, since labor abroad would no longer be as cheap as it is now.

Opponents of wage regulation assert that supply and demand should dictate the rate at which a person is employed. Their central argument is that imposing a minimum wage does nothing but put low-paid jobs in jeopardy. In other words, when asked to raise to a minimum level the payment for a job that previously paid less, certain companies will be unwilling or unable to do so and will simply eliminate the job. This basic rule applies to those earning less than $2

per day in a developing country, just as it does to those who earn $5.15 per hour in the United States. Furthermore, minimum wage critics claim, in the case of developing countries, to impose an international minimum wage would be to rob these countries of their only competitive advantage—cheap labor. Such a move would deprive millions of their jobs.

Critics also point out that the cost of living in developing countries is substantially cheaper than in the United States. An income of $2 per day in India might be worth far more to an Indian than $5.15 an hour in the United States would be to an American. Therefore it is very difficult to decide what an international minimum wage should be.

The following two articles explore different aspects of wage regulation. Michael Ardon, professor of chemistry at the Hebrew University in Jerusalem, argues in favor of an international minimum wage. He asserts that restrictions on the free flow of labor result in inequalities in the global economy. Since removing all barriers to immigration would result in an unacceptable level of migration from developing economies to the industrialized countries, "the only long-term solution lies in bridging the gap between the per capita income in the rich and poor countries."

Roger Koopman, the owner of an employment agency in Montana, opposes government interference in wage levels. He argues in the second article that the minimum wage "harms most the very segments of our society that it is intended to help." According to Koopman, "Government intervention in these matters distorts economic decision-making, misallocates scarce resources, and destroys personal liberty."

TO HEAD OFF MASS MIGRATIONS, SET A GLOBAL MINIMUM WAGE
Michael Ardon

YES

Enabling the free flow of trade through the lowering of trade barriers (notably tariffs, or taxes on imports) is one of the purposes of the World Trade Organization (WTO). For further information on the WTO and its perceived strengths and weaknesses see pages 86–87, The World Trade Organization (WTO).

JERUSALEM—The fact that globalization is widening the gap between the rich North and the poor South, and is increasing poverty in many developing countries, is used to discredit the very idea of globalization. This is confused thinking.

The term "globalization" is generally understood to mean the trend to enable a free flow of goods and capital by removing national and regional barriers. Such a definition is misleading, because it leaves out one of the most important elements of a truly competitive global economy—the free flow of work forces.

Globalization, as practiced today, is based on fundamentally contradictory elements: a free flow of goods and capital, coupled with a ban on the free flow of work forces from country to country. Globalization based on maintaining restrictions on immigration is self-contradicting.

Flawed ideology

The basic paradox of the current ideology of globalization is that without the freedom of laborers to work anywhere, free competition and the rule of market forces in the global economy are mere fictions.

What is more, most of the negative results of globalization, as it is now practiced, originate from this restriction on the free flow of work forces.

It is this restriction which maintains wages of less than a dollar a day in developing countries. It is this restriction which leads to the coexistence of very poor and very rich countries in the world of today. It is this restriction which nourishes feelings of hatred and revenge in poor countries toward the affluent North.

Repetition of a phrase is a common debating device for emphasizing a point.

The long-term answer

But of course the North cannot afford to lift all restrictions on immigration.… That would result in migration to the rich countries by hundreds of millions of poor laborers. Such population movements could be seriously disruptive.

Should multinationals be forced to pay local workers a recognized minimum wage?

A blind child in India stitches together a souvenir soccer ball. For this work she is paid about 10 cents a ball; the balls are sold in the West for about $15.00 each.

COMMENTARY: Globalization and migration

In conditions of true free trade goods, services, capital, and labor are all able to move from one country to another with little or no restriction. This state of affairs exists within a common market such as the European Union. Generally, though, while goods, services, and capital can come and go freely, the movement of labor is closely controlled by immigration policies. Even so, economic globalization has been accompanied by migration of large numbers of people. According to a 2000 report by the International Organization for Migration, one in 50 people across the globe is in the process of migrating. Economic migration is nothing new, but globalization has apparently made western culture more familiar to people in developing countries and to move less daunting than it once might have been. Similarly, worldwide transportation and communications networks have made the practicalities of migration easier, and going abroad to find work now need not necessarily be a one-way trip.

The push–pull effect

Commentators cite the push–pull effect as being greatly responsible for this level of migration. Wide disparities in wages between developing and developed countries "push" workers into leaving the former and seeking their fortunes in the latter. At the same time, there is a demand for these people's labor in the wealthier countries—often in the service sector—which "pulls" them in to do jobs that native citizens do not want to do. According to a 1996 survey of about 500 undocumented Mexicans in the United States, they earned nine times as much north of the border as in their previous jobs at home—$278 per week against $31 per week.

The connection between migration and relative economic conditions in different countries is suggested by evidence that undocumented migration from Mexico to the United States rises and falls according to the strength of Mexico's economy—the better Mexico is doing, the fewer the migrants. Furthermore, differences in economic strength between neighbors mean that migrants need not necessarily move to western industrialized countries to improve their earning power. According to a report published by the International Labor Organization (ILO), in 1997 Indonesian workers could earn seven times as much in nearby Malaysia as they could at home—around $2 per day compared with 28 cents per day.

There is no rapid solution to the inherent contradiction between restricted immigration and globalization. The only long-term solution lies in bridging the gap between the per capita incomes in the rich and poor countries.

Only when this income gap is narrowed will a global free flow of labor be possible without massive migration.

People do not tend to leave their homelands for a differential increase in income. Language, cultural and social barriers, the high costs of migration and of finding alternative living quarters, all this tends to discourage people from leaving home unless they have to.

Given the choice between $20 a day at home and $40 a day in a distant developed country, most people will choose to stay at home. Not so, though, if the choice is between staying at home hungry on $1 a day and emigrating to a developed country where a minimum wage and social benefits are secured.

Do you think the minimum wage has encouraged immigration to the United States from, for example, Mexico?

Results of closing the gap

A reasonable gap in incomes between South and North that would minimize the drive to emigrate would have two positive results:

• A 20-fold increase in wages in the South would eliminate hunger and extreme poverty for billions of people, and would simultaneously eliminate the global dangers that result from these conditions.

• Foreign capital would continue to flow to the South, even if the ratio of labor costs between South and North were 1-to-2 instead of 1-to-40.

Would multinational corporations still build factories in developing countries if wages there increased by 2,000 percent? Do you think foreign investment and jobs would dry up as companies decided it was as cost effective to employ domestic labor and resources instead?

How to close the gap

But by what mechanism could such a substantial narrowing of the gap be achieved? One of the options is a comprehensive global minimum wage.

The minimum wage might initially be only slightly higher than the present low wages in some developing countries, so as not to disrupt their economies, but it would be increased annually. Ultimately it should reach 40 to 50 percent of the average minimum wage in the industrialized nations.

Compliance with such a minimum wage might be achieved by a ban on imports from countries that fail to adopt it.

In the aftermath of Sept. 11, the time has come to realize that a deluxe globalization for the rich, without globalization of the labor force, is not sustainable, and that until some equity is attained between poor and rich countries, no true globalization will be achieved.

Furthermore, if the gap between the two worlds is not narrowed, the poor countries will continue to breed forces that endanger the very existence of our civilization.

The author seems to imply that globalization, by creating a wealth gap, was at least partly to blame for the Al Qaeda terrorist actions of September 11, 2001. Do you agree with him?

THE MINIMUM WAGE—GOOD INTENTIONS, BAD RESULTS
Roger Koopman

Richard M. Weaver (1910–1963) was a philosopher and a professor of English at the University of Chicago. His book Ideas Have Consequences was published in 1948.

NO

Ideas have consequences, Richard Weaver once wrote. They pace the course of human history—both good ideas and bad. And while intentions may be honorable, the passing of time has proven that, in the long term, you can't get good results from bad ideas.

The minimum wage is a classic example of a good intention and a bad idea. The idea behind minimum wage legislation is that government, by simple decree, can increase the earning power of all marginal workers. Implicit in this idea is the notion that employment is an exploitive relationship and that business owners will never voluntarily raise the wages of their workers. Businesses, we are told, must be coerced into paying workers what they deserve, and only politicians know what this is.

Illogical reasoning

Not only does this line of thinking run contrary to the most basic economic principles of a free society, but it is also patently illogical. If government could raise the real wages of millions of Americans by merely passing a law announcing that fact, then why stop at $3.35 per hour, or $4.65, or even $10? Isn't $500 per hour more compassionate than $50? Absurd, you say, and I would agree. But the "logic" is perfectly consistent with the idea of a minimum wage, once you have accepted the premise that political decrees can raise wages.

What does make wages rise? It is most certainly not government edicts that simply rearrange and redistribute existing wealth. Wages rise in response to the creation of new wealth through greater productivity. The more that a society produces per capita, the more there is to distribute through the marketplace in the form of higher wages, better benefits, and lower prices.

The author is referring to a standard means of explaining the idea of economic growth. Imagine the economy as a pie. The more a society produces, the bigger the pie gets, so each individual slice also gets bigger.

The "bigger economic pie" concept is not complicated in the least, and yet it is a principle that seems to elude us time and again in matters of public policy. We know instinctively that government cannot create or produce anything. It regulates, confiscates, and consumes, all at the expense of the

COMMENTARY: The U.S. minimum wage

Minimum wage legislation in the United States began at the state level, in Massachusetts in 1912, and covered only women and children. The next year eight further states enacted similar laws, and by 1923 sixteen states plus the District of Columbia had minimum wage provisions. In the same year, though, the Supreme Court declared the District of Columbia law unconstitutional, a decision that brought state minimum wage legislation temporarily to an end.

Federal legislation

As part of the New Deal program in 1933 President Franklin D. Roosevelt (1933–1945) included minimum wage provisions for men and women in the National Industrial Recovery Act (NIRA), only for the Supreme Court to declare the NIRA unconstitutional in 1935. Three years later, however, Roosevelt proposed the Fair Labor Standards Act (FLSA), establishing a federal minimum wage of 25 cents an hour. FLSA, though amended many times, has remained the federal minimum wage law ever since.

Besides uprating the minimum wage numerous times, amendments to FLSA over the years have also extended the act's provisions to further sectors of the workforce. The initial 1938 legislation covered only those people employed in interstate commerce—that is, about 20 percent of the workforce of the time. In 1949 workers in the air transportation industry were included in the scope of FLSA, and in 1961 an extra 2 million workers in the retail sector were granted the minimum wage. Yet the employees newly taken under the act's wing were not awarded the full minimum wage at once. In 1961, for example, the minimum wage was set at $1.15, but newly included sectors received only $1.00, reaching parity over a period of four years in order to ease the burden on employers. FLSA was not opened to agricultural workers until 1966. But while nonfarm employees found themselves with a minimum hourly wage of $1.60 by 1971, that for farmworkers was capped at $1.30. Parity between farm and nonfarm labor was not reached until 1977, when both received a minimum of $2.30.

Amendments: 1996–1997

The most recent round of FLSA amendments came into effect in 1997, when the minimum wage of $5.15 was adopted. This 1996–1997 round also included a subminimum wage of $4.25 per hour for workers under 20 years during their first 90 days of employment, a $2.13 per hour minimum for workers whose wage would be made up in tips, and an enforcement clause under which violations of the act can be punished by a fine. Over and above federal law, most states have legislation of their own. As of January 2003, 11 states plus the District of Columbia had minimum wages that were above the federal level. Alaska had the highest, at $7.15 per hour.

private economy. And yet we still believe that government can wave its magic wand with laws like the minimum wage, and we all will be better off.

Politicians engage in this deception to buy political favor from special interest groups. We keep falling for these deceptions because our focus is on short-term personal gains rather than on the long-term consequences to the entire nation. We see the apparent benefit of having our own wages increased. But we don't consider the nameless victims of the minimum wage hike who will lose their jobs because the government has priced them out of the labor market....

The author uses the words of renowned economist Henry Hazlitt (1894–1993) to explain and reinforce his argument. Hazlitt believed in free markets rather than government intervention in the economy, and his book Economics in One Lesson (1946) was a bestseller.

All harm, no good

Commenting on the minimum wage, economist Henry Hazlitt put it succinctly:

You cannot make a man worth a given amount by making it illegal for anyone to offer him less. You merely deprive him of the right to earn the amount that his abilities and situation would permit him to earn, while you deprive the community even of the moderate services that he is capable of rendering. In brief, for a low wage you substitute unemployment. You do harm all around, with no comparable compensation. The net loss to society that results … is staggering. Those losses include: (1) The loss of employment to the individual himself, (2) the shrinking of the economic pie by the loss of his productive contribution, (3) the financial loss to society in supporting him in his idleness (unemployment compensation, welfare, etc.), (4) the financial loss in funding useless job training programs and other government efforts to get him re-employed, and (5) the net loss to society in having consumer prices driven up to cover the higher labor costs, and the loss of market share to foreign competition that may occur.

This article was originally published in 1988. According to 2001 figures, 29 percent of black teenagers (16–19 years old) in the workforce were unemployed, compared with 12.7 percent of white teenagers.

The cruel irony of the minimum wage is that it harms most the very segments of our society that it is intended to help— the unskilled poor and the inexperienced young. The evidence to support this is overwhelming, and it is the black community that is the hardest hit. In the 1950s, black teenage unemployment was roughly that of white teens. Following years of steady increases in both the level and coverage of the Federal minimum wage, over 40 per cent of the nation's black teenagers are now unemployed.

Just look at all the jobs that have been abolished by the minimum wage—good and worthwhile jobs for those who are taking their first step on the economic ladder. Movie ushers, gas station attendants, caddies, fruit pickers, dishwashers, fast food help, and a wide variety of other entry-level job opportunities have been either cut back or eliminated because the minimum wage has rendered them unaffordable. How tragic this is, when you consider the value of these low-level jobs to young and unskilled workers....

Do you agree that for some people even a low-paid job is better than no job at all? Or do you think that is just exploitation?

Do politicians have the right?

If a young person is willing to wash cars for $2.50 an hour to gain work experience and self-esteem, is it the right of Congress to tell him he can't do it? Is it, in fact, the right of any politician to make these kinds of economic choices for a free people?

Commenting ... on the minimum wage, [black economist Walter] Williams makes this critical observation:

It is important to note that most people acquire work skills by working at "subnormal wages" which amounts to the same thing as paying to learn. For example, inexperienced doctors (interns), during their training, work at wages which are a tiny fraction of that of trained doctors. College students forego considerable amounts of money in the form of tuition and foregone income so that they may develop marketable skills. It is ironic, if not tragic, that low skilled youths from poor families are denied an opportunity to get a start in life. This is exactly what happens when a high minimum wage forbids low skilled workers to pay for job training in the form of a lower beginning wage.

The author refers to a quote that likens low-paid work for young people to a medical internship or college education, inasmuch as it provides a gateway to greater things. Do you agree with this analogy?

In a free society, people must have the right to offer their services in the marketplace for whatever price they choose, whether they are workers serving employers or businesses serving consumers. It is by this process that productivity, wage rates, and prosperity are maximized. Government has no more business objecting to a low wage rate for a menial job than it has objecting to a business that offers its services or products for a low price. Government intervention in these matters distorts economic decision-making, mis-allocates scarce resources, and destroys personal liberty.

See Topic 1 Is a free market the best way to organize world trade?

If we are to remain a free people, we need to start trusting freedom, and jealously guard our right to make our own choices about our own lives. Repealing the minimum wage law would be an excellent place to start.

Summary

Whether multinational companies should be forced to pay local workers an internationally recognized minimum wage is a key question in the continuing debate about economic globalization. Michael Ardon and Roger Koopman put forward two fundamentally different viewpoints. The former believes that for the global economy to be truly competitive, it is not enough that there is free flow of goods and capital—there must also be free flow of labor. Removing all barriers to migration is not currently an option because of the mass movement from the poor South to the rich North that would result. Ardon proposes offering workers in the South an annually increasing minimum wage that over time would narrow the wealth gap and make migration less inviting if barriers to it were lowered. "A 20-fold increase in wages in the South would eliminate hunger and extreme poverty for billions of people," but would keep foreign investment flowing into developing countries, where labor costs would still be lower than elsewhere.

Koopman takes a completely different view of the minimum wage, arguing strongly for its abolition. In his opinion wage levels must not be manipulated: "Wages rise in response to the creation of new wealth through greater productivity. The more that a society produces per capita, the more there is to distribute through the marketplace in the form of higher wages, better benefits, and lower prices." He quotes the economist Henry Hazlitt: "You cannot make a man worth a given amount by making it illegal for anyone to offer him less. You merely deprive him of the right to earn the amount that his abilities and situation would permit him to earn, while you deprive the community even of the moderate services that he is capable of rendering."

FURTHER INFORMATION:

Books:

Cavanagh, John, et al., *Alternatives to Economic Globalization: A Better World Is Possible.* San Francisco, CA: Berrett-Koehler, 2002.

Friedman, Thomas L., *The Lexus and the Olive Tree.* New York: Anchor Books, 2000.

Neumark, David, *How Living Wage Laws Affect Low-Wage Workers and Low-Income Families.* San Francisco, CA: Public Policy Institute of California, 2002.

Stiglitz, Joseph E., *Globalization and Its Discontents.* New York: W.W. Norton & Company, 2002.

Useful websites:

www.policyalmanac.org/economic/minimum_wage.shtml
Almanac of policy issues page on the minimum wage.

The following debates in the Pro/Con series may also be of interest:

In this volume:

Topic 1 Is a free market the best way to organize world trade?

Part 2: Globalization and its effects

In *Economics*:

Topic 7 Is the minimum wage fair?

SHOULD MULTINATIONALS BE FORCED TO PAY LOCAL WORKERS A RECOGNIZED MINIMUM WAGE?

YES: Even if labor were more expensive than before, it would still be cheaper than at home

YES: By reducing North–South inequality, a minimum wage would make a mass migration less likely once movement restrictions were lifted

DIFFERENTIAL
Would companies still produce abroad if wages rose in poor countries?

GLOBALIZATION
Would a minimum wage aid transition to the free flow of labor?

NO: Introducing an international minimum wage would safeguard jobs in developed countries. It would equate to a protectionist measure.

NO: An international minimum wage would only make matters worse. Imposing a minimum wage would rob developing countries of their only competitive advantage—cheap labor.

SHOULD MULTINATIONALS BE FORCED TO PAY LOCAL WORKERS A RECOGNIZED MINIMUM WAGE?

KEY POINTS

YES: Huge wage differentials between workers in rich and poor countries should not be tolerated in a civilized world

YES: Developing countries are involved in a "race to the bottom," outbidding each other to pay the lowest wages to secure foreign investment

EXPLOITATION
Would it be morally right to increase the wages of workers in developing countries?

NO: Cheap labor is often the only competitive advantage that developing countries have when it comes to attracting investment from multinationals

NO: It is an affront to freedom and the general good to impose a value on someone's labor—especially if that value is too high

Topic 11

SHOULD COMPANIES BE PUNISHED FOR FOR SUPPLYING ARMS TO REGIMES THAT SUPPORT TERRORISM?

YES
"CHINESE COMPANIES SANCTIONED FOR PROLIFERATION"
ARMS CONTROL TODAY, SEPTEMBER 2002
ROSE GORDON

NO
"ECONOMIC FORCES, NOT HYPOCRISY, SHOULD GOVERN THE ARMS TRADE"
WWW.ROSENHAUER.COM
DEXTER P. ROSENHAUER

INTRODUCTION

The regulation of the arms industry to prevent weapons falling into the hands of repressive regimes or terrorist organizations has always been a controversial subject, but never more so than in the wake of the terrorist attacks of September 11, 2001. President George W. Bush (2001–) has pledged that the government will "direct every resource at our command … to the disruption and to the defeat of the global terror network." In so doing, the government is focusing on not only terrorists but also the regimes that harbor and support them. As part of the "War on Terror," it is building on existing policies to target terrorism. They include embargoes (bans) on the trading of arms to countries that foster terrorism and sanctions against foreign arms manufacturers that do business with terrorists and the regimes that support them.

The arms trade is currently the second largest global industry. According to a Congressional Research Service report published in 2002, in the preceding year U.S. companies signed deals to supply $12 billion worth of arms, while the Russians signed $5.8 billion worth of contracts, the French $2.9 billion, and the Germans $1 billion.

If imposing penalties on companies reduces or eliminates the threat of terrorism, or terrorism itself, then few people would contest that governments have a moral duty to take such action. However, the situation is not clear-cut.

The arms trade was contentious long before September 11. Some people believe that it is intrinsically bad, while others consider it inevitable because conflict is a reality in human affairs. They see the arms trade as a business like any other, satisfying laws of supply and demand. As such, they believe it should be allowed to operate in a free market without limitations imposed by governments.

However, many commentators argue that governments have an obligation to control the arms trade because of the effect it can have on national and world stability. Countries and international organizations like the United Nations (UN) impose arms controls to ensure that weapons are not sold to powers that threaten world peace and security. However, constantly shifting political allegiances make this a difficult task—as the cases of Afghanistan and Iraq show.

"[A]ll states shall … refrain from providing any form of support, active or passive, to entities or persons involved in terrorist acts, including by … eliminating the supply of weapons to terrorists…."

—UN SECURITY COUNCIL RESOLUTION 1373 (2001)

While some people believe that terrorism—using violence to instill fear in order to achieve a goal—is always indefensible, others argue that it depends on the end to which violence is directed: Some people's terrorists are other's freedom fighters. In the 1980s the United States supported the Nicaraguan Democratic Force in its fight against the Marxist Sandinista government, even though the international community recognized the legitimacy of that government.

Although there are often problems associated with agreement on terrorist organizations, in many cases there is widespread consensus. The United Nations condemns any form of terrorism and since 1989 has placed 14 arms embargoes on state governments or opposition groups that pose a threat to world peace for reasons including the support of terrorism. On September 28, 2001, the UN Security Council adopted a wideranging antiterrorism resolution (Resolution 1373). UN member countries are required to pass national laws in line with embargoes to make it a criminal offense for any of their citizens to break the embargoes. Governments also impose their own sanctions. The Department of State had designated 36 foreign terrorist organizations as of March 2003.

While the aim of arms embargoes is to remove the supply of arms to hostile powers and thereby reduce the threat they pose, many commentators believe that such measures are ineffective. They argue that if there is demand for weapons, and that if terrorists or their supporters have funds to buy them, then the trade will continue. Most commentators recognize that sanctions of any type are difficult to monitor and enforce. Critics also maintain that sanctions can have a negative effect, forcing the arms trade underground. At least if the trade is legal, it can be monitored. There are also practical problems associated with deciding what items should be included under sanctions and embargoes. While finished weapons are easy to identify, components and substances are more difficult to control—it is not always possible to know to what end a product will be used. The following articles examine the debate further.

CHINESE COMPANIES SANCTIONED FOR PROLIFERATION
Rose Gordon

YES

On July 9, the Bush administration sanctioned nine Chinese entities and an Indian individual for knowingly contributing to the efforts of Iran and possibly Iraq to acquire weapons of mass destruction or advanced conventional weapons.

Effective immediately, the sanctions, levied under the 1991 Chemical and Biological Weapons Control and Warfare Elimination Act and the 1992 Iran–Iraq Arms Nonproliferation Act, prohibit the United States from conducting business with or providing financial or technical assistance to any of the 10 entities. The sanctions, in place for a year under the Chemical and Biological Weapons law and two years under the Iran–Iraq law, also bar the United States from providing the 10 entities with military and dual-use technology, items on the U.S. Munitions List, and certain other items requiring a government-issued export license.

First use of law

These are the first entities to be sanctioned under the 10-year-old Iran–Iraq law, which applies to entities that transfer goods or technology that could assist either Iran or Iraq in acquiring "chemical, biological, nuclear, or destabilizing numbers and types of advanced conventional weapons." The Chemical and Biological Weapons law applies to entities transferring goods or technology that could help any country or group to "acquire, use or stockpile chemical or biological weapons."

State Department officials declined to specify which entities were transferring what types of items to which country, but in a July 19 press briefing State Department spokesman Richard Boucher said that eight of the entities were being sanctioned for transfers to Iran, and two were being sanctioned for helping Iran develop chemical weapons.

As listed in the July 25 Federal Register, these Chinese companies were sanctioned under both the Iran–Iraq law and the Chemical and Biological Weapons law: Jiangsu Yongli Chemicals and Technology Import and Export Corporation,

COMMENTARY: The weapons industry

Since the end of World War II in 1945 there have been roughly 150 major armed conflicts in the world, leading to the deaths of tens of millions of people. Spending on weapons to fight these wars remained high. At the same time, the United States and the Soviet Union spent enormous sums developing and procuring new tanks, ships, aircraft, guns, and missiles in the quest for technological superiority in the Cold War.

The Cold War and the growth of the arms industry
In 1961 President Eisenhower (1953–1961) warned Americans that U.S. industry was becoming dangerously dependent on military spending—that a "military–industrial complex" was being created that would have its own agenda in trying to sustain growth in weapons spending regardless of the political climate. These concerns were addressed at an international level by the United Nations, which initiated a series of nonproliferation measures to deescalate the arms race (see page 147). Despite nonproliferation treaties, by the mid-1980s global military spending reached an all-time high, equivalent in 1987 to $271 per person on Earth. With the end of the Cold War in 1990–1991 many observers hoped that resources—the so-called "peace dividend"—would be freed up for spending on more socially constructive projects. Some critics of current U.S. foreign policy believe that the threat of international terrorism would be more effectively reduced through spending of this kind than through the policy of security assistance, whereby military training and arms are provided to countries considered to be of strategic importance.

New conflicts and increased spending
Although the global weapons industry had lost about a third of its value by the mid-1990s, by 1997 world arms spending began to rise again. One effect of the ending of the Cold War was the reactivation of old quarrels—mostly rivalries fueled by ethnic nationalism—that had previously been kept in check by the superpowers. Ethnic tensions ignited in major wars in Chechnya, between Armenia and Azerbaijan, and in the former Yugoslavia. Following the 1995 assassination of Yitzakh Rabin, prime minister of Israel, the peace process between Israel and the Palestinians deteriorated, increasing tensions and instability in the Middle East as a whole. All of these conflicts, and many others, increased violence, or the threat or fear of violence, resulting in increased markets for arms. Following 9/11 this effect has been intensified even further. The U.S. policy of providing security assistance has led to a substantial increase in the U.S. arms trade. The military response in Afghanistan was a multibillion dollar effort, while estimates of the final cost of the war in Iraq in 2003 range as high as $100 billion. The global arms trade seems likely to continue its upward trend.

A client testing a Russian-made gun at a weapons trade fair in Abu Dhabi in February 1993.
Russia has been a major supplier of arms to Middle Eastern countries, including Iran and Iraq.

China Machinery and Equipment Import Export Corporation, China National Machinery and Equipment Import Export Corporation, CMEC Machinery and Electric Equipment Import and Export Company Ltd., CMEC Machinery and Electrical Import Export Company Ltd., China Machinery and Electric Equipment Import and Export Company, Wha Cheong Tai Company Ltd., and Chinese citizen Q.C. Chen.

Sanctioned exclusively under the Iran–Iraq law were the China Shipbuilding Trading Company and the Indian individual Hans Raj Shiv, who the State Department believes resides in the Middle East.

Chinese companies have been sanctioned three times this year for helping Iran to develop chemical or biological weapons....

Not the first time

Five of the 10 entities have been previously penalized by U.S. sanctions. Under the Iran Nonproliferation Act, which bans the transfer of equipment that could aid Iran's "development of nuclear, biological or chemical weapons, or ballistic or cruise missile systems," the Jiangsu Yongli Chemicals and Technology Import and Export Corporation was sanctioned in June 2001, the China Machinery and Electric Equipment Import and Export Company in January 2002, and the Wha Cheong Tai Company Ltd. and the China Shipbuilding Trading Company in May 2002. This is the fourth time Chinese citizen Q.C. Chen has been charged with violating U.S. nonproliferation laws since 1997.

If an entity is currently under previous sanctions, the new sanctions extend the time they are subject to penalty, Boucher said.

China's Foreign Ministry expressed opposition to the U.S. decision, calling the sanctions "unreasonable," Agence France-Presse reported July 22. China also called the sanctions levied in January and May "unreasonable." The sanctions do not apply to the Chinese government.

Do you think that the willingness of companies from developing countries such as China to supply weapons to states blacklisted by other nations demonstrates that arms sanctions are unworkable?

Unless these companies would normally do business with the United States, these laws will have no effect. Can you think of any more effective legal method of trying to prevent certain countries from acquiring dangerous materials?

Should U.S. action against China have international backing? If so, is it primarily a political matter that should be addressed through the UN, or is it mainly a trade issue that should be dealt with by the World Trade Organization?

ECONOMIC FORCES, NOT HYPOCRISY, SHOULD GOVERN THE ARMS TRADE
Dexter P. Rosenhauer

> Neoclassical economics is the free market system, which has been the dominant trend in economic policy since World War II (1939–1945).

> The author launches into his argument immediately. This approach is a good way to attract and keep the reader's attention.

NO

Any neo-classical economist worth his or her salt can put forward a good argument against barriers to trade, be these tariffs (taxes) imposed by a government on certain imports, or subsidies paid to domestic companies to help them compete on international markets. There really can be no justification for such policies, most economists rightly argue, because they ultimately lead to the reduced efficiency and competitiveness of firms at home, retaliatory policies by foreign governments, and the subsequent slowing down of international trade to the detriment of all concerned.

However, what about sanctions imposed on a particular country or firm for political reasons? Surely barriers of this sort can be justified under certain moral circumstances, or where there is a question of national security? In these days of the so-called "war on terror," for example, shouldn't we be using every means at our disposal to prevent weapons, particularly chemical, biological, and nuclear, getting into the wrong hands? Shouldn't we be imposing sanctions on governments, or at least fining (in the case of domestic arms firms) or restricting our own involvement with (foreign) arms manufacturers, who are selling weapons to regimes known to be supporters of terrorism? Surely imposing a barrier to such unethical trade can be justified?

Well, actually, no, not necessarily; sanctions applied under even these exceptional circumstances are not only an exercise in breathtaking hypocrisy in most cases, but often serve no purpose other than to adversely affect the competitiveness of domestic firms in the global arms market.

> Do you agree with this statement? Is all violent action wrong? See Volume 1, Individual and Society, Topic 10 Is violent protest ever justified?

Subjective application of terms

First, what a government defines to be the "wrong hands" or a "supporter of terrorism" is entirely subjective; it is entirely open to the interpretation of the politicians making the decision whether or not to impose a particular sanction, restrict the import or export of a particular weapon, or fine a particular arms company. The United States' 1992 Iran–Iraq Arms Nonproliferation Act legislates for sanctions to be

COMMENTARY: Arms controls and terrorism

Embargoes and sanctions are part of a wider framework developed by the international community to prevent weapons from getting into the hands of powers that threaten world peace and security. During and since the Cold War the United Nations has sought to reduce and regulate weapons of mass destruction—nuclear, biological, and chemical. Such strategies have assumed new importance following Osama Bin Laden's stated aim to acquire and use weapons of mass destruction against the West.

Nonproliferation and threat reduction

Key nonproliferation measures include the international Nuclear Non-Proliferation Treaty (1970), the Biological Weapons Convention (1975) and the Chemical Weapons Convention (1992), which aim to eliminate these categories of weapons, and the Global Partnership against the Spread of Weapons of Mass Destruction (2002). The United States and Russia have also signed the Strategic Arms Reduction treaties—START I (1991) and START II (1993)—to reduce their stockpiles of nuclear weapons, and in 1991 Congress enacted the Nunn-Lugar program, an initiative to secure and eliminate weapons of mass destruction and related materials.

Many military experts emphasize the importance of making existing weapons of mass destruction and associated technologies secure to prevent them from falling into the hands of terrorists. The Department of Energy recently estimated that enough nuclear material exists in Russia alone to make more than 100,000 nuclear weapons. There are widespread concerns about security at facilities housing this material in all the republics of the former Soviet Union and the ease with which terrorists might get hold of it and smuggle it across borders. Critics argue that Western governments need to devote far more resources to recording, protecting, and destroying such nuclear materials as part of the war on terrorism.

Security assistance and counterterrorism

The United States has also provided countries of strategic importance with security assistance (such as military training and provision of arms) in order to counter the threat of international terrorism. Shortly after the September 11, 2001, attacks the Bush administration lifted sanctions on Pakistan, a country of strategic importance for the subsequent U.S. campaign against Al Qaeda in Afghanistan. Embargoes had been imposed after Pakistan tested nuclear devices in 1998 and after President Pervez Musharraf came to power in a military coup. Many observers have criticized U.S. action in Pakistan and the other countries to which it has given security assistance. They argue that U.S. actions often contradict international counterterrorism and nonproliferation measures, and in many cases exacerbate existing regional hostilities.

applied to companies supplying arms to Iran and Iraq (prior to the invasion this year by the United States and its allies and the subsequent fall of Saddam Hussein's regime). But how is it that George W. Bush's administration has decided that the regimes in Iran and Iraq are (or in the case of Iraq, were) supporters of terrorism while that in Saudi Arabia, say, whose nationals made up 15 of the 19 hijackers on September 11, 2001, and from where Osama bin Laden himself heralds, has no case to answer?

Do you think this inconsistency is an argument for not sanctioning Iran and Iraq? Or is it an argument for sanctioning Saudi Arabia as well?

Then to take the other member of Bush's "axis of evil," while North Korea may be pressing ahead with its nuclear weapons program, in what way is that more of a threat to the West (or any other country) than Pakistan's, India's, or indeed Israel's undoubted nuclear capability?

Meanwhile, as the old adage goes, one person's terrorist is another's freedom fighter. Many Irish-Americans used to lend political support and, it is often alleged, weapons and money as well, to what most people would describe as a terrorist organization. The Irish Republican Army (IRA) may be winding down operations these days, but many argue that it would not have survived this long without U.S. support.

In 1981 the Reagan administration authorized the payment of $19 million in military aid to the FDN (Nicaraguan Democratic Force), armed opponents of Nicaragua's Sandinista government. Covert CIA operations followed providing, for example, finance, weapons, and training to the FDN and other contras ("counter revolutionaries"). Given the level of popular support that the Marxist Sandinistan government enjoyed in Nicaragua at that time, many people (including the World Court) interpreted U.S. action in this instance as support for terrorism.

How do these by no means isolated instances sit, then, with arguments that say the American, the British, and other governments should apply sanctions to those who supply weapons to regimes that support terrorism?

The "right hands"?

How important do you think it is that arms manufacturers do "remain in business"? Are the benefits they bring to a nation's economy, such as increased employment and revenue, outweighed by their potential use in contravention of international law?

If arms manufacturers are going to remain in business, they must be allowed to sell their goods. The world's largest arms trader is the United States; U.S. weapons producers made new agreements worth $12.1 billion in 2001, and delivered $9.7 billion worth of arms in that year. The United Kingdom, Russia, France, Germany, and Italy also have massive arms industries. The vast majority of these companies' multimillion dollar turnovers depend on export markets overseas. So what constitutes selling only into the "right hands"?

A number of recent reports have found that while the United States, the United Kingdom, and other governments may be clamping down on arms exports to a small number of specific ("terrorist") regimes, these governments have on the whole loosened controls on arms exports since the attacks of September 11, supplying increasing amounts of weapons to countries seen as being "on side" in the "war on terror."

For example, in 2002, the Group of Eight (G8) nations were responsible for more than 80 percent (some $19 billion each year) of all new weapons reaching the developing world. Many of these weapons were certainly destined for highly unstable regions and nations, and for regimes with poor records in terms of human rights, and for those that can barely feed their own populations.

Where do we draw the line, then? In controlling arms exports to "terrorist" regimes are we merely serving to direct ever increasing supplies of armaments toward governments that will use them for torture or to suppress dissent within their own populations? Or toward poor countries who often purchase such weapons at the expense of public health systems, or education? Taking a broader perspective, there really aren't many "right" hands for armaments.

A futile exercise

What is more, the arbitrary application of sanctions and fines upon those companies and nations who supply weapons to "terrorist" regimes is, essentially, pointless. As with the trade in illegal drugs, where there is a demand, there will always be a supply. Fines and legislation aimed at arms manufacturers only serve to force such companies to find new and more complex routes through which they will direct their goods; ultimately those goods will find their way into the hands of those who desire them, be they the "wrong" or the "right" ones. As recently as 2001, supporters of Osama bin Laden were able to buy U.S.-made missiles and arms in the Pakistani city of Peshawar.

Time to dispense with hypocrisy

As with any other barrier to trade that we look at in detail, those that are applied to international weapons transfers have more to do with the politics of the day than any ethical, moral, or, indeed, economic argument. While this is the case, we should dispense with hypocrisy and let the economic laws of supply and demand in a free trade environment govern this trade, as with any other.

Is it better for Western countries to supply arms to the developing world because if they do not, other countries will? Or would it be better not to supply them and to put pressure on other countries, through the UN, not to do so either?

The author compares the arms trade to the drugs trade. Crops to produce drugs can be grown in the poorest countries of the world, whereas armaments are complex pieces of machinery that need technical knowledge and an advanced industrial infrastructure to produce. Do you think this affects the validity of his argument?

If it is hypocritical to apply a rule inconsistently, is it better not to attempt to apply it at all, as the author suggests? Or is it better to try to apply it more consistently?

Summary

Should companies be fined for supplying arms to regimes that support terrorism? The Bush administration has stressed the grave potential dangers in the post-Cold War world of so-called "rogue states"—states that support terrorism—acquiring weapons of mass destruction. An important part of the Bush administration's war on terrorism is to halt the proliferation of such weapons. To this end, the Bush administration has used economic sanctions to restrict trade in technologies and other exports that have potential military applications, as discussed by Rose Gordon. Such sanctions are controversial. Among the controversies they raise is their subjective application. Dexter Rosenhauer argues that what a government defines as the "wrong hands" or a "supporter of terrorism" is subjective: He questions why Saudi Arabia is supported rather than targeted and points to past American support for the terrorist activities of the Irish Republican Army in Northern Ireland and the Nicaraguan Democratic Force in Nicaragua. He also argues that wealthy G8 nations have increased their trade in weapons to poor, unstable developing countries, often with bad human rights records. Considering these factors, Rosenhauer concludes that the United States does not have a sound moral argument for restricting the arms trade, and that it should "let the economic laws of supply and demand in a free trade environment govern this trade, as with any other."

FURTHER INFORMATION:

Books:

Keller, William W., and Kenji Hakuta, *Arm in Arm: The Political Economy of the Global Arms Trade*. New York: Basic Books, 1995.

O'Prey, Kevin P., *The Arms Export Challenge: Cooperative Approaches to Export Management and Defense Conversion*. Washington, D.C.: Brookings Institution, 1995.

Speier, Richard H., Brian G. Chow, and S. Rae Starr, *Nonproliferation Sanctions*. Santa Monica, CA: RAND, 2001.

Useful websites:

www.globalpolicy.org/security/sanction/
Global Policy Forum's page of links to articles on sanctions.
www.armscontrol.org/
Arms Control Association homepage, including articles from its journal *Arms Control Today*.
www.smartsanctions.se/
The Stockholm Process page on targeting sanctions.

The following debates in the Pro/Con series may also be of interest:

In this volume:

Topic 8 Do transnational corporations have more influence on the world economy than national governments?

Topic 16 Should the United States trade with countries with poor human rights records?

In *Human Rights*:

Topic 6 Do threats to national security ever justify restrictions on human rights?

SHOULD COMPANIES BE PUNISHED FOR SUPPLYING ARMS TO REGIMES THAT SUPPORT TERRORISM?

YES: Sanctions hit countries and companies where it hurts most, in their pockets, forcing them to reassess and change their policies

YES: In discouraging the supply of arms to terrorist regimes, the U.S. government is making a moral stand against the unethical use of arms to instill terror and force change

SANCTIONS
Do sanctions work?

MORALITY
Is the U.S. government taking a moral stand?

NO: Trade sanctions are rarely a successful method of effecting change because there will always be suppliers willing to satisfy market needs for a product—sanctions might even make the arms trade more profitable by limiting supply

NO: The United States is not taking a moral stand; in the past it has supported terrorist regimes—such as the Nicaraguan Democratic Force. It is simply protecting its own interests.

SHOULD COMPANIES BE PUNISHED FOR SUPPLYING ARMS TO REGIMES THAT SUPPORT TERRORISM?

KEY POINTS

YES: Certain goods have a detrimental effect on world stability if they fall into the wrong hands; arms are one of them and should be exempt from free trade

YES: Merriam-Webster's dictionary defines terrorism as "the systematic use of terror as a means of coercion." The U.S. government maintains a list of terrorist organizations as part of its War on Terror.

FREE TRADE
Is enforcement of sanctions and fines possible?

DEFINITIONS
Is it easy to define who is a terrorist?

NO: Companies should be free to sell their goods where ever there is demand; if some countries impose restrictions, others will quickly take their place

NO: The evaluation of whether the objectives of an organization are in the common interest is subjective; such a group's use of arms might be the most viable way to achieve its goals

151

Topic 12
DOES THE INTERNET MAKE IT DIFFICULT TO ENFORCE COPYRIGHT LAW?

YES

FROM "DIGITAL PIRACY SAPS MUSIC INDUSTRY"

CNBC, MAY 4, 2003

DAVID FABER

NO

"THE ILLUSTRATED STORY OF COPYRIGHT"

GIGALAW.COM, 2001

DOUG ISENBERG INTERVIEW WITH EDWARD SAMUELS

INTRODUCTION

Copyright is the right of the author of a creative work to control the copying and use of that work. Copyright has two main purposes: to protect the author's right to make commercial gain from valuable work, and to protect the author's general right to control how a work is used.

There are exceptions to copyright law in certain circumstances. You can make limited use of a copyrighted work without permission for the purposes of parody, commentary, news reporting, research, and education. This is known as "fair use." For example, if someone is teaching a class about an author, they are allowed to photocopy short extracts of the author's work as part of the class. Certain types of information are also exempt if they are considered to be in the public domain. For example, anything produced by the United States government cannot be copyrighted.

At one time all work had to have a copyright notice attached to it to be protected. However, most countries now follow the Berne Convention, under which all creative work is protected from the time it is fixed in a tangible form. In the United States nearly everything created after April 1, 1989, is copyrighted automatically.

The idea of copyright originated after the introduction of the printing press in Europe in the late 15th century. The first modern copyright law, establishing the principles of authors' ownership of copyright, was passed by the British Parliament in 1710. Since that time copyright law in most countries has evolved and reformed in an effort to widen the terms of copyright and to address the new technologies that affect copyright.

The advent of computers has had major implications for the issue of copyright, particularly in music. Computer technology and sound-recording technology use the same digital method of storing information, so the Internet—which allows computers to exchange digital information—has been accused of being the biggest single threat to copyright in its history.

"As to telling [Americans] they will have no literature of their own [if copyright is not respected], the universal answer (out of Boston) is, 'We don't want one. Why should we pay for one when we can get it for nothing? Our people don't think of poetry, sir. Dollars, banks, and cotton are our books.'"

—CHARLES DICKENS,

BRITISH NOVELIST (1842)

Since the early 1990s software standards such as MP3 have enabled people to download music files from the Internet without payment. As a result, musicians and music companies are losing millions of dollars in copyright revenue as well as being the victims of intellectual theft. There are also now websites, such as Grokster, that give away software that allows users to send music files from person to person. This is known as peer-to-peer (P2P) file sharing, of which Napster is also an example.

Critics of the music companies feel that the music industry is the victim of its own failure to address the problems that new technology has created. If the price and quality of their product were more competitive, people might not take music from the Internet instead.

However, music companies say that they invest in artists and recordings, and have the right to earn money. They point out that they have to pay for marketing campaigns for their artists and have to be able to recoup their costs.

Traditionally, copyright law has fallen within the realms of civil law. However, new legislation means that copyright violation is increasingly being treated as a criminal offense. Under the NET act of 1997 unauthorized downloading of music from the Internet is a felony. The Recording Industry Association of America (RIAA) has sued several websites for aiding copyright infringement. However, a federal judge has since ruled that these sites are not breaking copyright laws. Some people fear that the music industry may prosecute individual computer users themselves.

Commentators argue that copyright law has to adapt to the arrival of new technologies. They say that history has shown that markets can adjust to new technology, just as they did when radio, television, photocopying, video recording, and other forms of new technology first arrived. Lawmakers cannot predict the behavior of computer users or the makers of new technologies. Other critics would like new copyright laws to protect digital works. Congress has responded to such calls with the Digital Millennium Copyright Act of 1998, which allows copyright owners to encrypt their work to identify when someone is illegally accessing or copying it.

The following two articles discuss the question of whether the Internet makes it difficult to enforce copyright law.

DIGITAL PIRACY SAPS MUSIC INDUSTRY
David Faber

YES

Jack is a typical college student: his room is a little messy, and like most kids on campus with a high speed Internet connection, Jack—who asked to be identified by his first name only—is stealing from the entertainment industry. "I pirate," he said. "I download music that I don't pay for."

Jack has access to 33,000 songs on the system he uses. He's one of thousands upon thousand of pirates who download 2.6 billion songs a month. "You've got everything from Mozart to the Beastie Boys [and] Michael Jackson," he said. He says he does it because he was tired of paying for music he didn't like. "I can listen to music that I know is good, instead of having to pay for music that isn't really that good that's marketed to me," he said.

> *Could Jack achieve exactly the same result by listening to a radio station that plays the music he likes?*

Sites such as Grokster and Kazaa give away software that enables you to trade music with anyone that has downloaded that software. So the copyrighted material—the files containing music—is never put on a Web site; it's traded from one person's computer to another. It's known as "peer-to-peer"—or simply "p2p."

> *Is there any difference in principle between trading files with another user and downloading them from a central site?*

But people who produce the downloaded content don't see a dime.

"It's a giant problem," said Howard Stringer, Chairman and CEO of Sony Corporation of America. He says that while there are other problems facing the music industry, piracy is the biggest.

> *Sony is a large corporation. How do you think the drops in profits might affect small labels producing more experimental, less mainstream work?*

"When you're losing two and a half billion files to the pirates every month, then you have to ask yourself that this is bound to have an impact. And the fact that we're down 10 percent in sales this year and 10 percent last year, seven percent the year before—there's obviously a correlation. How big it is—it's very hard to be precise. But there is no question that it's eating away at the revenues of the industry."

Titanic struggle

John Malone is one of the country's largest investors in media companies. "We now have essentially in the hands of the consumer at relatively low cost the ability to steal every piece of intellectual property that's out there," he said.

Malone says we are in the middle of a "Titanic struggle" between the record and movie companies that make content; the telephone and cable companies that deliver content, and the people who build the computers and CD burners into which that content is received and stored.

> *"You have the entire computer and consumer electronics industry basically saying it ought to be stealable, you know, we shouldn't be responsible ... because it will sell more computers,"* said Malone. *"We are all going to sell more hardware if the content is free ... and you have the cable guys and the satellite guys in the middle who aren't really sure which side of that equation they're on. You know, are they going to sell more subscriptions to their high-speed data service if people can steal what goes over it?"*

What responsibility do you think makers of computer hardware should take for the situation? Should there be a levy on hardware to compensate providers of content?

Malone says the entertainment industry has failed to respond effectively to a challenge that could wipe out its business. "I think we have been slow in the music industry to come to grips with it," said Stringer.

Sony's Stringer says the music business may have been overtaken by technology but it is now addressing the issue. There are now Web sites, such as AOL's Musicnet, where you can download music legally: $8.95 a month allows you to listen on your computer [to] all the music you want....

Outdated model

But Wayne Rosso, President of Grokster, one of the more popular file sharing sites, says music companies "are living in the 20th century."

> *"They're out of their minds, and they're going to go down in flames if they don't get with the program fast,"* he said. *"They are hanging on to an old business model that is completely outdated. And it's not our fault or file sharers who are causing the big problem with the record industry. It's clearly issues of pricing, competition for the entertainment dollar and quality."*

Can the music industry be blamed for piracy because it has overpriced its products? Should not consumers just accept that music is expensive to create and record?

Cary Sherman is President of the Recording Industry [Association] of America, known as RIAA. It's the record industry's lobbying group. "How many other businesses could survive if they're competing with free versions of the same product?" he said.

The RIAA sued Grokster and two other sites for aiding copyright infringement. Rosso says they are not breaking any laws—they are just giving away software. "All we do is distribute a software product that allows access to a network," he said. "They know full well what's going on," said Sherman. "And they know they're facilitating it."

Late last month [April 2003], a federal judge ruled against the recording industry, finding that Grokster and another site are not breaking copyright laws. How will the recording industry react? Some believe they will go after those doing the pirating—students like Jack. "The user is doing any infringing," said Rosso. "So if you, the record company wants to stop infringing, go after the user."

> *Judge Stephen Wilson gave his decision on April 25, 2003, saying that Grokster was in the same position as makers of video recorders, which could also be used to infringe copyright. See http://news.com.com/2100-1027-998363.html for the full text of the ruling.*

"People have a sense that when they engage in pirate activity, that somehow it's anonymous—but it's not," said Sherman. "They are actually doing this in a public network on the Internet, here anybody can come and figure out who they are. So, they're not anonymous and they can be prosecuted and we want people to understand that illegal activity can be prosecuted."

> *Do you think users need to be made more aware of the implications of Internet piracy? Would they continue to do it if they thought there was a chance they might be prosecuted?*

While the RIAA can't arrest anyone itself, it can take them to court. In fact, just last month the RIAA sued four college students for $150,000 over copyright infringement.

Michael O'Leary is the man who could arrest a pirate. He prosecutes computer crimes for the Justice Department. O'Leary says unauthorized downloading of music is a felony under the NET act of 1997.

"The way Congress wrote the law is that you have to infringe either through the unauthorized distribution or reproduction of a certain amount of pirated product within 6 months, and that pirated product has to exceed a certain monetary value," he said.

In other words, it's a felony if you download 10 copies of copyrighted work, valued at $2,500 or more in a 180-day period.

But asked if he planned to put teenagers in jail for downloading music, O'Leary said "I don't want to deal with hypothetical situations."

O'Leary says his focus is on what's known as Warez groups—teams of individuals involved in downloading and distributing large amounts of copyrighted material.

"But individuals using peer to peer networks, any mechanism they're using—we haven't ruled any of those things out," he said. "There's a lot of factors we have to look at. Can we meet the statutory requirements? Is the person's conduct of such a level that it triggers the criminal law? Or is this something which would better be handled civilly? These are all factors."

What about the parents of kids who download music illegally?

"Parents would be a good alternative as well," said O'Leary. "Part of what we find is that parents, for a lot of different reasons—they're not necessarily fully understanding what is going on online—they are certainly not understanding the scope of it."

O'Leary says what really concerns him is that a generation is growing up which assumes that if it's on the Internet, it's free....

Do you think parents should be legally accountable for the actions of their children if the children are too young to be prosecuted? See Volume 11, Family and Society, Topic 8 Should parents be held responsible for the actions of their children?

THE ILLUSTRATED STORY OF COPYRIGHT
Doug Isenberg interview with
Edward Samuels

NO

Isenberg: Legal observers often have commented that, despite new technologies such as the Internet, existing copyright laws are adequate. Others have said new copyright laws are needed to protect digital works. What do you think?

Do you think the Internet has created new ways of infringing copyright? Surely copying has been easy for a long time?

Samuels: There are some observers who claim that the Internet "changes everything," and that the prior laws of copyright are obsolete. I think that such an assessment is just wrong, and that's the whole point of my book. I try to trace some of the prior technologies—photocopying, music, radio, movies, television, computer programs—and show how the Internet is just one in a series of new technologies to which the law is adapting, not one that will destroy the existing system.

Of course, the prior laws are not "adequate" in the sense that the Internet makes possible a lot of copying of works that are virtually undetectable and unenforceable under any law. But I don't have to predict what Congress will do; it's already acted, in the form of the Digital Millennium Copyright Act of 1998. Under that act, if copyright owners encrypt their copyrighted works, it's now highly illegal—in many cases criminally illegal—to break through the encryption system to get access to or to make unauthorized copies of the works. The law is incredibly complicated, and it remains to be seen whether it's workable. Stay tuned for future developments.

The DMCA is the first major piece of legislation aimed at bringing U.S. copyright law up to date with the new situations created by digital information technology. See www.arl.org/info/frn/copy/dmca.html for a page of links that give background and analysis of the act's implications.

Isenberg: In 2001, the great copyright debate involves MP3 files. A few years ago, it was computer software applications. Before that, it was the VCR. What new technologies do you think will create the greatest copyright conflicts in five or 10 years?

Samuels: If I knew that one, I'd invest in the technology ahead of the curve, and make a fortune.

In 1992, the entire music industry predicted that the great new technology that would change everything was the digital audio tape [DAT] recorder. The various interested companies got together and proposed a remarkable compromise to deal with the issue of digital audio home recording, by providing for a "serial copy management chip" to prevent multiple generation copying, and a compulsory licensing fee to generate money for musical copyright owners. The industries got Congress to pass the compromise, and many of us thought it was probably workable. The only problem was that the digital audio technology was stillborn. Nobody bought the recorders that were supposed to generate the money for copyright owners, but instead moved to the downloading of [lower-quality] MP3 files from the Internet. If the industries themselves can be totally blindsided by the new technology, then how can a law professor be expected to call this one? The recent technologies that have raised the most serious problems for copyright are all digital technologies. The problems arise from the incredible ease with which we can copy, transform, distribute and "perform" digital works, all of which are supposed to be exclusive rights of the copyright owner. I assume that the next problematic technology, whatever it is, will be digital, but that's about as far as I can predict.

DAT is a format still used in the recording industry to archive the master recordings from which CDs are reproduced. However, the cost of machines for the high-quality medium meant it never took off as a format for end users, who were satisfied with the lower quality of MP3 files.

Isenberg: In your book, *The Illustrated Story of Copyright*, you focus on the evolution of copyright law in the United States. On the Internet, where there are no borders, what role do the copyright laws (or lack of laws) in other countries play?

Professor Edward Samuels is an expert in copyright law and teaches at New York School of Law. His book The Illustrated Story of Copyright was first published in 2000.

Samuels: I know it's chic to say that the Internet has no borders, but recent cases dealing with child pornography or credit card fraud or bomb threats or other criminal activity, as well as copyright, suggest that Internet activity is very much based in the real world. Things still don't pop up on the Internet unless someone, somewhere, puts them there.

Many of the copyright reforms are international. The Digital Millennium Copyright Act, for example, was passed in response to recommendations and treaties adopted under the auspices of the World Intellectual Property Organization [WIPO]. The European Community is in many ways at the cutting edge of copyright developments. In the last chapter of the book, I outline how the developments in the copyright law of the United States parallel developments that are taking place in other countries. So, yes, it does require international cooperation, but, yes, we seem to be getting it from most countries around the world.

The WIPO, based in Switzerland, is an organization "dedicated to promoting the use and protection of works of the human spirit." See www.wipo.org/ for further information.

Isenberg: Based on your research for your book, *The Illustrated Story of Copyright*, and your other education as a copyright law professor, what historical copyright dispute is most instructive for today's cyberspace environment?

Samuels: I was particularly struck by one book, *Musical Plagiarism*, by Alfred Shafter, written in 1932. He describes the copyright law of the day, but when it comes to the effects of radio, he can only speculate about how the law will develop.

Do you think the situation is the same with the Internet? Hearing records on radio was perhaps like downloading an audio file, but in the 1930s users had no means of recording the radio signal to play back later.

In the early days of radio, it wasn't clear whether the money would be made from subscription services or from advertising, or whether it was possible to make money from the new medium at all. Some copyright owners thought it was great to get "play time" on the new medium, and others were hysterical that the new medium would destroy audiences for their live shows or for their sound recordings. All you have to do is plug in the word "Internet" for the word "radio," and some of the passages could have been written last week.

In fact, the sales of sound recordings took a big nosedive during the Depression, precisely when people were buying up radios and listening to music "for free." The same thing happened again in the 1950s and 1960s, as movie revenues plunged while the sales of television sets took off. As Sam Goldwyn quipped, why would anyone pay to see a lousy movie when they could see a lousy movie for free? Well, ultimately the markets adapted, and the sound recording and movie industries recovered by developing markets alongside radio and television. I can't predict exactly how it's going to come out, but I'd be awfully surprised if the existing industries don't manage to adapt somehow to the new environment.

Isenberg: What do you tell frustrated copyright owners— photographers, for example—who say, "I will not publish my works on the Internet because, once I do so, I cannot prevent them from being copied"?

Samuels: I doubt that the copyright owners have much choice. If they don't "publish" on the Internet, someone else will scan their works and post them on the Internet.

The solution suggested by the Digital Millennium Copyright Act is to put your work in digital form, and either protect it by an encryption system, or embed in the work so-called copyright management information that at least informs users who the copyright owner is and how to go about getting permission to make copies.

There's no doubt that there are more opportunities than ever for copying other people's works; but there are also more opportunities for developing new markets. There are some people who say that the more an artist distributes free copies, the more that artist will be able to sell. That's true sometimes. If it is true, then, of course, the creators are going to be giving some of their works away for free, or figuring out ways of building up their customer base. But it's up to each creator, each copyright owner, to make the choice about how to distribute their works; I don't think it should be the end-user who gets to decide what they take for free (except in very limited contexts). A copyright owner may very well decide to give away some samples in order to get people to buy some of their other works. But it's awfully hard to compete with other people if they just take your works for free, when they want.

Do you agree that the more an artist gives away, the more he or she will sell? Why would people pay for material they can get easily for free?

Summary

In the first article David Faber argues that the Internet does make it difficult to enforce copyright law. He says that piracy—especially the illegal downloading of music from the Internet—is the biggest threat the music industry faces. The seriousness of the problem can be seen, he says, in the increasing willingness of the music industry to take legal action against those infringing copyright laws. Faber concedes that it is still not clear what the legal position is on the websites that aid copyright infringement, but he predicts that record companies may instead decide to prosecute directly those who are breaking the law—computer users who download the material. Many of them are teenagers and college students, a few of whom have already been prosecuted by the Recording Industry Association of America (RIAA). Faber suggests that bearing in mind the age of the piracy offenders, parents may be able to play a role in solving the problem.

In the second article copyright law professor Edward Samuels contends that copyright law can adapt to the Internet just as it has adapted in the past to other new technologies. He says that despite movie revenues dropping when television sales first took off in the 1950s and 1960s, they later recovered. Samuels says that he would be surprised if existing industries cannot adapt to new technology and points out that while there are more opportunities than ever before to copy other people's work, there are also more opportunities to develop new markets. He concludes that it is up to each copyright holder to decide how to distribute their work, but that it should not be the end user who decides what they can take for free.

FURTHER INFORMATION:

Books:

Alderman, John, *Sonic Boom: Napster, MP3, and the New Pioneers of Music*. Cambridge, MA: Perseus, 2001.

Biegel, Stuart, *Beyond Our Control? Confronting the Limits of Our Legal System in the Age of Cyberspace*. Cambridge, MA: MIT Press, 2001.

Isenberg, Doug, *Gigalaw Guide to Internet Law*. New York: Random House, 2002.

Useful websites:

www.nlc-bnc.ca/9/1/p1-261-e.html
The National Library of Canada's Information Technology Service's page on MP3 overview and issues.
www.gigalaw.com/articles/copyright-napster.html
Gigalaw's page of links to articles on various aspects of the MP3 copyright/download controversy.

www.house.gov/judiciary/72613.pdf
Transcript of the House of Representatives hearing on "Music on the Internet," May 2001.

The following debates in the Pro/Con series may also be of interest:

In this volume:
Topic 3 Is a free market the best way to organize world trade?

In *Education*:
Topic 16 Are universities doing enough to prevent plagiarism?

DOES THE INTERNET MAKE IT DIFFICULT TO ENFORCE COPYRIGHT LAW?

YES: The Internet enables the illegal copying of material on a massive scale. New copyright laws are needed to deal with the problem.

YES: Unauthorized downloading of music is a felony under the law. Music companies need to protect themselves and their artists from intellectual theft.

NEW TECHNOLOGY
Does digital technology pose a serious threat to copyright law?

CRIMINAL VS. CIVIL OFFENSE
Should the illegal downloading of music be a criminal offense?

NO: Existing copyright laws are sufficient to protect digital works. The law can adapt to the new technology as it has done to other technologies in the past.

NO: Most offenders are teenagers and students who need to understand why it is wrong to infringe copyright rather than be prosecuted. Recent federal rulings prove that the law is still not clear about whether this should be a criminal offense.

DOES THE INTERNET MAKE IT DIFFICULT TO ENFORCE COPYRIGHT LAW?

KEY POINTS

YES: The music business has provided sites where music can be legally downloaded in return for a monthly fee

YES: The industry is taking legal action against websites aiding copyright infringement and computer users directly infringing the law

ADEQUATE RESPONSE?
Has the music industry responded adequately to the copyright problems caused by the Internet?

NO: The music companies will be destroyed if they do not address the real issues. They need to be more competitive with their pricing if they want to stop people taking music from the Internet for free.

NO: The industry has not shown the same degree of prevention it did, for example, when it responded to the threat of the digital audio tape recorder with a chip to stop serial copying

163

PART 4
THE UNITED STATES

In March 2003 Robert B. Zoellick, the U.S. Trade Representative, reported the commitment of President George W. Bush "to ignite a new era of global economic growth through a world trading system that is dramatically more open and more free." As part of this move Bush submitted what some observers saw as progressive trade proposals to the World Trade Organization (WTO), the organization created to promote international free trade. Bush's proposals included plans to remove all tariffs on manufactured goods by 2015 and to open agriculture and services markets, and suggestions on how to address the problems and trade needs of poor nations. The U.S. administration presented its proposals as a positive step to addressing disparities in the world economy. Critics, however, remained skeptical, arguing that the United States has a record of entering into trade agreements only out of self-interest.

U.S. trade

The United States comes under particular scrutiny because its economy is the largest and most influential in the world. In 2000 the United States purchased $1.223 trillion of imports such as foodstuffs, crude oil, and machinery. Its exports, generated from selling aircraft, armaments, and grain, among other things, totaled around $776 billion.

Historically the United States has been a supporter of free trade, in which business is regulated by economic factors of supply and demand rather than by government legislation or interference. Critics argue, however, that western nations that traditionally espouse free trade, such as the United States, do not always practice what they preach. For example, in the late 1920s, during a period of isolationism from the rest of the world, the United States imposed tariffs on imports in an attempt to protect domestic producers, such as coal mines and steel plants, from foreign competition. The reciprocal imposition of similar tariffs by many other countries strangled international trade and contributed to the severity of the Great Depression during the 1930s. Today the United States still uses tariffs and quotas to protect certain industries, such as steel.

The comparative merits of a free market or protectist system—one of the fundamental debates in economics—continues as fiercely today as it did throughout the 20th century. Some commentators argue for "economic nationalism," in other words, making the United States as self-supporting as possible. Others, however, fear that any limitation of imports would lead to reduced competition, higher prices, and less consumer choice. Despite the U.S. commitment to free trade, trade is often closely linked to politics. At home, corporations buy influence through political contributions and lobbying activities. Abroad, some commentators see U.S. foreign policy as being dictated, both historically and today, by trade considerations.

In the early decades of the 20th century, U.S. troops were sent to Central American nations such as Nicaragua to create stable conditions for U.S. businesses such as fruit growing. Some commentators argue that the United States' involvement in

Trade agreements

Topics 14 and 15 examine different aspects of the free trade debate. Topic 14 considers whether the United States has benefited from protectionism. Topic 15 examines the specific effects of the North American Free Trade Agreement (NAFTA). The agreement between the United States, Canada, and Mexico was ratified in 1993 to reduce trade barriers and increase investment and economic growth in all three countries. Together with other free trade agreements,

> *""America is back in the business of promoting open trade to build our prosperity and to spur economic growth."*
> —GEORGE W. BUSH, 43RD PRESIDENT (2001)

the Persian Gulf War in 1991 was influenced by a desire to gain control of Middle East oil supplies. Similar accusations were leveled against the U.S.-led 2003 invasion of Iraq.

High or low

The U.S. dollar is the most important currency in the world. Its influence has long been debated. Some economists and politicians believe that a strong dollar—one that is expensive relative to other currencies—enhances U.S. prestige and reflects a strong economy. Imports become cheaper because the dollar is worth more in terms of other currencies. Equally, however, a strong dollar can limit the export trade. U.S. exports become comparatively expensive in other countries, and U.S. manufacturers suffer as a result. Topic 13 examines the main issues in the high dollar debate in greater detail.

advocates believe that such measures will benefit the average U.S. family by $1,300 to $2,000 a year. Critics argue, however, that NAFTA has cost the U.S. economy much-needed jobs and that any benefit has come only at the expense of Mexico, whose lower labor costs and environmental legislation U.S. firms exploit.

Topic 16, the last topic in this book, asks if America should trade with countries with poor human rights records. Many people believe that the United States, as a champion of human rights, should bring pressure to bear by stopping trade with such nations. Others believe that trading with countries such as China is the only way in which the United States can promote change. Skeptics, however, claim that this view is based more on the profits to be made from the Chinese economy rather than human rights concerns.

Topic 13

DOES A HIGH DOLLAR HARM THE U.S. ECONOMY?

YES

"GOOD NEWS! THE DOLLAR IS DOWN"

BUSINESSWEEK ONLINE, MAY 16, 2003

RICH MILLER AND PETER COY, WITH CHRISTINE TIERNEY, DAVID FAIRLAMB, ET AL.

NO

HEARING ON "RISKS OF A GROWING BALANCE OF PAYMENTS DEFICIT"

SUBCOMMITTEE ON ECONOMIC POLICY, JULY 25, 2001

ROBERT RUBIN

INTRODUCTION

The value of a country's currency relative to the value of other currencies is generally taken as a sign of the health of that country's economy. If the dollar is high, it means that every dollar has a high value against other currencies. So, for example, when the dollar is high, it is cheaper for Americans to travel to Europe because one dollar buys more of other currencies such as pounds or euros. Economists spend much of their time trying to figure out whether a high or low dollar would be best for the economy and adjusting economic policy to reflect this. There are both advantages and disadvantages to a high dollar.

Many economists believe that a strong dollar is a sign of a healthy economy. That is because it is normally taken as a sign of high productivity (profitability per worker), strong consumer demand (people spending money on things, so creating and sustaining jobs), and high foreign investment because foreign investors are eager to invest their money in a country with a strong currency. The strong dollar brings prestige and diplomatic influence. It also makes imports cheaper and so acts to offset inflationary pressures: Domestic goods cost less, so people spend less, and inflation is kept down.

Yet some economists believe that there is a downside to having a high-valued currency, even in strong, thriving economies. A high dollar makes it increasingly difficult for U.S companies to sell their goods abroad because export goods are more expensive for foreign buyers. This particularly affects manufacturers and farmers—in 2002, for example, there was a 7 percent decrease in the value of wine exports caused by the strong dollar. A high dollar also means that foreign goods are cheaper for U.S. consumers; manufacturers may thus lose vital business in the domestic market, since most consumers will buy

166

cheaper foreign goods instead of home-produced ones. Another important disadvantage is that a high dollar will normally lead to a balance-of-payments deficit. This happens when the value of goods imported exceeds that of goods exported. For as long as such a deficit lasts, the difference between the value of what is sold and what is bought must be borrowed (whether by individuals, corporations, or governments), and interest must be paid on the loan.

"A strong currency provides a reliable medium of exchange and serves as a stable store of value that people choose to hold."

—JOHN SNOW, SECRETARY OF THE TREASURY, JANUARY 28, 2003

During the recession of the 1980s the dollar had a relatively low value, and the long economic upturn that began in the early 1990s saw the dollar's value steadily rise. In the boom of the late 1990s the strong dollar was a cornerstone of President Bill Clinton's economic plan. From the late 1990s until 2001 the dollar maintained a very high value against both European currencies and the Japanese yen.

However, by 2002 the U.S. trade deficit (the country was importing more than it was exporting) amounted to 22 percent of the country's gross domestic product (GDP), an all-time record. This problem led some observers to feel that the value of the dollar was too high, especially in

relation to the euro, the currency of the European Union. Stephen Roach, chief economist at Morgan Stanley merchant bank, claimed that "The world is out of whack, and we need a shift in relative prices." In May 2003 the administration of President George W. Bush made it clear that it would not intervene to sustain a high dollar. This led investors to sell dollars at an accelerating rate, which left the dollar worth nearly a quarter less against the euro than 18 months before.

Manufacturers welcomed the news, believing that U.S. firms now had a much greater chance of exporting their goods at lower prices, thus helping reduce the balance-of-payments deficit. They also predicted that foreign goods would become more expensive in the U.S. domestic market, giving American producers an advantage on the home front they had previously lacked.

Other observers, such as the currency trader George Soros, were more pessimistic. Soros said the fall in the dollar "had some very negative implications." He and others pointed out that consumer spending in Europe and Japan was weak compared to the United States, and that any spending increase in those countries was more likely to go on domestic goods than U.S imports. The historian Robert Brenner also noted that since the 1970s the economic fortunes of all three trading blocs (Europe, Asia, and the United States) had risen and fallen together. It was therefore unlikely that the U.S. economy would recover because the low dollar would make the export-led economies of Europe and Japan falter.

The following two articles by Rich Miller and others and Robert Rubin respectively examine the high dollar debate further.

GOOD NEWS! THE DOLLAR IS DOWN
Rich Miller and Peter Coy, with Christine Tierney, David Fairlamb, et al.

A bubble economy refers to an economy with rapidly rising equity prices. In this type of economy the price of equities reaches a point at which they can no longer continue to rise and "burst." The price of equities then declines rapidly.

YES

The rip-roaring stock market wasn't the only bubble that ballooned to unsustainable levels in the 1990s. The U.S. dollar did, too. Enamored of high growth rates, and a world-beating stock market, foreign investors poured money into the U.S., snapping up companies and equities. The influx of foreign funds drove the dollar inexorably higher, and with it, the trade deficit, as cheaply priced imports flooded the country and more pricey U.S. exports abroad sagged.

Now, the day of reckoning looks to have finally arrived. A dollar drop that began early last year has picked up speed. The greenback has suffered its biggest drop against the euro, losing 23% since January, 2002—7% since mid-March alone. Although less severe, the dollar has also tumbled 12% against the yen and 8% against a broader basket of currencies of America's trading partners over the last 17 months. And further declines are in store, experts say.

Unlike the bursting of the stock-market bubble, however, the dollar's drop is good news, on the whole, for the U.S. economy. Sure, over the short term, it will raise the cost of imports into the U.S. and act as a temporary tax on consumers.… Rising job worries are already hampering spending: Excluding autos, retail sales dropped an unexpectedly sharp 0.9% in April, according to the Commerce Dept.

"Deflation" refers to a sustained decrease in the general price level. It can be caused by a reduction in personal spending, government spending, or investment. Deflation often leads to a lower level of demand in the economy, and that can then cause an increase in unemployment.

Globalization

GLOBAL GAIN. Still, a rise in import prices will have a silver lining since it helps stave off the risks of deflation. Longer term, the weaker dollar should help put a dent in the trade deficit, which soared 8% in March, to $43.5 billion, the second-highest monthly total ever.

Just as important, the dollar downdraft is already having a salutary effect on profits—and the stock market—by raising the overseas earnings of Corporate America. In the last few days alone, a string of companies, from Wal-Mart Stores (WMT) and Procter & Gamble (PG) to farm-equipment maker Deere (DE), have joined the parade of companies reporting sharply higher foreign sales and earnings thanks to dollar-induced gains.

What's more, while the dollar's drop is causing deep pain for European, Japanese, and many other foreign exporters right now, eventually, it could be a net plus for the global economy if America's trading partners respond by cutting interest rates or loosening fiscal policy. Such steps would keep their currencies from rising much more against the dollar while stimulating their domestic growth.

NO PANIC YET. The result: worldwide economic expansion —a kind of "competitive reflation"—and a move away from the global economy's dangerous dependence on the U.S. for virtually all of its growth. "What we want in a deflationary environment is for all the central banks to assume a little bit of the burden" of spurring growth, says University of California at Berkeley economist Barry Eichengreen.

> *The authors stress that the health of the world economy is dependent on the health of the U.S. economy. Can you think of ways in which this situation would benefit the United States?*

Of course, there's always the risk that the dollar decline could turn into a rout, with skittish foreign investors yanking money out of U.S. stock and bond markets, sending Wall Street plunging and interest rates skyrocketing. But so far, "We haven't seen any panic," says David Gilmore of Foreign Exchange Analytics.

Indeed, as the dollar has dropped in recent weeks, both the stock and bond markets have risen strongly. While foreign investors are more nervous about new purchases of U.S. assets, they aren't selling off the stocks and bonds they have already bought. What seems to be happening, says former Federal Reserve official Edwin M. (Ted) Truman, is that foreign investors are keeping their money in U.S. stocks and bonds but hedging some of their exposure to the dollar by selling greenbacks in the global currency market.

DEFLATION WORRIES. In some sense, the dollar's decline couldn't come at a more opportune time for the U.S. economy. Normally, a fall in the currency would be a concern because it would push up inflation, forcing the Fed to raise interest rates in response. But now, that's not the case because there's so much slack in the economy, with manufacturing companies operating at just 73% of capacity, a four-decade low. Indeed, as Fed policymakers signaled on May 6, they're worried about deflation—a broad decline in prices that would wreck corporate profits, crash the stock market, and drag down the economy.

> *The Fed, or Federal Reserve Bank, monitors the health of the U.S. economy. The bank's seven-member board establishes monetary policy, including the setting of interest rates.*

It was that signal—and with it the implicit promise to keep interest rates low for an extended period—that helped kick off the dollar's latest slide. Treasury Secretary John W. Snow gave it another push on May 11, when comments he made on

TV were interpreted by the markets as lukewarm support for a strong dollar. Yet as far as the Fed and many in the Administration are concerned, the dollar's fall is a welcome tonic for the economy.

Is good news for "Corporate America" necessarily good news for all Americans?

It's certainly good news for much of Corporate America, especially multinational companies. About a quarter of the sales of companies in the Standard & Poor's 500-stock index come from their foreign units, estimates Merrill Lynch & Co. The biggest reason for the immediate profit gains that many are starting to see isn't rising exports or better protection from cheap imports but simply from translating foreign earnings from more valuable foreign currencies into dollars.

Winners and losers

MULTINATIONAL BOOST. Of course, some sectors stand to do better than others. The biggest winners from a typical dollar decline are suppliers of consumer staples, energy, materials, and technology, while laggards tend to be financial services, utilities, and telecom, Merrill says.

Better results are already showing for U.S. multinationals such as McDonald's Corp. (MCD), which reported on May 13 that its sales in Europe rose 19% in April. Most of that was the result of foreign-currency translation, not because the Oak Brook (Ill.) giant sold more burgers and fries in Europe.

One of the most obvious ways to cut costs is to cut jobs, resulting in higher unemployment. Do you think that such social priorities should play a part in economic decisions?

With higher profits have come an improved stock market and increased investor wealth—another plus for the economy. Fatter corporate profits should also relieve some of the pressure on companies to slash costs to boost earnings.

COMPETITIVE ADVANTAGE. Over time, manufacturers in a host of industries from steel to office machines should also enjoy improved pricing power, as the weaker dollar forces foreign rivals to raise prices in the U.S. That's what U.S. carmakers are hoping. For Chrysler Group, "the very strong dollar we've had since about 1997 gave foreign manufacturers … a pricing advantage," says DaimlerChrysler (DCX) economist Van Jolissaint in Auburn Hills, Mich. A weaker dollar "will help us—if not today, then later this year and next year, because it will reduce the ability of foreign manufacturers to offer discounts."

Many large U.S. companies have factories throughout the world. Do you think a stronger dollar could also be beneficial?

U.S. exporters of consumer and capital goods should also benefit from a weaker currency. The dollar's fall will allow them to cut local currency prices and grab market share abroad without having to take a hit to their dollar-denominated earnings.

Indeed, while it will take some time to play out, a weaker dollar should help trim the record U.S. current account deficit—the widest measure of trade. That, in turn, should boost U.S. economic growth. Last year, U.S. domestic demand grew 3%, but about a half-percentage point of that was effectively filled by foreign companies thanks to America's insatiable demand for imports.

UNEVEN TUMBLE. This year, the foreign-trade sector should again be a drag on growth, but less so than it was in 2002, says former International Monetary Fund Chief Economist Michael Mussa. In 2004, it should be a small plus for the economy, as the trade deficit finally starts to turn down.

Even with the steep decline of the dollar, though, not all import prices are headed higher—and not all of the U.S.'s trade problems will be resolved. In part, that's because the dollar's fall has been uneven and mostly concentrated against the euro.

> The euro is the standard currency of most of the European Union. It was introduced into circulation in 2002 in countries such as France, Germany, and Italy.

Asian nations have acted to prevent their currencies from appreciating against the greenback. Japan sold $20.5 billion worth of yen in the first quarter in a move that limited the dollar's slide. And China, whose first-quarter trade surplus in goods with the U.S. soared from $7 billion in 1996 to $25 billion today—giving it the world's biggest surplus with the U.S.—has kept its carefully controlled currency steady against the dollar.

SLOW LEAK. That means there's no pressure on China to raise the prices of its exports. And if those prices don't rise, there's no reason to believe U.S. buyers will cut back on their purchases of Chinese goods or that the trade surplus will diminish.

> China has become one of the United States' most important trading partners. In 2001 the United States was China's largest source of foreign investment outside of Hong Kong.

Europe, on the other hand, is suffering the brunt of the dollar's fall. So far, European policymakers have reacted with equanimity to the euro's steep rise. Wim Duisenberg, president of European Central Bank, says the euro's strength is not yet a real concern. But it's a big worry for European companies, which are urging the ECB to cut interest rates.

That would be welcome in Washington. The Administration has been pestering America's trading partners to do more to boost global growth. It's also privately putting pressure on Beijing to allow its currency to float upward against the dollar in order to rein in surpluses. But that strategy is unlikely to bear fruit any time soon, especially since the spread of SARS threatens to slow China's economic growth substantially.

> SARS (Severe Acute Respiratory Syndrome) is a potentially lethal infectious disease. In 2003 (when this article was written) an epidemic had broken out in southern China, spreading from there to Hong Kong and then onward to the West. See Volume 17, New Science, pages 72–73.

Letting the air out of a bubble is never easy. There's always the risk that too much will come shooting out too fast. But in the case of the deflating dollar, so far, so good.

HEARING ON "RISKS OF A GROWING BALANCE OF PAYMENTS DEFICIT"
Robert Rubin

In July 2003 the G8 (the eight major industrial nations—France, Germany, Italy, Britain, Canada, Russia, the United States, and Japan) met in Genoa for an economic and political summit. During the summit there were violent demonstrations by antiglobalization protestors, one of whom was shot dead by police.

In the 1990s the U.S. economic boom was helped by low inflation, growth in the high-tech sector, investment in the stock market, and economic expansion. From 1991 to 1997 the proportion of families earning $50,000 a year rose from 40.7 percent to 44.1 percent.

NO

Mr. Chairman and Members of the Committee:

I think it is both useful and timely to develop further Congressional focus on our country's current account deficit. Thus I think this hearing is a very good idea. Moreover, recent events in Genoa and elsewhere suggest that the full range of issues around globalization merit great focus by this body.

The current account deficit is basically the trade deficit plus the deficit in net payments, including interest, dividends and the like, but public discussion of our deficit has, I think, become a symbol for concern about the whole area of trade related matters. I will try to very briefly express my views on these matters, and related policy issues, and hopefully that will be responsive to the four questions in the Chairman's letter outlining this hearing, as well as very summarily suggesting an approach to the broader issues around globalization.

Good economic growth

To begin, the U.S. has had remarkably good economic conditions over the past 8 years, with far stronger growth and far greater productivity increases than Europe or Japan, and far lower unemployment than Europe. At the same time, our markets have been more open to imports than Europe or Japan, our currency has been strong, our capital markets have been open, and our trade and current account imbalances have grown substantially.

I have no doubt that our economy has benefited enormously from both sides of trade, not only exports, but, even though it is not popular to say this, also very powerfully from imports. Imports lower prices to consumers and producers, dampen inflation (and thereby lower interest rates), provide a critical role in allocating our resources to the areas where our competitive advantage is greatest, and, maybe most importantly, create competitive pressure for productivity improvement. All this has contributed greatly of the very low unemployment and rising incomes at all levels.

The imbalance between exports and imports has occurred because of vast net capital inflows from around the world into the United States, motivated by the relative attractiveness of the United States for investment and as a repository for capital. That vast net inflow has allowed our consumption plus our investment to exceed what we produce. The consequence has been a lower cost of capital in our country and greater investment, which helped increase the rate of productivity growth.

Another consequence of the net capital inflows has been a strong dollar, which has lowered costs to consumers and producers for what we buy abroad, and more favorable terms of exchange between what we sell and buy abroad. The result is lower inflation, lower interest rates, higher standards of living, and greater productivity. The strong dollar has also helped attract capital from abroad.

Current account deficit

The next question is, even if our open markets, imports and a strong dollar are beneficial, is the imbalance itself a problem.

While a current account deficit reduces aggregate demand, in recent years we have had fully adequate demand, and, in any case, monetary and fiscal policy (such as the current tax rebate) are far preferable means of generating demand, if this is desired.

The claims against future output from the vast net capital inflows is like any other borrowing or raising of equity capital: if the funds are well used for investment, then the future contributions to growth will exceed the cost of repayment or other forms of return to foreign investors.

The remaining concern is that, in various ways, the current account deficit could contribute to future instability, as, for example, by adversely affecting confidence in the dollar or making us more vulnerable to a change in perception abroad about our economic prospects or the soundness of our policy regime (which, parenthetically, is another reason why maintaining fiscal discipline is so critically important for our economic well-being). While we should be able to sustain this deficit for an extended period because of the relative size and strength of our economy, it would be desirable over time to greatly reduce this imbalance.

There are some policy measures that could promote this purpose… and there are some policy measures that are more frequently advocated, which might help reduce the current account deficit but could have other severe adverse economic effects and on balance would be most unwise.

Monetary policy refers to the regulation of money through interest rates. It is used to control inflation and stabilize currencies. Fiscal policy is made by the president and Congress, and usually has to do with taxation or government spending. Traditionally the objectives of fiscal policy are stable prices, full employment, and economic growth.

What do you think could be the main economic disadvantages of a country having a current account deficit, or spending more than it earns?

Doing whatever we can to promote structural reform and trade liberalization in Europe and Japan would contribute to greater growth with more attractive investment opportunities in those areas, thus increasing our exports and increasing investment flows to Europe and Japan. This is good for us in many ways, including reduction of our current account deficit, and exemplifies why strongly engaging in international economic issues is greatly in our interest.

The personal savings rate is the amount individuals save of their income. Some countries, such as Japan, have a reputation for high personal savings. Why do you think the United States might have a low personal savings rate?

At home, increasing savings over the full business cycle would reduce imports and reduce the inflow of capital and would be the most constructive approach to reducing the current account deficit. While our low personal savings rate seems to be a cultural phenomenon—and there is a real question about how much net effect some savings tax credits have—I do think carefully crafted tax credits for subsidizing saving is a useful approach to explore if Congress at some point revisits the recently enacted 10 year tax, which is itself a significant diminution of future national savings and, in my view was most unwise.

Two frequently mentioned correctives for the current account deficit that might have some impact but on balance would be highly detrimental to our economic well-being are increased trade barriers and modifying our country's strong dollar policy.

In 1930 the U.S government introduced the Smoot–Hawley tariff, which led to 60 countries enacting retaliatory tariff increases. As a result, U.S. trade fell by a third, and the Depression worsened. In 2002 (a year after this piece had been published) President George W. Bush imposed tariffs on steel imports. See Topic 14 Is protectionism good for U.S. business?

Trade barriers and a strong dollar policy

Increased trade barriers would increase prices, lessen the comparative advantage effects, and reduce competitive pressures for productivity. Also, history suggests that protectionist measures here could lead to retaliatory trade measures in other countries.

Modifying our strong dollar policy could adversely affect inflation, interest rates and capital inflows and would lessen the favorability of our terms of exchange with the rest of the world.

Having said all this, as our administration made clear over the past decade, trade liberalization, though highly beneficial on balance for industrial and developing countries, can create dislocations—just as technology does to a far greater degree – and there are critically important matters, in our country and around the globe, such as poverty and the environment.... The demonstrators this past week were sometimes strident—and we must condemn violence—but there are underlying concerns about globalization that are serious and need to be addressed....[T]here should be a parallel agenda to promote productivity and equip people to deal with change, including education, effective re-training, programs to equip the poor to

COMMENTARY: The "greenback"

The dollar was officially adopted as the U.S. currency in 1792. Dollar bills did not go into circulation until the Civil War (1860–1865): After its gold reserves ran out, the United States was forced to fund the conflict by issuing huge quantities of nonconvertible paper money, known as "greenbacks." In 1900 the country officially adopted the gold standard linking the dollar to the price of gold, but after the Great Depression of the 1930s all countries abandoned the gold standard. The Bretton Woods Agreement, which established the dollar as the international standard, was abandoned in 1971. Today the values of all currencies are determined by the market.

Strength of the dollar

Since World War II (1939–1945) the dollar has dominated international trade mainly because of its enduring strength and stability. The dollar is the world's most actively traded currency and is used more than any other currency in international commercial contracts. European countries use dollars to buy oil from the Middle East, Japan often pays for its imports from Southeast Asia in dollars, and the dollar is the world's favored "third currency" (when one country sells its own currency for dollars and then uses dollars to buy another foreign currency).

The birth of the euro

However, the supremacy of the dollar in the international financial system is now threatened by a new currency, the euro. The euro was launched on January 1, 1991, as an electronic currency and became legal tender on January 1, 2002. It replaced the domestic currencies of 12 of the 15 European Union countries, including France, Germany, Italy, and Spain. By 2003 non-European countries, such as Indonesia, had begun to use the euro rather than the dollar in import–export transactions and for foreign exchange reserves. As a balance to this trend there has been increasing interest among parts of Latin America in adopting the dollar as their domestic currency in a process that is know as "dollarization."

join the economic mainstream, environmental protection and much else. And the industrial nations, in their own self-interest, should greatly increase assistance to developing nations.

Mr. Chairman, let me conclude where I started. The current account deficit is a complex issue that immediately leads to the whole range of trade-related issues, and I think that this committee performs a great public service by this hearing and whatever other processes it employs to provide serious public examination of these issues.

Summary

Is a high value for the dollar good for the U.S. economy? Or is a low dollar better for American manufacturing? The two preceding articles, although they do not disagree on what has happened in the past, have very different outlooks on what the future results of these trends will be.

In the first article Rich Miller and his coauthors concentrate on the positive aspects of a low dollar. A low dollar, they argue, increases the value of foreign earnings when converted into dollars, thus making U.S. corporations more profitable. It gives U.S. manufacturers a competitive advantage in pricing their goods both at home (where they can undercut imports that are now more expensive) and abroad (where they can now offer discounts without reducing their dollar earnings). The authors take an upbeat view that European and Japanese financiers can be persuaded to reduce their interest rates and take other measures to stimulate consumer spending in their countries, boosting U.S. exports and allowing a reflation of the economy.

In the second article—part of a congressional hearing from before the dollar's fall in value in May 2003—President Clinton's former Treasury Secretary Robert Rubin takes a more cautious view. He agrees that reducing the trade deficit is a worthwhile goal, since a current account deficit could make the dollar less stable and the U.S. economy less attractive to foreign investors. However, in his view not every means of achieving a reduction is equally good. Increased consumption abroad, and saving at home, would be beneficial, but a low dollar could result in a worsening situation for inflation, interest rates, and capital inflows.

FURTHER INFORMATION:

Books:

Brenner, Robert, *The Boom and the Bubble: The U.S. in the World Economy*. New York: Verso Books, 2002.
Duncan, Richard, *The Dollar Crisis: Causes, Consequences, Cures*. Hoboken, NJ: John Wiley & Sons, 2003.
Soros, George, *The Alchemy of Finance*. Hoboken, NJ: John Wiley & Sons, 2003.

Useful websites:

www.lrb.co.uk/v25/n03/print/bren01_.html
Article by Robert Brenner on the crisis of the U.S. economy.
www.ex.ac.uk/~RDavies/arian/northamerica.html
Money in North American history.
www.mtholyoke.edu/acad/intrel/eurodol.htm
Euro as potential rival to the dollar.

The following debates in the Pro/Con series may also be of interest:

In this volume:
Topic 14 Is protectionism good for U.S. business?

In *Economics*:
Topic 1 Is the free market the best form of economic organization?

Topic 5 Does government intervention do more harm than good?

DOES A HIGH DOLLAR HARM
THE U.S. ECONOMY?

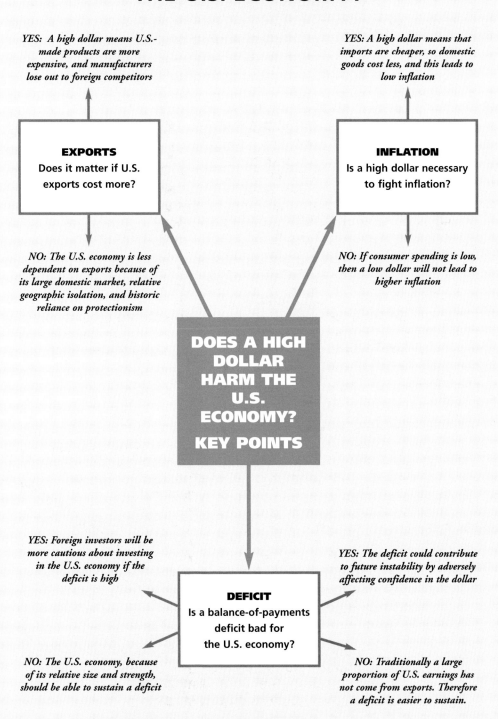

YES: A high dollar means U.S.-made products are more expensive, and manufacturers lose out to foreign competitors

YES: A high dollar means that imports are cheaper, so domestic goods cost less, and this leads to low inflation

EXPORTS
Does it matter if U.S. exports cost more?

INFLATION
Is a high dollar necessary to fight inflation?

NO: The U.S. economy is less dependent on exports because of its large domestic market, relative geographic isolation, and historic reliance on protectionism

NO: If consumer spending is low, then a low dollar will not lead to higher inflation

DOES A HIGH DOLLAR HARM THE U.S. ECONOMY?

KEY POINTS

YES: Foreign investors will be more cautious about investing in the U.S. economy if the deficit is high

YES: The deficit could contribute to future instability by adversely affecting confidence in the dollar

DEFICIT
Is a balance-of-payments deficit bad for the U.S. economy?

NO: The U.S. economy, because of its relative size and strength, should be able to sustain a deficit

NO: Traditionally a large proportion of U.S. earnings has not come from exports. Therefore a deficit is easier to sustain.

Topic 14

IS PROTECTIONISM GOOD FOR U.S. BUSINESS?

YES
"WHEN PROTECTIONISM IS A GOOD THING"
PCDFORUM COLUMN #67, JANUARY 25, 1994
HERMAN E. DALY

NO
"IMPORT QUOTAS 'STEEL' FROM US ALL"
WWW.CAPMAG.COM, SEPTEMBER 10, 2001
JEFF JACOBY

INTRODUCTION

Protectionism is when restrictions are placed by a government on foreign imported goods in order to protect domestic producers from competition. These measures typically take the form of bans, tariffs (taxation on imported goods), or quotas (limits on the amount or value of goods allowed to be imported). But do they work? Common sense suggests that protectionism must benefit business; but some economists believe that it encourages inefficiency, puts jobs at risk, and forces consumers to pay higher prices.

Although some critics argue that opposition to the protectionist policy of Great Britain was significant in causing the American Revolution, successive U.S governments up until World War II (1939-1945) continued to favor protectionism as the system that best served the country's economic interest.

In 1791 Alexander Hamilton, the first secretary of the Treasury of the United States, urged in his "Report on Manufactures" that tariffs be used to foster the growth of manufacturing and thus strengthen the American economy. Tariffs continued to be deployed throughout the 19th century. The 1930 Smoot–Hawley Act raised the average tariff rate by 53 percent. However, global economic depression and high unemployment during the 1930s culminated in a collapse in international trade. In the aftermath of World War II a reassessment of the world economy resulted in the abandonment of the protectionist policies that many maintained had contributed to prewar economic unrest.

The international community turned instead toward a policy of free trade, an economic system popularized by the 18th-century British economist Adam Smith in his book *The Wealth of Nations* (1776). Smith proposed that all nations become better off when each concentrates on manufacturing products in which its natural resources or labor skills give it an advantage. This ensures that each nation's goods are produced with the greatest efficiency and thus at the lowest price the market will bear; this in turn maximizes the amount of those goods that each unit of currency is able to buy. When governments impose tariffs to raise prices above their market level, the buying power of each currency unit is reduced. Since all nations would match others' tariffs with their own, the overall effect would be to reduce the wealth—the buying power of currencies—of all nations. Great Britain pursued a rigorous free-trade policy, imposing no tariffs of any kind, from the 1840s to the 1930s.

"Free trade, one of the greatest blessings which a government can confer on a people, is in almost every country unpopular."

—LORD MACAULAY, BRITISH HISTORIAN (1824)

In 1947 the United States was key in establishing the General Agreement on Tariffs and Trade (GATT), whose aim was to facilitate international trade by regulating and reducing tariffs on traded goods and by providing a common mechanism for resolving trade disputes. Policymakers increasingly favored free market economic policy over protectionism. Free-trade areas (groups of countries that have no tariffs or other restrictions on trade with each other) were established, including the

European Union (EU) and in 1993 the North American Free Trade Area (NAFTA), which is made up of Canada, the United States, and Mexico. In 1995 GATT was succeeded by the World Trade Organization, whose stated goal is "to ensure that trade flows as smoothly, predictably, and freely as possible."

However, as the world economy slows down and consumer confidence and investment falter, the idea that protectionist measures would benefit U.S. business is again being vigorously proposed. Supporters of protectionism point to the history of the United States and argue that the use of tariffs was instrumental in the rapid growth of the U.S. economy in the 19th century. They maintain that supporting domestic industries in this way protects U.S. jobs and wages. Some argue that industries essential to national security, such as steel, oil, and shipbuilding, must be protected.

Those who take an antiprotectionist view, such as Paul Nathanson of the American Institute for International Steel, who criticized President Bush's decision to impose tariffs on imported steel in 2002, argue that free trade is essential if the United States is going to compete in the global market. They maintain that protectionist measures encourage industries to rely on government support and so discourage them from innovating, eventually making them uncompetitive. Critics also point out that protectionist measures can bring about similar measures from foreign governments in retaliation, and that it is inconsistent to expect other countries to be open to U.S. exports when those countries' goods are themselves subject to U.S. tariffs.

The following two articles consider the question further.

WHEN PROTECTIONISM IS A GOOD THING
Herman E. Daly

NAFTA was signed on December 17, 1992, and came into effect on January 1, 1994. The final round of GATT negotiations concluded in 1994, paving the way for GATT to be superseded by the World Trade Organization (WTO) in 1995.

YES

Most public discussions of free trade treat "protectionism" as a dirty word. The recent debates on the North American Free Trade Agreement (NAFTA) and current debates on the General Agreement on Tariffs and Trade (GATT) are a case in point. Protectionism to economists usually means protecting an inefficient, lazy and often monopolistic national industry against really efficient foreign competition to the detriment of consumers....

This does not mean, however, that protectionism is always bad. To the contrary, there are important instances in which protectionism is an essential precondition even to economic efficiency. The most fundamental rule of economic efficiency ... is that the full costs of producing a product must be included in its price. There must be no subsidies.

Protecting efficiency

This argument is often made in regard to nuclear energy, for instance. Some people argue that electricity from nuclear plants is only competitively priced if the costs of decommissioning the plant at the end of its life are ignored. Governments thus often intervene to subsidize electricity produced by nuclear plants.

When the environmental costs of producing a product are passed on to the larger society, this constitutes a form of subsidy by the society to the producer. When a country requires that environmental costs be internalized in prices, this is a step toward greater economic efficiency. However, when a country with policies that support this form of economic discipline engages in free trade with one that does not, the tendency will be for more and more production to shift to the latter. This reduces economic efficiency and should be resisted as vigorously as the protection of inefficient national monopolies.

Free trade also has enormous consequences for the standards a society chooses for itself, that must be treated separately from questions of pure economic efficiency. Standards regarding the distribution of income exemplify the issue. Whether intended or not, free trade between the countries of North American under NAFTA represents an active commitment to a low wage policy. While NAFTA was often presented as a generous act by Canada and the United States to share their great wealth with Mexico, proponents

A U.S. steelworker. In 2002 President George W. Bush imposed tariffs of up to 30 percent on imported steel to protect U.S. steelworkers.

COMMENTARY: The U.S. steel industry today

Throughout the 1980s and 1990s U.S. steelmakers struggled to hold their own, as foreign producers made increasing inroads into the domestic market. The economic boom conditions of the 1990s fostered a strong construction industry in the United States, which in turn was bolstered by the low price of steel available on the world markets. During that time countries with well-established steel industries, such as Japan and Germany, were joined in the steelmaking business by newly developing industries in countries such as South Korea, India, and Brazil.

Commentators have listed a number of reasons why U.S. manufacturers have found it difficult to respond to this competition. As a mature industry, they claim, its infrastructure of fixed plant and equipment, built up over decades, is becoming progressively outdated and cannot compete with the high-tech equipment available in more recently constructed mills in the developing world. Investment in costly infrastructure has been discouraged by norms of corporate governance in the United States that favor the distribution of dividends to stockholders over the reinvestment of profits into modernizing equipment. As a long-established heavy industry, U.S. steelmaking also has a strongly unionized workforce, reluctant to abandon favorable pay and working conditions negotiated during more prosperous times. Defenders of U.S. steelmaking have countered that many foreign producers benefit from assistance from their governments in setting up or modernizing their plants, or in providing guaranteed markets for their products, effectively subsidizing them in a way that they claim is contrary to the rules of the World Trade Organization (WTO). They also claim that national security concerns make it imperative that the United States retain a strong steelmaking capacity—though in fact the amount used by the defense industry is only about 1 percent of total production (most steel is used in the construction and automobile industries).

American steel manufacturers lobbied the government throughout the 1990s to impose tariffs on foreign steel imports as a way of redressing what they saw as these hidden subsidies, but the Clinton administration (1993–2001) did not consider such action to be compatible with a commitment to free trade. On June 5, 2001, however, President George W. Bush announced that he was launching a wideranging investigation into allegations of dumping (see first sidebar on p. 185) against foreign steel producers. In March 2002 he announced tariffs aimed at the producers deemed guilty of dumping, which included most of Europe, Asia, and South America. Governments around the world strongly criticized the move and challenged it through the WTO, which found against the United States in March 2003. As the *Wall Street Journal* commented: "The steel dispute has cast the U.S. in the awkward role of defending protectionist practices even as it preaches free trade to those criticized for their closed markets."

made little mention of who was to do the sharing. In fact, it is the laboring class, which in the United States has already suffered a seventeen percent decline in real wages since 1973. Lower wages mean that returns to those who own capital in all three countries will go up. In reality the workers in the United States and Canada will not be sharing their declining wages with underpaid Mexican workers so much as with the owners of capital.

The author suggests that NAFTA tends to encourage the relocation of manufacturing to Mexico from Canada and the United States. See www.utexas.edu/ depts/bbr/tbr/Dec. 98.Gruben.html for a discussion of whether or not this is actually taking place.

Back to child labor?

We have come to speak of global competition as a major value. Are we competing for a good standard of living for most of our people? Eighty percent of the U.S. labor force is classed as non-supervisory employees. What is the value of competing to lower the incomes of eighty percent of U.S. working people? We could do many unwise things to make ourselves more internationally competitive, such as moving back to child labor. That doesn't mean we should. There are two ways to make products cheaper for the consumer. One is to increase efficiency. Everyone favors that. The other is to reduce environmental and employment standards. Reducing the wages paid for a given amount of productive work represents a lowering of standards, not an increase in efficiency.

Since developed nations like the United States cannot compete with the low wage rates of developing nations, should the United States even try to compete for business in the international marketplace?

Free trade encourages a standards lowering competition as much as it motivates increases in real efficiency. It is important to distinguish between the two. There are real gains from trade, but there are also benefits in maintaining a degree of local self-sufficiency which is very different from autarky. Let me close with a quote from John Maynard Keynes, who in 1933 wrote an overlooked essay on national self-sufficiency. I've heard this referred to as the aberration of a great mind. But I think it was the clear thinking of a great mind. He said the following: "I sympathize therefore, with those who would minimize, rather than with those who would maximize, economic entanglement between nations. Ideas, knowledge, art, hospitality, travel, these are the things which should of their nature be international. But let goods be homespun whenever it is reasonably and conveniently possible. And above all, let finance be primarily national."

John Maynard Keynes (1883–1946) was one of the most influential economists of the first half of the 20th century.

IMPORT QUOTAS "STEEL" FROM US ALL
Jeff Jacoby

NO

Free trade across international borders is not just good for business or good for job-creation. It is good—period.

So said President Bush in a remarkable speech earlier this year, when he made the case for free trade on unabashedly moral grounds. "Open trade is not just an economic opportunity, it is a moral imperative," he told the Council of the Americas in May.

> *Do you think that economic arguments should be subject to morality?*

> *President Bush made this address to the Council of the Americas in Washington, D.C., on May 7, 2001. Go to www.white house.gov/news/ releases/2001/05/ 20010507-6.html to see the full text of the speech.*

Trade creates jobs for the unemployed. When we negotiate for open markets, we are providing new hope for the world's poor. And when we promote open trade, we are promoting political freedom. Societies that open to commerce across their borders will open to democracy within their borders—not always immediately, and not always smoothly, but in good time.

You would expect a president who speaks so stirringly about the virtues of free trade to be impervious to pleas for protectionist measures like import quotas and tariffs. Yet barely a month after Bush's paean to free trade, he invoked Section 201 of the U.S. trade law and announced that he would move to punish foreign steel producers for engaging in "unfair trade practices." Their sin? Selling steel at a good price to Americans who want to buy it.

The case of steel

In recent years, as the world price of steel has dropped, steel imports to the United States have more than doubled. That has been a boon to American consumers, holding down the price of everything from trucks to tools to "tin" cans. Of course, no American company is compelled to buy steel from a foreign supplier; every imported bar and ingot has been purchased by a willing buyer from a willing seller at a mutually agreed price.

You wouldn't know that to listen to the domestic steel lobby, though. For years, U.S. steelmakers and steelworkers have been accusing overseas producers of "dumping" steel on the American market—and demanding that Washington intervene to stop them. The chairman of U.S. Steel, Thomas Usher, is thrilled that Bush has yielded to this pressure. (Bill Clinton, to his credit, resisted it.) The administration's new protectionist stance, Usher crowed, "sends a message to our trading partners that the United States will no longer be a dumping ground for the world's excess steel."

But the Korean, Italian, Japanese, and Indian steel being imported to the United States is hardly being "dumped." It is going into new houses and new cars, into filing cabinets and food containers, into industrial machinery and home appliances. It is adding value to the nation's economic output and contributing to the employment of countless men and women. And it is doing so at a lower cost than if the steel were coming from Usher's company.

Losing out to competitors

Naturally, the steel industry isn't happy to be losing business to foreign competitors. It's understandable that Big Steel lobbies the government to beat up on its competitors. What is not so understandable is why a president who knows how immoral protectionism is— and Bush certainly seemed to know in May—would agree to do it.

The "Section 201" action Bush has set in motion is supposed to help U.S. steelmakers by limiting the amount of foreign steel sold in the United States. Last week, the Commerce Department announced new "antidumping" duties of up to 33 percent on imported steel.

But if that's a good idea, why not help U.S. wineries by limiting imports of French and Italian wine? Why not help U.S. weavers by slapping a quota on imported Oriental rugs? Why not help U.S. filmmakers by imposing punitive duties on foreign movies?

Because in every case, far more people would be hurt than the small number who are helped. Artificially hiking the price of domestic steel (wine/rugs/movies) might be good for a few steel mills (vineyards/ rugmakers/studios) and their workers. But it would be bad for the thousands of manufacturers whose costs would rise, the tens of thousands of employees whose jobs would be made less secure, and the millions of American consumers who would be forced to pay higher prices.

In any case, quotas only delay the inevitable. "Erecting barriers to imports will only postpone needed consolidation of the U.S. steel industry," says Daniel Griswold, a trade

> *"Dumping" is usually defined as selling an item for less than its cost of production. However, U.S. Customs defines it as selling for less than the market price of the exporting country (which will always be higher, assuming the maker has a profit margin). This means that more imports are classified as "dumping" in the United States than they would be in most other countries.*

> *Do you think there are any important differences between steelmaking and these other industries that would weaken this argument?*

THE CONSUMER CONSUMED.

The front cover of the magazine Harper's Weekly *from 1888. The U.S. Customs, depicted as Uncle Sam, and "Monopoly" are begging for money from the "Consumer."*

scholar at the Cato Institute. "The industry hasn't been losing jobs because of unfair imports, but because of relentless technological change"—particularly in "mini-mills" that can produce steel more cheaply from scrap than the big integrated mills can from coke and iron ore. It is the oldest rule of the market: adapt or die.

Another name for theft

Protectionism distorts markets, hurts importers, kills jobs, and sows distrust between nations. But the foremost reason governments should refuse to impede free trade is that it is theft. It steals from the many to enrich the few. It deprives individuals of the right to control their own property—to choose for themselves where to buy the products they want and to sell the goods they own.

"Every citizen who has produced or acquired a product," wrote Frederic Bastiat, the great 19th-century economist and philosopher of freedom,

should have the option of applying it immediately to his own use or of transferring it to whomever on the face of the earth agrees to give him in exchange the object of his desires. To deprive him of this option … solely to satisfy the convenience of another citizen, is to legitimize an act of plunder and to violate the law of justice.

Why do you think it might be harder for countries like the United States to adopt recent technological innovations in steelmaking than other countries that have developed their steel industries more recently?

Do you think there are any legitimate reasons why governments might seek to limit the freedom of individuals to buy whatever they like from whoever is willing to sell it to them?

Summary

The question of whether protectionism is good for U.S. business provokes heated debate among commentators, and two very different approaches are taken by Daly and Jacoby. Daly takes economists to task for assuming that protectionism "usually means protecting an inefficient, lazy, and often monopolistic national industry against really efficient foreign competition to the detriment of the consumer." He believes that that kind of protectionism "should always be resisted," but goes on to look at instances in which protectionism is necessary in order to maintain economic, environmental, and social standards set by society. He quotes John Maynard Keynes: "… let goods be homespun whenever it is reasonably and conveniently possible. And above all, let finance be primarily national."

Jeff Jacoby argues passionately for the free-trade position. He begins by quoting from President George W. Bush's speech in May 2001, in which, Jacoby says, the president "made the case for free trade on unabashedly moral grounds." However, in a clearly protectionist move the Bush administration shortly thereafter agreed to support the steel lobby by limiting the amount of foreign steel sold in the United States. Jacoby draws a parallel with other industries and asks why the government does not afford the same support to other U.S. industries. He argues that falsely supporting U.S. steel means that it remains inefficient and is therefore financially nonviable. The result of this protectionism, he points out, is that it will be bad for the U.S. economy because it will increase costs for thousands of manufactures, put thousands of jobs at risk, and force American consumers to pay more for domestic goods.

FURTHER INFORMATION:

Books:

Bhagwati, Jagdish N., *Protectionism*. Cambridge, MA: MIT Press, 1989.

Gomory, Ralph E., and William J. Baumol, *Global Trade and Conflicting National Interests*. Cambridge, MA: MIT Press, 2000.

Rothgeb, John M., Jr., *U.S. Trade Policy: Balancing Economic Dreams and Political Realities*. Washington, D.C.: CQ Press, 2001.

Useful websites:

www.steelnews.com/companies/chapter11/steel_trade_cases.htm
Site summarizing steel trade disputes from 1998 to 2002.
www.wto.org/english/tratop_e/dispu_e/dispu_subjects_index_e.htm
The World Trade Organization page listing disputes.

internationalecon.com/v1.0/ch20/20c010.html
A comparison of tariff rates in various countries.

The following debates in the Pro/Con series may also be of interest:

In this volume:

Topic 1 Is a free market the best way to organize world trade?

Topic 6 Does the World Trade Organization need reforming?

IS PROTECTIONISM GOOD FOR U.S. BUSINESS?

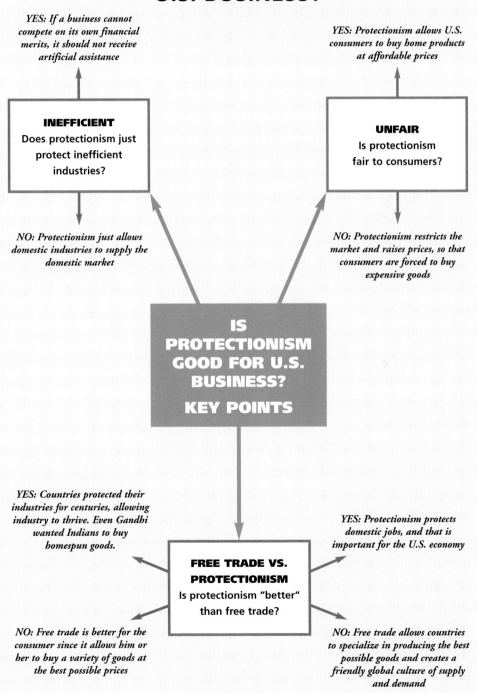

YES: If a business cannot compete on its own financial merits, it should not receive artificial assistance

YES: Protectionism allows U.S. consumers to buy home products at affordable prices

INEFFICIENT
Does protectionism just protect inefficient industries?

UNFAIR
Is protectionism fair to consumers?

NO: Protectionism just allows domestic industries to supply the domestic market

NO: Protectionism restricts the market and raises prices, so that consumers are forced to buy expensive goods

IS PROTECTIONISM GOOD FOR U.S. BUSINESS?
KEY POINTS

YES: Countries protected their industries for centuries, allowing industry to thrive. Even Gandhi wanted Indians to buy homespun goods.

YES: Protectionism protects domestic jobs, and that is important for the U.S. economy

FREE TRADE VS. PROTECTIONISM
Is protectionism "better" than free trade?

NO: Free trade is better for the consumer since it allows him or her to buy a variety of goods at the best possible prices

NO: Free trade allows countries to specialize in producing the best possible goods and creates a friendly global culture of supply and demand

189

Topic 15

HAS NAFTA COST THE UNITED STATES JOBS?

YES
FROM "NAFTA'S BROKEN PROMISES: FAILURE TO CREATE U.S. JOBS"
PUBLIC CITIZEN'S GLOBAL TRADE WATCH, JANUARY 1997
PUBLIC CITIZEN

NO
"BUSH NEEDS TRADE PROMOTION AUTHORITY TO RECHARGE
ECONOMY AND SPUR GROWTH"
HTTP://WWW.NCPA.ORG/BOTHSIDE/KRT/KRT053101A.HTML
NATIONAL CENTER FOR POLICY ANALYSIS

INTRODUCTION

One of the most intense current debates concerning U.S. economic policy centers on the North American Free Trade Agreement (NAFTA). The United States, Canada, and Mexico signed up to NAFTA in 1992, and the agreement went into effect on January 1, 1994. Since then its supporters and critics have argued over NAFTA's effects on the U.S. economy, in particular its impact on American jobs.

The purpose of NAFTA was to eliminate trade barriers such as tariffs (taxes on imports) between the three signatories, thereby creating the world's largest free-trade area. According to free-trade theory, markets without barriers stimulate economic activity. Because companies acquire new export markets into which they can sell their goods unimpeded, they can step up production, which leads to more export-related jobs at home, more workers earning wages, and an

increased demand for goods to buy. Meanwhile, for the public the competition for sales that free trade generates makes a wider range of goods available and at lower prices.

However, free-trade agreements also enable corporations to invest in the economies of their trading partners— for example, by building factories abroad and shifting production from plants at home. Such a course of action may be attractive when workers in one of the countries in a trade agreement are accustomed to lower wages than a company's domestic labor. In the case of NAFTA this means Mexican workers. Opponents of NAFTA believed that many U.S. jobs would be lost south of the border when it came into effect. Texas businessman and 1992 presidential candidate H. Ross Perot (1930–) graphically predicted that the coming of NAFTA would create a "giant sucking sound" as millions of jobs were drawn out of the United States and into Mexico. What was more, according to critics of NAFTA, further American jobs would also be on the line when cheap imports began flooding into the United States from Mexico. U.S. manufacturers simply would not be able to compete with low labor costs and would be forced to close.

"NAFTA is a major stepping stone to the New World Order."

—HENRY KISSINGER (1923–),

DIPLOMAT

So what effect has NAFTA had on the U.S. labor market?

Critics of the agreement maintain that their fears about job losses have been vindicated. They point to an April 2001 report by the Economic Policy Institute, which claimed that NAFTA had been responsible for the disappearance of more than 700,000 American jobs from 1994 to 2000. According to the paper, every state and the District of Columbia were affected. The report blamed the high rise in U.S. imports for the job losses—fewer American workers were needed to make things because more goods were coming from Mexico and Canada. NAFTA critics also claim that at least some of those imported goods came from factories that had at one time been operated by American labor before being transplanted to Mexico.

NAFTA supporters acknowledge that some jobs have been lost or put at risk because of the agreement—about

316,000 by 2001, according to the Department of Labor. However, they argue that the U.S. economy has also created some 20 million new jobs overall since NAFTA came into effect, many of them high-paying positions in export-related industries.

NAFTA proponents also refute talk of a stampede of American manufacturers to Mexico. According to an article published in December 2002 by the pro-free market Cato Institute, U.S. manufacturers invested in Mexican factories on average only about one-hundredth of what they spent on investment at home. The same piece also claimed that between 1994 and 1998 the number of people working in U.S. manufacturing rose by 700,000.

The following articles take opposing sides on the effects of NAFTA. The first piece is from Public Citizen, a nonprofit organization that represents consumer interests. It accuses the government of understating NAFTA job losses and estimates that the movement of U.S. jobs to Mexico has increased employment in border plants by 48 percent. It argues that what new jobs have appeared since NAFTA are mainly in low-paid sectors.

The second article, from the National Center for Policy Analysis (a nonprofit research organization), takes issue with the assertion that NAFTA has cost 700,000 American jobs, claiming that even the auto industry, which shows a trade deficit with Mexico, "employs over 100,000 more workers today than before NAFTA." It also rejects the assertion of a mass exodus of U.S. manufacturers south of the border. At the same time, though, the article agrees that some U.S. workers have lost their jobs and states that "we have to do a better job of retraining them."

NAFTA'S BROKEN PROMISES: FAILURE TO CREATE U.S. JOBS
Public Citizen

NAFTA TAA (NAFTA Trade Adjustment Assistance) was introduced to help workers who have lost their jobs as a direct result of imports from Canada or Mexico, or because of a shift of U.S. production to those countries. The NAFTA TAA was replaced under the Trade Adjustment Assistance Reform Act of 2002. Go to www.doleta.gov/ tradeact to find out more.

YES

As of February 19, 1997, the U.S. Department of Labor had certified 109,384 workers as having lost their jobs due to NAFTA under the narrow terms of NAFTA TAA. These numbers represent only the tip of the iceberg of NAFTA job losses because the NAFTA TAA program is only available to some workers in some industries, and many workers file for assistance under other, better known and less complicated trade unemployment assistance programs. Indeed, only workers who know about and choose to apply for the new NAFTA TAA program are even considered, and only certain types of workers in certain types of companies can qualify. For instance, only workers involved in the production of an actual product—such as assembling a car—damaged by NAFTA trade can qualify. Workers producing auto parts used by that NAFTA TAA certifiable assembly plant would not qualify. A vivid example of how the NAFTA TAA job loss data understates actual NAFTA job loss involves the case of jeans maker Guess Inc. According to the *Wall Street Journal*, Guess has cut the percentage of its clothes sewn in Los Angeles from 97% prior to NAFTA to 35% as of February 1997 as it sent work to five sewing factories in Mexico, and to plants in Peru and Chile. More than 1,000 Los Angeles Guess workers lost their jobs in August and September 1996 alone. None of these Guess jobs that shifted to Mexico—either directly with Guess or with its U.S. contractors—show up as having even applied to NAFTA TAA, much less as being certified for assistance. The Department of Labor's TAA program lists only one clothing manufacturer in Los Angeles as having laid off workers because of a shift in production to Mexico. That company, Lee Thomas, is not and has not been a Guess contractor.

Peru and Chile are outside NAFTA. Does that suggest that the movement of jobs was inevitable anyway?

NAFTA and Florida tomatoes
Another example of NAFTA TAA's gross understatement of NAFTA job loss involves Florida tomatoes. According to a June 14, 1996 University of Florida Institute of Food and Agricultural Sciences press release, "... Before NAFTA,

tomatoes were a $700 million industry for Florida with more than 200 growers. By 1995, with the NAFTA provisions in place and a peso devaluation of more than 50 percent, revenues shrank to $400 million and growers numbered less than 100." Yet, with 100 Florida tomato firms wiped out, only one company associated with Florida tomatoes, Regency Packing Company of Naples, has been certified by the Department of Labor's TAA program. That one firm's closing resulted in over 1,000 workers being certified under NAFTA TAA.

The NAFTA TAA program also does not apply to U.S. retail workers harmed by the peso devaluation. For instance, as reported in a January, 1996 *Miami Herald* story on the impact of the devaluation on U.S. border retail outlets, in Calexico, California, 1,322 jobs were lost due to the December, 1994 peso devaluation. The loss of cross border retail business by newly impoverished Mexicans gave the town of 18,600 the highest unemployment rate in the state (40.6%). Not a single NAFTA TAA petition was filed from the town of Calexico and Calexico's newly unemployed would not qualify for NAFTA TAA if they did file.

In December 1994 Mexico devalued its currency, the peso. At that time the exchange rate was about 3.5 pesos to the dollar. By the end of April 1995 the value of the peso against the dollar had halved. This meant that 100 pesos, for example, bought Mexicans only half as much at border stores as before devaluation.

NAFTA job losses: The big picture

A full three years have passed since NAFTA was implemented in January 1994 and over two years have passed since the December 1994 peso devaluation. Since mid-1996, the Clinton Administration and the Mexican government have been declaring that the Mexican economic crisis is over, a point most Mexican citizens living in economic despair would strongly contest.

However, the Mexican peso's value remains at nearly a third of its pre-NAFTA value. This exchange rate, which makes the U.S. $5 per day pre-NAFTA wages of Mexico's border assembly plants worth less than $3 U.S....

Thus, now the combination of NAFTA and the new post-devaluation peso value has spurred relocation of high-paying U.S. jobs into the Mexican border maquiladora factory sector. Employment in the Mexican border plants has increased 48% since NAFTA's start.

Since NAFTA, companies relocating U.S. jobs to Mexico are now also equipping their border plants with state-of-the-art equipment, guaranteeing productivity rates comparable to those in U.S. plants. Thanks in part to NAFTA's built-in investment insurance, guaranteed by the U.S. Treasury, businesses can now obtain $3 per day wages without risk. Indeed, under NAFTA's Chapter 11 investment rules, any

Since the 1960s Mexico has invested in the creation of maquiladoras, factories in the borderlands where Mexican labor assembles products for U.S. firms. At the end of the 20th century there were about 3,000 small factories.

investor from a NAFTA country will be reimbursed … if a NAFTA country "directly or indirectly nationalizes or expropriates" the investor's property or assets.…

The effects of NAFTA's investment guarantees and Mexico's low wages have been dramatic. Before NAFTA, Mexico was the only major trading partner with whom the United States did not have a trade deficit. In NAFTA's first three years, the $1.7 billion U.S. trade surplus with Mexico that existed in 1993 has been transformed into a record new NAFTA trade deficit. The 1996 U.S. trade deficit with Mexico is the largest ever at $16.3 billion, breaking the record $15 billion deficit of 1995. If the U.S. trade deficit with Canada is added, the overall NAFTA trade deficit from January 1994 to January 1997 is over $85 billion, according to U.S. Department of Commerce data.

This article was published in January 1997. The U.S. trade deficit with NAFTA countries has continued to rise. The deficit with Mexico for 2002 was $37.2 billion, while that with Canada was almost $49.8 billion. Go to www.census.gov/ foreign- trade/balance for current and past U.S. international trade figures.

Auto and electronics exports to blame

Mexican exports in automobiles and electronics are almost entirely responsible for this U.S. trade deficit. In 1996, the United States had a $27.7 billion trade deficit in automobiles, light trucks and parts with Mexico and Canada—$15 billion with Mexico, $12.7 billion with Canada. The composition of the NAFTA trade flow is particularly damaging to U.S. jobs in another way. According to unpublished Census Bureau Data, only 11.7% of U.S. goods exported to Mexico consisted of consumer goods for the first eleven months of 1996. U.S. exports to Mexico are overwhelming[ly] "outsourcing"—assembly which used to be done in the United States.

If assembly jobs are so low paid, would Americans want them? Is it not better if the jobs go abroad?

NAFTA boosters argue that without NAFTA the damage to the United States from Mexico's economic crisis would have been even worse. Yet, when Mexico's economy last crumbled in 1982, the U.S. trade deficit at its worst was less than half of the current deficit the U.S. has suffered in each of two of NAFTA's three years. What's more, while the United States has been walloped with a new NAFTA trade deficit (about which *Business Week* reported under the headline "Singing the NAFTA Blues"), Mexico's other major trade partners, including the European Union, Japan and China, have maintained trade surpluses with Mexico throughout this latest economic crisis.

In May 1993, then U.S. Trade representative Mickey Kantor predicted "Export jobs related to Mexico" will reach 200,000 "by 1995 if NAFTA with the supplemental agreements is implemented." However, the economic models used by the Administration and the pro-NAFTA lobby to create the

200,000 new-jobs-per-year promise to sell NAFTA to the American public, including the so-called "Hufbauer-Schott model," were methodologically flawed. These flawed predictions have no relation to the present reality. For instance, these models—used by NAFTA's promoters both in and outside the Administration—predicted that by the end of 1995 the United States would enjoy a $9 billion trade surplus with Mexico. The reality, of course, is that the post-NAFTA surge in imports from Mexico resulted in a $15-plus billion trade deficit with Mexico for 1995 and an even larger deficit in 1996.

If the U.S. trade deficit is plugged into the job creation formulas created by NAFTA advocates, approximately half a million U.S. jobs have been lost under NAFTA. Most of the U.S. jobs lost are high paying jobs in automobiles, trucks and auto parts. The Washington D.C. based think tank found that the U.S. trade deficit with Mexico in these areas has quadrupled since 1993.

In 1993 Gary Hufbauer and Jeffrey Schott of the Institute for International Economics, a Washington-based research institution, created a formula for linking trade with job creation and loss. They reckoned that for every $1 billion change in exports, about 19,000 jobs would be created or lost.

New jobs are lower paid

Confronted with such data, NAFTA's boosters scramble towards general U.S. job creation figures, arguing that if the U.S. economy is creating jobs, then NAFTA cannot be doing any real damage. Of course, the vast majority of new jobs now being created in the United States are in low paying sectors of the economy. According to the Labor Department's Bureau of Labor Statistics, the top four occupations having the largest numerical increase over the next decade are, in order, cashiers, janitors, retail sale clerks and waiters and waitresses. As well, studies show that the chances are 2 to 1 that a laid off U.S. worker will not find an equal or higher paying job. The median annual pay drop of a worker who was hired after being laid off in the early 1990's was $4,420. As ugly as the NAFTA job loss data is, NAFTA's downward pressure on wages may be even more damaging.

Does it matter what sort of jobs are created? Is not any job better than no job?

In NAFTA's three years, real wages have continued to drop. The lack of real wage growth during a period of economic recovery is unique in over one hundred years of U.S. wage data. Now, a Cornell University report commissioned—and then suppressed for over four months—by the U.S. Labor Department shows that NAFTA is being used to bust unions and thwart labor organizing. "NAFTA created a climate that has emboldened employers," says the study's author, Cornell Professor Kate Bronfenbrenner, in a January 27, 1997 *BusinessWeek* story entitled, "NAFTA: A New Union-Busting Weapon?"...

Among the study's findings was that employers were using the threat of plant closure and relocation to Mexico as a way of diluting employees' bargaining power in areas such as pay.

BUSH NEEDS TRADE PROMOTION AUTHORITY TO RECHARGE ECONOMY AND SPUR GROWTH
National Center for Policy Analysis

NO

America needs more trade. Imports bring lower priced goods into our stores—reducing the cost of living, while exports create high-paying jobs for American workers. Trade-intensive industries pay an average of $60,000 a year—one-third more than other industries. We have the highest wages and living standards in history, and trade has been an important reason.

The problem is that many other countries are not as open to our trade as we are to theirs. U.S. tariffs (taxes on imports) average only 2 percent, but in Asia and South America our products face tariffs of up to 20 percent to 30 percent. Many markets are closed outright to America's farm products and services industries. This isn't fair, and it costs us exports and jobs.

Although the average is only 2 percent, tariffs on some goods are up to 30 percent.

We have to negotiate these barriers away—and quickly! We are falling behind. Our global competitors have 130 free trade agreements. We have two. That hurts.

One example: Canadian paper mills are displacing American paper exports to Chile because of the Canada—Chile free trade agreement.

Trade Promotion Authority, or "fast track," amounts to an agreement between the president and Congress on the goals U.S. trade negotiators will pursue with other countries. Congress may vote only yes or no on any deals reached—no amendments may be tabled—thus speeding up the process of getting trade deals into effect.

Trade agreements required

And things are about to get much worse. The Europeans are negotiating duty-free access to the huge South American market, and Japan is starting deals in Asia. We need a Free Trade Area of the Americas (FTAA), which would triple U.S. exports to South America to $200 billion within a decade.

We need a World Trade Organization (WTO) agreement allowing America's farm products into world markets. The President needs Trade Promotion Authority (TPA) to move ahead on these. Other countries won't negotiate with us unless they know Congress must simply vote yes or no on the whole package—with no amendments. It's the same principle that unions use to reach labor contracts.

COMMENTARY: Alternatives to NAFTA

The alternatives to the North American Free Trade Agreement (NAFTA) fall into three broad categories: maintaining NAFTA levels of cooperation but with more partners, achieving closer cooperation than under NAFTA between existing partners, or moving away from free trade.

Free Trade Area of the Americas (FTAA)

Since the first Summit of the Americas, held in Miami, Florida, in 1994, efforts have been under way to create a Free Trade Area of the Americas (FTAA), a "super-NAFTA" that is scheduled to come into effect no later than December 2005. Whereas NAFTA consists of three members, the FTAA is set to comprise no fewer than 34 states of North, Central, and South America and the Caribbean. As the name suggests, the aim is to create a free-trade area in which trade barriers between member states will be gradually removed.

Closer cooperation

It has also been suggested that the members of NAFTA might forge closer ties. Free-trade agreements may evolve through stages, of which the first is the free-trade area—internal tariffs between members disappear, but each state still has its own external tariff when it comes to doing business with nonmember countries. This is the case in NAFTA. The next stage is the customs union, in which the members of a free-trade area each agrees to charge a similar tariff on goods coming from outside the zone. Such a policy simplifies customs operations. In NAFTA, although goods produced in member countries can pass freely across other signatories' borders, external imports passing between members still need to be checked at customs. Otherwise they might be imported through a low-tariff member and then transported to a member charging a higher external tariff without the full duty being paid. In a customs union a uniform external tariff makes such checks unnecessary. Beyond the customs union lies the common market, in which goods, services, and investment are all free to move from member to member, and common work permits allow free movement of labor. The European Union (EU) is a common market. Unlike NAFTA, the EU also has bodies that can enact legislation enforceable in its member states. However, such levels of integration raise issues of loss of national sovereignty.

Protectionism

The third alternative to NAFTA is to move away from free trade and toward protectionism. Thus the government might impose tariffs on cheap imports to make them expensive to the public and therefore unattractive. It might also prevent the importation of goods from countries that do not allow in American exports. Opponents of free trade see these measures as a way of protecting jobs and bringing down the U.S. trade deficit.

In the 1992 presidential election U.S. workers show they think NAFTA would be a good thing.

Trade agreements work! NAFTA slashed Mexico's barriers, and this year our exports to Mexico will be $120 billion—triple their level before NAFTA. Mexico provides almost one-third of our global export growth, and we now sell as much to Mexico as to Japan, Germany, and France combined.

Imports from Mexico grew even faster, and some argue NAFTA cost 700,000 U.S. jobs. Not so.

One-third of our Mexican deficit comes from the oil imports we need. And except for automobiles, we sell more manufactured goods to Mexico than we buy—giving us an overall trade surplus in these goods.

True, we have a large automobile trade deficit with Mexico. But instead of losing jobs, our auto industry employs over 100,000 more workers today than before NAFTA—because U.S. production has grown so fast as well. And wages? Real U.S. manufacturing wages grew 50 percent faster after NAFTA than before!

For every factory that moved to Mexico, many more stayed and expanded U.S. production. Since NAFTA, our exports to Mexico skyrocketed by $80 billion while our manufacturing investment there grew to only $2.5 billion a year.

According to Census Bureau figures, in 2002 the United States imported $41 billion in cars, trucks, and parts from Mexico and exported goods of a similar type to Mexico to the value of about $15 billion—a deficit of about $26 billion.

No "race to the bottom"

There is no "race to the bottom" in search of the cheapest labor. Over 85 percent of all U.S. manufacturing investment overseas goes to high-wage areas like Europe. Even so, America's overall trade gain shouldn't come at the expense of those workers who are displaced, and we have to do a better job of retraining them.

Congress has stalled TPA for six years, debating labor and environmental issues. Meanwhile, every day that we sit behind our two percent barriers and permit others to keep theirs at up to 30 percent we make life more difficult for American workers.

President Bush has put forward a TPA plan that will help improve labor and environmental conditions abroad while avoiding protectionism. Congress should pass it quickly.

The term "race to the bottom" describes the perceived drive by companies to set up operations in countries with the lowest labor and environmental standards. In the competition to attract foreign investment, some people argue, countries may set these standards lower and lower.

Summary

A decade after NAFTA's implementation the debate continues over whether American jobs have been lost as a result of the agreement. The preceding two articles examine aspects of the argument.

In the first selection, from Public Citizen, the author argues that the narrow terms of the government's assistance program to workers displaced by NAFTA mask the true number of jobs lost. The author goes on to claim that the combination of Mexico's low wages and NAFTA, with its "built-in investment insurance," has led to high-paying American jobs moving to Mexico's border area and to the United States' trade deficit with Mexico. Moreover, the author contends that proponents of NAFTA were too optimistic about new job creation in the United States as a result of expanded export markets—"the vast majority of new jobs … are in low paying sectors of the economy." Finally, the piece asserts that NAFTA "is being used to bust unions and thwart labor organizing."

In the second article the National Center for Policy Analysis—a Texas-based public policy think tank—concedes there is a trade deficit with Mexico in automobiles. However, it argues that there are 100,000 more auto workers in the United States since NAFTA than before and that a trade surplus with Mexico exists in other areas of manufacturing. According to this article, although some American factories did move to Mexico, "many more stayed and expanded U.S. production." While calling for the better retraining of displaced American workers, the article insists that the president be allowed to negotiate more free-trade deals. Exports bring highly paid jobs for Americans but cannot do so while other countries retain high trade barriers.

FURTHER INFORMATION:

Books:

Hufbauer, Gary C., Jeffrey J. Schott, and Diana Orejas, *NAFTA: A Seven-Year Appraisal*. Washington, D.C.: Institute for International Economics, 2003.

MacArthur, John R., *The Selling of "Free Trade": NAFTA, Washington, and the Subversion of American Democracy*. New York: Hill and Wang, 2000.

Articles:

Fitzgerald, Sara J., "The Effects of NAFTA on Exports, Jobs, and the Environment: Myth vs. Reality." The Heritage Foundation, August 1, 2001.

Useful websites:

www.ustr.gov/regions/whemisphere/nafta.shtml
Office of the U.S. Trade Representative's NAFTA page.

The following debates in the Pro/Con series may also be of interest:

In this volume:
Topic 1 Is a free market the best way to organize world trade?

In *U.S. Foreign Policy*:
Topic 6 Does NAFTA work?

Topic 8 Should the United States be more open to exports from other nations?

HAS NAFTA COST THE UNITED STATES JOBS?

YES: NAFTA has led to a flood of imports and a huge trade deficit with Mexico and Canada

YES: Some 20 million jobs have been created in the United States since NAFTA, and many are in the high-paying export industry

TRADE
Has NAFTA adversely affected U.S. trade?

JOB CREATION
Has NAFTA lived up to its promise to generate jobs?

NO: NAFTA has generated new export business, but further trade agreements are required to open up more markets

NO: NAFTA supporters were too optimistic about the number of jobs that would be created; most new jobs are in the low-paying service sector

HAS NAFTA COST THE UNITED STATES JOBS? KEY POINTS

YES: Low wages have tempted American corporations to open factories in Mexico, with the loss of investment and jobs in the United States

YES: Cheap imports from Mexico have forced U.S. factories to close

COMPETITION
Has NAFTA made it difficult for the United States to compete?

NO: There has been no mass exodus of companies to Mexico. American investment in Mexico has been a fraction of investment at home.

NO: Employment in the U.S. manufacturing industry rose by 700,000 between 1994 and 1998

Topic 16
SHOULD THE UNITED STATES TRADE WITH COUNTRIES WITH POOR HUMAN RIGHTS RECORDS?

YES
FROM "U.S. SANCTIONS AGAINST BURMA: A FAILURE ON ALL FRONTS"
TRADE POLICY ANALYSIS NO. 1, MARCH 26, 1998
LEON T. HADAR

NO
"U.S. AND EU IMPOSE BURMA SANCTIONS"
ICEM INFO, VOL. 2, NO. 2, 1997
INTERNATIONAL COUNCIL OF CHEMICAL, ENERGY, MINE, AND GENERAL WORKERS' UNIONS

INTRODUCTION

In the aftermath of World War II (1939–1945) international concern with human rights led to the creation of the United Nations Universal Declaration of Human Rights (1948). This document marked the culmination of the campaign to establish a code of basic rights to which every individual was entitled. However, like other human rights proclamations, the declaration was a code of conduct. There was no mechanism to enforce it, and various nations continue to flout its provisions.

Although many countries acknowledge the need to improve human rights around the world, there is considerable debate about the best way to do so. One of the most obvious ways would appear to be restrictions on trade. Withholding or regulating trade could weaken the economy of a country and in this way undermine oppressive regimes. In the 1990s, following the Cold War, economic sanctions became an essential part of U.S. foreign policy.

Human rights activists argue that strong democracies like the United States have a moral duty to bring about change in abusive regimes through means such as trade embargoes. They believe that nations should not engage in trade with countries that violate the rights of their citizens, since by doing so they are promoting the economy and thereby supporting the ruling regime. Supporters of trade restrictions argue that they have been successful in ending human rights abuses in many countries. From the mid-1970s the United States and many other countries imposed trade and other restrictions on South Africa in protest against its oppressive system of apartheid. Their action contributed to the end of race separation in 1991.

However, some economists and politicians believe that trade sanctions are not an effective means of tackling human rights abuses. They say that the United States should be able to trade with all countries, even those with poor human rights records. The United States claims that having a trade relationship with countries like China enables them to apply pressure on the Chinese to improve their human rights situation. But some commentators contend that this policy is not working in practice.

> "We ought not to buy from countries who violate the child labor norms, we ought not to buy from companies that basically oppress their workers with labor conditions and lack of a living income."
>
> —PRESIDENT BILL CLINTON,
>
> DECEMBER 1, 1991

Others have accused the Americans of picking and choosing their trade partners in Asia. They point out that poorer countries, like Burma, have been subject to sanctions because of their human rights abuses, while it is considered appropriate to trade with richer countries, like China, which are also guilty of infringing human rights.

Opponents of sanctions argue that there are a number of cases in which sanctions have not worked, such as in Iraq. They claim that sanctions do more harm than good and impose greater restrictions on people living in the countries targeted. Many observers believe that the Iraqi people—rather than Saddam Hussein's regime—suffered most from the U.N. trade sanctions imposed after Iraq invaded Kuwait in 1990, even after the "oil for food" program was implemented in December 1996, which allowed Iraq to sell oil to buy essential supplies for its people. The trade sanctions limited the income of Iraq, but did not affect the way that Saddam Hussein's government administered the resulting profits.

While the main focus of sanctions is the power they have to effect change in the targeted country, they also have repercussions for the nations initiating them. Such consequences include loss of potential revenue, markets, and jobs, which can lead to increased unemployment and poverty at home. According to a study by the National Association of Manufacturers, between 1993 and 1996 the United States produced 61 laws and executive actions to impose unilateral economic sanctions. Sanctioned countries represented about 2.3 billion potential consumers of U.S. goods and $790 billion worth of export markets.

The arguments associated with the question of whether the United States should trade with countries with poor human rights records is examined in the following articles dealing with U.S. trade relations with Myanmar—the official name for Burma since 1989. In 1988 the Burmese military prevented the democratically elected National League for Democracy from taking office. The United States imposed trade sanctions on Burma in 1996 to try to force the government to end its repression of political opponents and to improve its human rights record.

U.S. SANCTIONS AGAINST BURMA: A FAILURE ON ALL FRONTS
Leon T. Hadar

Leon T. Hadar is a journalist and adjunct scholar of the Cato Institute, a nonprofit public policy research foundation based in Washington, D.C., for which this paper was written. The International Federation of Chemical, Energy, Mine, and General Workers' Unions was instrumental in lobbying the government, as were many smaller NGOs, including the Coalition for Corporate Withdrawal from Burma and The Burma Project. Go to http://www.soros.org/burma/welcome.html for more details.

A socialist military dictatorship has ruled Burma since 1962. International condemnation was triggered in 1988 when the regime killed thousands of prodemocracy protesters during uprisings that began in Rangoon on August 8. In September the military formed the State Law and Order Restoration Council to reestablish its rule.

YES

Introduction

…The successful campaign by American groups to force the U.S. government to impose economic sanctions against Burma highlights the damaging strategic, economic, and moral consequences of America's new approach to determining foreign policy. It is a trend that weakens U.S. ties with Asia, reduces American diplomatic and economic influence, and retards creation of a favorable balance of power in the region. Sanctions have already damaged the interests of American companies operating in the region by undermining their reputations as reliable suppliers and denied U.S. firms the ability to compete aggressively with rival foreign firms for market share and profitable investments.

Present U.S. policy toward Burma is not going to bring meaningful change in the human rights practices of the regime and will probably make the bad situation in Burma even worse. Sanctions strengthen the hand of the ruling authorities by creating a scapegoat for their own internal policy failures and narrowing the opportunity of private individuals in Burma to expand their economic, social, and cultural contacts with the citizens of the West.…

Burma becomes public enemy no. 1

Washington has sought to isolate Burma since the State Law and Order Restoration Council [SLORC] came to power in 1988, and especially since it refused to transfer power in 1990 to the National League for Democracy, which had defeated the SLORC in an open election. (Burma's ruling junta officially abolished the SLORC in November 1997, only to replace it with the equally repressive State Peace and Development Council.)

The United States has refused, among other things, to recognize the government's change of the country's name to Myanmar, but it has maintained limited diplomatic and economic ties as well as counternarcotics cooperation with Rangoon. In 1990 Washington withdrew its ambassador from

Rangoon, and since then it has opposed Burma's membership in various multilateral financial organizations, refused to approve licenses for the export of military-related items to Burma, and imposed limited economic sanctions on that country (for example, suspending Burma from the U.S. Generalized System of Preferences).

Since 1990 the U.S. policy of isolating Burma has been rejected by America's trade partners in Asia, who happen also to be Burma's major trade partners, but it has received some symbolic backing from Washington's Western allies....

America's limited leverage

America's potential leverage over Burma has always been marginal at best. The United States is only the fifth largest foreign investor in Burma (Britain, France, Thailand, and Singapore lead the list), with total investments of $226 million. U.S. investment accounts for less than 10 percent of total foreign direct investment, and the share may be even smaller because of Burma's large black-market economy. For example, in 1993 total imports and exports reached nearly $2 billion, but the value of black-market trade with India and China was about $1 billion. In 1994 the United States accounted for about 1 percent of Burmese imports and took in about 7 percent of that country's exports. China, Singapore, and the rest of the Asian countries were the origin of about 90 percent of Burma's imports; and India, Singapore, and China were the three main destinations for its exports.

Those figures suggest that the U.S. economic stake in Burma is limited and that Burma therefore is not susceptible to U.S. economic pressure. Cutting U.S. economic ties with Burma will only reduce the already limited leverage the United States has on Rangoon. Consequently, the failure of U.S. unilateral sanctions to change the behavior of Burma's rulers is inevitable.

U.S. policy alienates allies

The United States has failed to rally its allies to its campaign against Burma. In 1997 ASEAN admitted Burma as a member; the European Union has imposed only limited and symbolic sanctions on Rangoon, declining to go beyond suspending Burma's access to duty-free entry to its market, and Australia has refrained from doing even that....

The potential for long-term confrontation with ASEAN is one of the most troubling aspects of the Burma sanctions. Sanctions are seen in the region as part of a general U.S.-led Asia-bashing campaign, with Washington weighing economic

---

The Generalized System of Preferences (GSP) is a mechanism designed to benefit countries in the developing world by extending duty-free treatment to certain products they produce. The GSP first came into force in 1976 and is regularly reviewed.

Although U.S. trade is only of limited direct importance to the Burmese economy, do you think that the power of the United States in the wider global economy can exert pressure and therefore increase the effectiveness of its sanctions?

ASEAN, or the Association of Southeast Asian Nations, was established in 1967 to promote development and cooperation in Southeast Asia. Its members are Indonesia, Malaysia, the Philippines, Singapore, Thailand, Brunei, Vietnam, Laos, Burma, and Cambodia. See www.aseansec.org/ to find out more.

sanctions against another ASEAN member, Indonesia, to punish it for its repression in the former Portuguese colony of East Timor and for its lack of American standards of labor rights, as well as against China, Southeast Asia's neighboring economic powerhouse....

Sanctions fall hardest on people of Burma

What really matters is that the Burma sanctions have not worked to achieve their political goals of domestic change. The SLORC/SPCD junta remains in control and is not facing any serious challenge to its power. As many of the businesses operating in Burma have pointed out, the sanctions' main victims are the Burmese people themselves.

The U.S.–ASEAN Business Council is an organization representing the interests of U.S. companies in the ten member countries of ASEAN. Go to http://www. usasean.org/ Aboutus/index.htm for more information.

When it comes to advancing political and economic reforms, U.S. companies in Burma are part of the solution, not the problem. "The presence of U.S. companies abroad helps to promote the values we as a nation espouse, including human rights and fair labor standards," noted Ernest Bower, president of the U.S.-ASEAN Council and one of the leading opponents of sanctions. U.S. companies train workers and transfer technology more readily than do their Asian and European competitors. They promote democratic values, set a positive example, and improve the general quality of life by providing fair pay, safe working conditions, and health and education benefits....

The author advocates an approach often known as "constructive engagement," based on the view that by working within a country, foreign businesses can instill good practice by example. Do you agree that this is a more effective means of bringing about change than removing foreign business presence through trade embargoes?

One objection raised to U.S. investment in Burma is that foreign companies are often required to deal directly with government ministries and state-owned enterprises, including those tied to the defense ministry. Advocates of sanctions argue that those joint ventures do more to prop up the government than to nurture an alternative private sector. Dealing with the government is difficult to avoid in a country where socialism has guided government economic policy for decades. Even when working jointly with state-tied companies, American-owned investment brings higher wages, new technology, and Western-style labor practices to workers in Burma. Outside investment strengthens private institutions while exerting influence on the government to liberalize its economic policies....

Sanctions slow Burma's liberalization

In recent years, while continuing to maintain tight political control over the country, the military regime has allowed Burma to gradually emerge from decades of self-imposed isolation and open itself economically. Indeed, its economy has begun to grow and attract foreign investment. After several years of stagnation in the late 1980s and early 1990s, Burma's economy grew by an estimated 6 percent in 1994 and by an estimated 8.2 percent in 1995. Similarly, per capita income has risen modestly, from about $198 in 1993 to $224 in 1995. Under the regime's economic reform program, exports were expected to increase by 30 percent from 1994 to 1997. And the Privatization Commission … is … privatizing government-controlled enterprises. According to some figures, the private sector now accounts for close to 80 percent of gross domestic product and is expected to grow in the coming years. Japanese and South Korean experts are assisting in the creation of a stock exchange, and foreign currency regulations and tax regulations are being liberalized as the regime is approving larger amounts of foreign investment in the country. Such investments reached more than $2.5 billion in 1995, up from $735 million in 1992.

Burma's integration into ASEAN is expected to accelerate the process of economic growth and provide new opportunities for foreign businesses, although the economy will continue to face major problems. U.S. unilateral sanctions against Burma will have only a limited effect on that process, since other nations that already have substantial foreign investment in Burma will proceed with that investment. In fact, since a lack of managerial skills seems to be one of the major obstacles to the growth and reform of the Burmese economy, U.S. economic disengagement from that country is preventing Burma's Western-oriented business elite from acquiring the expertise needed to integrate Burma into the global economy. Hence, while Congress and the Clinton administration sing the praises of globalization, their policies toward Burma run contrary to that goal.

Finding the right policy

Advocates of sanctions point out that opposition leader Aung San Suu Kyi supports sanctions against her own country. If she favors sanctions, who are we to decide that sanctions would be bad for her countrymen? But that line of reasoning dodges the all-important question of whether sanctions are good policy. Aung San Suu Kyi's courageous opposition to a repressive regime deserves respect, but that does not necessarily mean that Western nations must endorse her choice of tactics. The fact that the opposition within a country has endorsed a policy that hurts nearly everyone involved and has little prospect of succeeding does not require the United States to follow the same questionable path….

Does the size and importance of the United States mean that even unilateral sanctions will have an important effect?

Aung San Suu Kyi (1945–) is the leader of the National League for Democracy, the party that won the general election in 1990 with an 82 percent majority. The military junta placed her under house arrest from 1989 to 1995 and from September 2000 to May 2002, and continues to limit her freedom. She has become the international focus for prodemocracy and human rights in her country. She was awarded the Nobel Peace Prize in 1991 and the U.S. Presidential Medal of Freedom in 2000. Go to http://www.dassk.com/ to find out more.

U.S. AND EU IMPOSE BURMA SANCTIONS
International Council of Chemical, Energy, Mine, and General Workers' Unions

This article, written in spring 1997, comes from ICEM Info, a publication produced by the International Federation of Chemical, Energy, Mine, and General Workers' Unions, an industry-based world labor federation. Go to http://www.icem.org/campaigns/burma/burindexen.html to find out about the ICEM Burma campaign.

The Association of Southeast Asian Nations, or ASEAN, admitted Burma as a member on July 23, 1997.

NO

The United States imposed economic sanctions on Burma (Myanmar) this April after a sustained campaign headed by ICEM American affiliate the Oil, Chemical and Atomic Workers' International Union (OCAW). The Clinton administration's move follows international lobbying by trade unions and others over the massive human rights violations committed by the Burmese military dictatorship, the SLORC. Forced labour is systematic under the Burmese regime.

The European Union has already withdrawn trading privileges from Burma over the same issue. This is the first time the EU has taken such action against labour rights violations … The next test of world resolve to isolate the SLORC is now likely to come in South-East Asia, where regional trading bloc ASEAN will soon have to decide on the junta's application for membership.

Fighting repression

OCAW President Robert E. Wages hailed the US sanctions as "a major victory in the struggle to make multinational corporations accountable for their actions at home and abroad. The repercussions of the decision to impose sanctions extend far beyond Burma and would not have been possible without an upsurge from workers, students and community activists, along with the brave actions of the Burmese people in fighting repression".

Three days for Burma

The sanctions were announced on the eve of the "3 Days for Burma" campaign on April 22–24, which was planned by the OCAW to take place at 400 workplaces around the country. The campaign was supported by the ICEM-affiliated United Mine Workers of America (UMWA) and had participation from over 60 college campuses and communities across the USA. A central focus of "3 Days for Burma" was a petition for sanctions. This February, Wages tabled a resolution on Burma adopted by the US national labour federation AFL-CIO. The resolution calls on US corporations to withdraw investment

COMMENTARY: Sanctions against Burma

To show its condemnation of the Burmese government's repression of the democratically elected League for Democracy and to try to effect change, the United States imposed trade sanctions on Burma. Similar sanctions against South Africa from the late 1970s were key in removing U.S. corporate presence from that country, contributing to the isolation of its government and the eventual ending of apartheid (race separation).

The Burma Act

In September 1996 Congress enacted the Burma Act, which imposed trade sanctions on Burma and granted the president discretionary powers related to these restrictions. It also banned aid to the Burmese government except for humanitarian and counternarcotics operations, and instructed U.S. members of international financial organizations to vote against loans or other forms of assistance to Burma. The statute states that the sanctions are to remain in place until "the president determines and certifies to Congress that Burma has made measurable and substantial progress in improving human rights practices and implementing democratic government." The act also gave the president power to impose more sanctions if the Burmese government committed further human rights abuses. To this end, in September 1997 President Clinton (1993–2001) issued an Executive Order banning new investment by U.S. companies in Burma.

The Massachusetts Burma Law

In June 1996, a few months before Congress passed the Burma Act, Massachusetts introduced state-level trade restrictions against Burma. An Act Regulating State Contracts with Companies doing Business with or in Burma, better known as the Massachusetts Burma Law, applied selective purchasing criteria against companies active in or with business links to Burma by imposing a 10 percent penalty on bids for state contracts—the state buys some $2 billion in goods and services a year. Massachusetts was one of more than 20 states and cities to adopt such measures against Burma. However, some companies with connections to Burma objected to the law. In April 1998 the National Foreign Trade Council (NFTC), a body representing companies engaged in foreign commerce, brought a legal case—*Crosby v. the National Foreign Trade Council*—against Massachusetts state officials. The NFTC claimed that the Massachusetts law conflicted with federal law, since it undermined the discretionary power granted to the president to control sanctions and contravened Congress's limitation of sanctions to new investments. On June 19, 2000, the Supreme Court upheld the NFTC's case, finding the Massachusetts Burma Law contravened the supremacy clause of the Constitution, under which everyone must follow federal law in the face of conflicting state law.

See page 209 for more information about selective purchasing legislation—notably the Massachusetts Burma Law—applied against companies with trading links with Burma.

from Burma and encourages unions to mobilize members to press the Clinton administration and the US Congress to take whatever steps necessary to restore democracy and civilian rule in Burma. Unions should also support selective purchasing legislation—already adopted in a number of US localities—barring the spending of public funds with companies that do business with Burma.

Oil multinationals Unocal, Arco and Texaco are providing the Burmese military regime with "large amounts of desperately needed hard currency," the AFL-CIO resolution points out. At the same time, these companies are engaged in "severe downsizing and cost-cutting which has compromised worker and community safety and is resulting in significant loss of high-skill, high-wage jobs in the United States."

Junta's mainstay: big oil

Go to http://www.free burmacoalition.org/ for more information about the Free Burma Coalition.

Zar Ni, a Burmese exile and founder of the Free Burma Coalition, cautioned that the imposition of limited economic sanctions, while a major victory, will not put an end to Burma's dictatorship and its atrocities. The new US sanctions do not affect existing investments in Burma. "We will now concentrate our efforts on the major oil companies who are providing a lifeline to the dictatorship as these companies downsize their US operations, lay off thousands of US workers and make oil refineries unsafe," Zar Ni said.

U.S. trade sanctions apply only to "new" investments made after 1997. Do you think that they should apply to all U.S. business interests in Burma regardless of when they began?

Certainly, global energy companies are a mainstay of the regime. The ICEM, to which the OCAW and the UMWA are affiliated, has consistently urged the oil multinationals either to use their great influence to end [human] rights violations in Burma or to close down their operations there.

But in fact, energy multinationals seem to have signed away their right to back democracy in Burma. A standard clause in contracts with the state-run Myanmar Oil and Gas Enterprise (MOGE) bans foreign partners from involvement "in any manner whatsoever with political activities detrimental to the Government of the Union of Myanmar". The punishment for offenders: termination of their lucrative contracts and seizure of their money and equipment by MOGE …

Drug money?

Particular controversy surrounds the Yadana pipeline project, a joint venture between global energy corporations Total and Unocal, MOGE and the Petroleum Authority of Thailand Exploration and Production Company. The pipeline will bring gas from Burma's offshore Yadana field to Thailand, where it will be used mainly for electricity generation. From the start, the project has been accused of serious human rights violations—notably the use of forced labour, which the multinationals continue to deny …

Apart from oil and gas, illicit drugs are probably the SLORC'S main hard currency earners. Burma is the largest producer of illegal heroin in the world. The US State Department says 60 per cent of the heroin seized in the US comes from Burma.

After a four-year investigation, the Paris-based organization "Geopolitical Drugwatch" last year charged that MOGE is the major channel for laundering SLORC revenues from heroin.

A shareholder resolution this June will call on Unocal to investigate the drugs allegations. To block discussion of the issue, Unocal had asked the US Securities and Exchange Commission (SEC) for a so-called "no-action letter", allowing the company to exclude the resolution from its annual proxy statement and prevent a vote.

But the OCAW revealed that the SEC had rejected the company's plea.

Unocal was subject to a legal action, John Doe v. Unocal, in the California Superior Court. The company defended itself against the charge of "vicarious liability," or whether it is responsible for human rights abuses allegedly committed by the Burmese military in connection with the construction of the Yadana natural gas pipeline. Unocal is based in California.

Unocal shareholder's investigation call

Submitted by a retired OCAW member, the resolution says outside or non-employee board members of Unocal should investigate the MOGE drugs link charge. If the allegation is true, board members should determine if Unocal officials had any knowledge of this matter, and should take appropriate action based on the findings. "We are pleased that the SEC acted judiciously in throwing out Unocal's objections," Wages commented.

"We hope that Unocal shareholders can now become better informed about the real cost of doing business with Burma's military regime, which may include a rise in drug use in the US. "Unocal has had plenty of time to present evidence that the allegation is false, but has done nothing," Wages said. This had "only added to growing suspicions that its partner is serving as a front for drug money laundering by Burma's narco-military regime."

Which do you think is more serious—the allegation that Unocal is linked to human rights abuses or that it is dealing with an organization alleged to be involved in the illegal drug trade?

Obstructive tactics

But he cautioned that further roadblocks can be expected from Unocal in a bid to ensure that the resolution does not pass at the shareholders' meeting in June. A "cover-up" investigation by Unocal would be no surprise, he said. "Corporations always have the upper hand in shareholder meetings and only a large shareholder and public outcry will produce a real investigation."

Visit Unocal's Yadana project website at http:// www.unocal.com/ myanmar/index.htm to find out about the company's policy on involvement in Burma.

Summary

The question of whether the United States should trade with countries with poor human rights records has caused much debate. While there is evidence that trade sanctions have helped end restrictive regimes, some critics argue that such measures actually make the situation worse. The preceding articles look at the issue in relation to whether sanctions against Burma have worked.

In the first article Leon T. Hadar, a Cato Institute academic and journalist, gives the background to U.S. policy, citing various studies to show that sanctions have cost the United States billions of dollars in revenue and the domestic economy consumer choice and jobs. Hadar asserts that trade sanctions in the case of Burma have alienated the United States in Asia, pushing Burma closer to China. He also argues that the people of Burma would benefit more from U.S. commercial collaboration and activity within their country, since such cooperation would enable them to learn from U.S. companies, and U.S. standards and systems would gradually permeate Burmese working practices and ways of life.

The second article, published by the International Council of Chemical, Energy, Mine, and General Workers' Unions, argues that trade sanctions imposed on Burma should be seen as a victory in making multinational companies accountable for their actions. The article focuses in particular on the involvement of international corporations in the Burmese oil industry. It emphasizes the importance of this business to the Burmese government and claims that the oil industry continues to be connected with human rights abuses and corruption. The authors of the article believe that dealing with a corrupt regime serves only to strengthen that regime and its abuses.

FURTHER INFORMATION:

Books:

Bales, Kevin. *Disposable People: New Slavery in the Global Economy*. Berkeley, CA: University of California Press, 2000.

Rodman, Kenneth A. *Sanctions beyond Borders*. Lanham, MD: Rowman and Littlefield, 2001.

Taylor, Annie, and Caroline Thomas (eds.). *Global Trade and Global Social Issues*. New York: Routledge, 1999.

Useful websites:

http://home.att.net/~slomansonb/burma.html
Edited version of the *Crosby v. National Foreign Trade Council* case on the Massachusetts Burma Law.
http://www.freeburmacoalition.org/
Free Burma Coalition site.

The following debates in the Pro/Con series may also be of interest:

In this volume:
Topic 9 Would banning imported goods made by children help stop child labor?

In *Human Rights*:
Topic 15 Should the United States have relations with regimes that abuse human rights?

SHOULD THE UNITED STATES TRADE WITH COUNTRIES WITH POOR HUMAN RIGHTS RECORDS?

YES: All countries have a moral obligation to try to stop human rights abuses; as a democratic superpower the United States is in a strong position of influence

YES: They are in a better position to change matters by helping improve the infrastructure of the country and showing by example how things should be done

MORALITY VS. REALITY
Does the United States have a duty to help stop abusive regimes?

COMPANY POWER
Can U.S. companies operating in countries with poor human rights records effect change?

NO: The United States has a duty to help its own citizens, and trade sanctions tend to lead to higher domestic prices and greater unemployment

NO: Companies operating in such countries often also adopt abusive tactics to maximize profits and minimize costs

SHOULD THE UNITED STATES TRADE WITH COUNTRIES WITH POOR HUMAN RIGHTS RECORDS?

KEY POINTS

YES: There are numerous examples of trade sanctions working, for example, U.S. action against South Africa helped end apartheid

YES: Trade sanctions are the most effective way to bring about change since they hit the targeted country where it hurts most

EFFECTIVENESS
Do sanctions work?

NO: Sanctions just make matters worse for local people living under abusive regimes; the elite rarely suffer

NO: Sanctions lead to retaliation and a breakdown of the international community

GLOSSARY

balance of payments a record of the value of a country's international trade, borrowing, and lending. *See also* export, import.

black market an illegal part of the economy that is not subject to regulation or taxation and that often deals in high-priced, illegal, or scarce commodities. *See also* tax.

boom and bust a period of wild swings in economic activity between growth and contraction. *See also* depression.

business cycle the periodic but irregular fluctuation in economic activity. Economists know that the business cycle exists, but they do not fully understand why.

capitalism an economic system based on private ownership and enterprise and the free market. Capitalism has been the dominant economic system in the western world since about the 16th century.

child labor widely regarded as work for children that harms or exploits them in some way —physically, mentally, morally, or by blocking access to education. International conventions also define "child labor" as activities such as soldiering and prostitution.

communism a political doctrine, based on the ideas of the philosopher Karl Marx, that seeks to establish social equality through central regulation of economic activity and communal ownership.

corporation a firm or business that is owned by shareholders.

deflation a downward movement in the general level of prices.

demand the desire for a particular good or service backed by the ability to pay for it.

depression a deep trough in the business cycle, usually marked by high prices and high unemployment. *See also* boom and bust; business cycle; Great Depression.

devaluation a reduction in the official rate at which one currency is exchanged for another currency.

developing country a poor country that is undergoing a process of economic modernization through the development of an industrial and commercial base.

export a domestic commodity sold to a foreign country.

fiscal policy government attempts to maintain economic balance by revenue-raising through taxation or altering spending on goods or services.

free market a market in which supply and demand are not subject to regulation by the government.

free trade international trade that is not subject to restrictions or barriers.

General Agreement on Tariffs (GATT) an organization established in 1948 designed to discuss and agree the easing of tariffs and trade restrictions on countries and to eliminate discriminatory treatment in international commerce. *See also* WTO.

globalization the worldwide expansion of private corporations and of the culture of the countries they come from.

Great Depression the worldwide depression throughout the 1930s that followed the collapse of the U.S. stock market in 1929. *See also* depression and recession.

gross domestic product (GDP) a measurement of a nation's economic performance. GDP is the total value of the financial output within the borders of a particular country.

gross national product (GNP) GDP plus the income accruing to domestic residents from investments abroad, less the income earned in the domestic market by foreigners abroad. *See also* GDP.

hangover theory part of the business cycle proposing that tight controls over money and credit policies trigger recessions. *See also* boom and bust; business cycle; recession.

import a commodity bought in from abroad.

Industrialization advances in production

methods and increased productivity brought about by technological innovation and change.

International Monetary Fund (IMF) an international organization of 184 member countries established in 1945. It promotes international monetary cooperation, exchange stability, and orderly exchange arrangements to foster economic growth, high levels of employment, and to provide temporary financial assistance to countries.

inflation an upward movement in the general level of prices.

laissez-faire a French term meaning "let it happen," used to describe an economy with no government intervention. *See also* free trade.

minimum wage a level of payment set by government legislation below which employers are forbidden to pay workers.

monetary policy the attempts to regulate inflation and economic activity by varying the money supply and interest rates.

monopoly a market in which there is only one supplier of a good or service for which there is no close substitute.

natural monopoly an industry in which technical factors such as infrastructure requirements prevent the efficient existence of more than one owner.

North American Free Trade Agreement (NAFTA) an accord the governments of Canada, the United Mexican States, and the government of the United States of America signed in 1992 which took effect on January 1, 1994 and established a free trade zone in North America.

nationalization transfer of a privately owned enterprise to government ownership.

patent a government-issued legal document that grants exclusive rights to the inventor of a product or service.

privatization transfer of a government-owned enterprise to private control and ownership. Privatization may involve subcontracting work to the private sector.

protectionism an economic doctrine that attempts to protect domestic producers by placing tariffs and quotas on imports.

recession a severe contraction of economic activity marked by two successive quarters of falling GDP. *See also* depression.

slump a short period of economic or financial weakness, such as a recession or depression. *See also* depression; recession.

supply the total amount of a commodity available to buy. *See also* demand.

tax a compulsory charge placed on economic activity by governments. Taxes might be placed on wealth or income, on business profits, or as license fees on activities such as driving.

terrorism the unlawful or threatened use of force or violence by a person or organized group against people or property with the intention of intimidating or coercing societies or governments, often for ideological or political reasons.

transnational corporation (TNC) an enterprise that operates in a number of different countries, and that has production facilities outside its home country.

unions organizations of workers united by the desire to protect their common interests and improve their working conditions.

World Bank a group of five financial organizations including the International Bank for Reconstruction and Development (IBRD), the International Development Association (IDA), and the International Finance Corporation (IFC). They provide low-interest loans, interest-free credit, and grants for Third World countries.

World Trade Organization (WTO) an international organization founded in 1995 after the Uruguay round of the General Agreement on Tariffs and Trade (GATT) negotiations. The WTO monitors national trading policies, handles trade disputes, and enforces the GATT agreements. *See also* GATT.

Acknowledgments

Topic 1 Is a Free Market the Best Way to Organize World Trade?

Yes: From "The Case for Free Trade and Lower Taxes" by Adam Smith in *An Inquiry into the Nature and Causes of the Wealth of Nations*, 1776. Public domain.

No: "Free Trade Is Not Free, Mr. President" by Patrick J. Buchanan, The American Cause, May 2001. Copyright © 2001 by Patrick J. Buchanan and Creators Syndicate, Inc. Used by permission.

Topic 2 Are Recessions Inevitable?

Yes: From "When the Economy Goes South: What Happens in a Recession" by Jane Katz in *Regional Review*, Vol. 9, No. 1, 1999. Used by permission.

No: From "The Hangover Theory: Are Recessions the Inevitable Payback for Good Times?" by Paul Krugman, *Slate*, December 3, 1998 (www2.gol.com/ users/coynerhm/hangover_theory.htm). Copyright © 1998 by Slate.com. Used by permission.

Topic 3 Are Monopolies Always Bad?

Yes: "Drug Makers Hiding behind Financial Fig Leaf" by Russell Mokhiber and Robert Weissman, FinalCall.com, February 7, 2002. Used by permission.

No: "Threatening Pharmaceutical Innovation" by Doug Bandow, Copley News Service, May 22, 2002. Used by permission.

Topic 4 Do Unions Adversely Affect Economic Growth?

Yes: "Union Tactics Cost Jobs" by Stephen Moore, *The Washington Times*, March 13, 2003. Used by permission.

No: "Labor Unions Good for Economies and Equity, Says World Bank" by Jim Lobe for OneWorld U.S. (us.oneworld.net). Used by permission.

Topic 5 Has Globalization Hindered the Economic Growth of Developing Countries?

Yes: "Global Trade Is Against Developing Nations—Kenneth Kaunda" by Brighton Phiri, *The Post* (Lusaka), November 26, 2002. Used by permission of *The Post* of Zambia.

No: "ICC Brief on Globalization" by International Chamber of Commerce, November 22, 2000. Courtesy of ICC: the world business organization (www.iccwbo.org).

Topic 6 Does the World Trade Organization Need Reforming?

Yes: From "Rethinking Liberalisation and Reforming the WTO" by Martin Khor, World Economic Forum, Davos, Switzerland, January 28, 2000. Used by permission of Third World Network (www.twnside.org.sg).

No: "The World Trade Organization Works for You" by Charlene Barshefsky (www.usr.gov/html/wto4you.html). Public domain.

Topic 7 Are International Monetary Fund Financial Assistance Policies Harmful?

Yes: "The IMF Strikes Out on Brazil" by Brett D. Schaefer and John P. Sweeney, Heritage Foundation Memorandum 569, February 4, 1999 (www.heritage.org/research/labor/). Used by permission.

No: "Debt Relief for Poor Countries, (HIPC): Progress Through March 2003" by International Monetary Fund, IMF Factsheet, April 2003. Used by permission.

Topic 8 Do Transnational Corporations Have More Influence on the World Economy Than National Governments?

Yes: From "Mega-Mergers, Mega-Influence" by Jeffrey Garten, *New York Times*, October 26, 1999. Copyright © 1999 by The New York Times Co. Reprinted with permission.

No: "Countries Still Rule the World" by Martin Wolf, *Financial Times*, February 6, 2002. Copyright © 2002 by *Financial Times*. Used by permission.

Topic 9 Would Banning Imported Goods Made by Children Help Stop Child Labor?

Yes: "Measure to Ban Import Items Made by Children in Bondage" by Steven Greenhouse, *New York Times*, October 1, 1997. Copyright © 1997 by The New York Times Co. Reprinted with permission.

No: "Child Labor" Issue Briefs, www.heritage.org/research/labor/. Used by permission.

Topic 10 Should Multinationals Be Forced to Pay Local Workers a Recognized Minimum Wage?

Yes: "To Head Off Mass Migrations, Set a Global Minimum Wage" by Michael Ardon, *International Herald Tribune*, January 23, 2002. Copyright © 2003 by International Herald Tribune. Used by permission.

No: "The Minimum Wage Good Intentions, Bad Results" by Roger Koopman, *The Freeman*, Vol. 38, No. 3, March 1988. Copyright © 1988 by The Foundation for Economic Education, Inc. Used by permission.

Topic 11 Should Companies Be Punished for Supplying Arms to Regimes that Support Terrorism?

Yes: "Chinese Companies Sanctioned for Proliferation" by Rose Gordon, *Arms Control Today*, September 2002. Used by permission.

No: "Economic Forces, Not Hypocrisy, Should Govern the Arms Trade" by Dexter P. Rosenhauer. Copyright © 2003 by Dexter P. Rosenhauer. Used by permission.

Topic 12 Does the Internet Make It Difficult to Enforce Copyright Law?

Yes: From "Digital Piracy Saps Music Industry" by David Faber, CNBC, May 4, 2003. Courtesy of CNBC.

No: "The Illustrated Story of Copyright," Doug Isenberg Interview with Edward Samuels, gigalaw.com, 2001. Used by permission.

Topic 13 Does a High Dollar Harm the U.S. Economy?

Yes: "Good News! The Dollar Is Down" by Rich Miller and Peter Coy, with Christine Tierney, David Fairlamb, et al, BusinessWeek Online, May 16, 2003. Reprinted from 05/16/03 issue of Business Week by special permission. Copyright © 2003 by the McGraw-Hill Companies, Inc.

No: Hearing on "Risks of a Growing Balance of Payments Deficit" by Robert Rubin, U.S. Senate Committee on Banking, Housing, and Urban Affairs, July 25, 2001. Public domain.

Topic 14 Is Protectionism Good for U.S. Business?

Yes: "When Protectionism Is a Good Thing" by Herman E. Daly, PCDForum Column #67, January 25, 1994. Used by permission.

No: "Import Quotes 'Steel' from Us All" by Jeff Jacoby, Capitalism Magazine.com, September 10, 2001. Used by permission.

Topic 15 Has NAFTA Cost the United States Jobs?

Yes: From "NAFTA's Broken Promises: Failure to Create U.S. Jobs," Public Citizen's Global Trade Watch, January 1997. Used by permission.

No: "Bush Needs Trade Promotion Authority to Recharge Economy and Spur Growth," National Center for Policy Analysis (www.ncpa.org). Used by permission of the NCPA.

Topic 16 Should the United States Trade with Countries with Poor Human Rights Records?

Yes: From "U.S. Sanctions Against Burma: A Failure on all Fronts" by Leon T. Hadar, Trade Policy Analysis No. 1, March 26, 1998. Used by permission of the Cato Institute.

No: "U.S. and EU Impose Burma Sanctions" by International Council of Chemical, Energy, Mine, and General Workers' Unions, *ICEM Info*, Vol. 2, No. 2, 1997. Used by permission.

The Brown Reference Group plc has made every effort to contact and acknowledge the creators and copyright holders of all extracts reproduced in this volume. We apologize for any omissions. Any person who wishes to be credited in further volumes should contact The Brown Reference Group plc in writing: The Brown Reference Group plc, 8 Chapel Place, Rivington Street, London EC2A 3DQ, U.K.

Picture credits

Cover: Corbis: Macduff Everton; **Corbis:** Wally McNamee, 6/7, 198; **Corbis Sygma:** Baitel Esaias, 117, Thomas Hartwell, 144, Wyman Ira, 18; **Digital Vision:** 181; **Empics:** Matthew Ashton, 103; **Getty Images:** 13, 55; **Richard Jenkins:** 46/47; **Library of Congress:** 52, 186; **Rex Features:** Nick Cobbing, 86/87, Jean Guyaux, 66, Eric C Pendzich, 122, 126/127, Sipa Press, 91; **Still Pictures:** 131